ISBN 978-1-330-36134-4
PIBN 10040722

1 MONTH OF
FREE
READING

at

www.ForgottenBooks.com

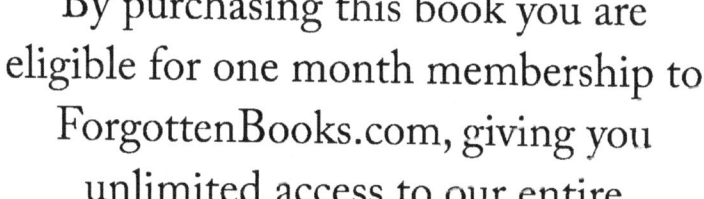

By purchasing this book you are eligible for one month membership to ForgottenBooks.com, giving you unlimited access to our entire collection of over 700,000 titles via our web site and mobile apps.

To claim your free month visit:

www.forgottenbooks.com/free40722

THE LIFE AND LETTERS OF
ROBERT G. INGERSOLL

ROBERT G. INGERSOLL

THE LIFE AND LETTERS OF
ROBERT G.
INGERSOLL

Edited with a Biographical Introduction by
EVA INGERSOLL WAKEFIELD

Edition for the English Reader
Edited with a Preface by
ROYSTON PIKE

WATTS & CO.
JOHNSON'S COURT, FLEET STREET, LONDON, E.C.4
WEHMAN BROS.

To the memory of my beloved Mother
Eva R. Ingersoll Brown
elder daughter of Robert G. Ingersoll
who first suggested the publication of her father's letters and
who was the editor's devoted aid and abiding inspiration
this book is lovingly dedicated

Eva Ingersoll Wakefield

First published 1952

*Printed in Great Britain
by Richard Clay and Company Ltd., Bungay, Suffolk,
and Published by C. A. Watts & Co. Ltd.,
5 & 6 Johnson's Court, Fleet Street, London, E.C.4*

FOREWORD

BY EVA INGERSOLL WAKEFIELD

I HAVE TRIED AS editor of this book to present an informal
but revealing portrayal of the man Ingersoll—his personality, ideas, interests, life-work, and influence—through the
medium of some of his characteristic personal letters. The
vast majority of the letters I obtained through the two daughters
of Colonel Ingersoll, Eva Ingersoll Brown (my mother) and
Maud Ingersoll, who were thoughtful and foresighted enough to
copy before mailing many of the letters which their father
wrote at home. Some letters were available through the files
of Ingersoll's law office. A few were secured by means of
requests for Ingersoll letters in various newspapers and journals.
A few more were sent to me by old admirers, acquaintances,
and friends of the Colonel. A number of valuable letters
were quoted by permission of Doubleday & Company, publishers, from *With Walt Whitman in Camden*, edited by Horace
Traubel; several were graciously contributed by Mrs. Harry
Houdini, from her late husband's collection of Ingersolliana.
All the letters written to Dr. John Livingston Ingersoll form a
part of the large and important Ingersoll collection in the
Illinois State Historical Library, at Springfield, Illinois, and
cordial appreciation is hereby extended to this Library for its
generous co-operation. Much of the original material that has
gone into this book was donated to the Library of Congress in
Washington, D.C., by the Editor and her brother, Robert Ingersoll Brown.

The Family, or Ingersoll—Husband, Father, and Friend
section of the book may well overwhelm, and even antagonize,
many a modern reader who is conditioned to looking down his
nose at any expressions of human affection and tenderness.
Love has long been out of fashion in literature, and biographies
nowadays are seldom written out of love for their subjects.
While this Editor is quite unashamedly in love with her subject,
she has at the same time tried to keep herself within bounds.
Small boys of all ages have always scoffed at sentiment as
" mush " and nonsense until they, too, fall victim to the tender

v

passion in one or another of its manifestations. Is the Inger-sollian capacity for love to be considered undesirable and out-moded in the present world, or is it not precisely this capacity for love that is most needed today?

The reader also may well be surprised by the omission of letters to Colonel Ingersoll's wife. The reason for this is that his younger daughter, Maud Ingersoll, felt very strongly that these letters were too intimate for publication, while her sister, Eva Ingersoll Brown, believed that their father and all his thoughts and works belonged not only to the family but to the world. As for Mrs. Ingersoll's attitude, her death occurred before the question was raised. The reader will readily appreciate that this situation left the Editor in a very delicate and difficult quandary, which she finally resolved by the aforesaid omission.

It will be obvious from the text that the Editor has in no wise attempted to write a genuine and thorough-going biography of Robert Ingersoll, but merely a biographical out-line or sketch. She has simply presented some of the important materials upon which to base biographies and appraisals by future students of Ingersoll.

The Editor wishes particularly to thank her Husband, Sherman D. Wakefield, for his invaluable assistance in re-search, editing, proof-reading, and indexing.

New York, N.Y
January, 1951

PREFACE

By Royston Pike

MORE THAN FIFTY years have passed since the supremely compelling voice of Robert G. Ingersoll was stilled, and with each of the years that have gone more and more of those who were thrilled by his oratory have joined him in the great silence. Yet his voice still makes its powerful contribution to the cause of truth, of reason, of human enlightenment.

On both sides of the Atlantic, Ingersoll's *Lectures and Essays* have been and are widely read and as widely appreciated and enjoyed. Through their pages the reader cannot fail to form a picture of the Man; but it is only now, in the Letters that have been so carefully garnered and presented by one who as a little girl learnt to know and love him in the family home in New York, that the Colonel's rich and many-sided personality is revealed in something like totality. Here we meet Ingersoll the inquiring youth and struggling law student, the rising advocate and trusted politician, the brave soldier, the bold thinker and the impassioned orator, the humanist and lover of his kind, the epicure and bon-vivant—and the man who in all the intimate relations of domestic life was loved as he himself loved, with something approaching adoration.

Famed as he was in so many different walks of life, highly regarded and esteemed as he was in all of them, it is as the Great Agnostic that Ingersoll was most generally and widely known; and in Britain as in America hosts of thoughtful men and women have owed to him their intellectual emancipation. As a smasher of idols, as an exposer of moral shams, as a smiter of religious hypocrisy, as a relentless foe of superstition, there has been none like him in the modern age.

Perhaps there will be some who will argue that he was *too* successful for his lasting fame—that he triumphed so largely that the worst extravagances of the Christian creed have been pushed away into the background since he assailed and exposed them with such devastating force.

To some extent this is true, of course. Only among the extremer sects of Bibliolaters and—but even here there is a toning down of horrors to suit modern susceptibilities—in the Church of Rome is there an insistence on the material reality of a hell with its undying worms and unquenchable flames, an eternity of damnation for the wicked and those most sinful of all fallen creatures, the unbelievers. As a young man Ingersoll made this, the most awful and horrible of all the beliefs engendered by the fecund fancy of the religionists, the principal target of his oratory; and more than any man, perhaps, he might claim the credit for having had it relegated to the theological attic if not lumber-room.

But when this has been said and admitted, we may do well to remember that the great mass of Ingersoll's critique is as valid as it ever was. The why and wherefore of the Universe, the meaning of life (if, indeed, it has any meaning), the existence of God and the spirit world, the problems of causation and of necessity, the mystery of pain and the even greater mystery of death—these, the subjects that awakened his genius, that inspired his thinking and the majestic flights of his oratory, are still contained within the sphere of the Unknown, perhaps the Unknowable. We are in very deed encompassed by question-marks, and Ingersoll's agnostic attitude is as rationally compelling as it has been since our remoter ancestors first flung questions at the unanswering sky.

As will be clear from Mrs. Eva Ingersoll Wakefield's Foreword, this edition of her Grandfather's *Letters* was published in the U.S.A. in 1951. For publication in this country a certain abridgment was imperative, and my task as editor has consisted in the main of the removal of those passages, chiefly dealing with Colonel Ingersoll's political and legal career, which would have come strange to the English reader. But I have striven to ensure that nothing is omitted that is essential to the understanding of a great American, a great man, whose influence was always exercised on the side of the Good, the True, and the Beautiful. And it is my most sincere hope that there will be many who will come to know better through these present pages the man who, with the most genial and profound commonsense, proclaimed as his creed:

> Happiness is the only good,
> The time to be happy is now,
> The way to be happy is to make others happy.

CONTENTS

CONTENTS

PART ONE

Biographical Introduction

"THAT WHICH HAS happened to all, happened to me," wrote Robert G. Ingersoll. "I was born, and this event, which has never for a moment ceased to influence my life, took place, according to an entry found in one Bible, on the 12th day of August in the year of grace 1833, according to another entry in another Bible, on the 11th of August in the same year. [The latter date is the correct one.] "So you will see," he continues, "that a contradiction was about the first thing I found in the Bible, and I have continued to find contradictions in the Sacred Volume all my life.

"The great fact of my being born happened at Dresden, near Lake Seneca, in the County of Yates, in the State of New York. My father was at that time trying to save the souls of the people in that neighbourhood by preaching the gospel for a consideration of about three hundred dollars a year. Four children had preceded me, two boys and two girls. I was the fifth and the last.

"My father was born in Rutland, Vermont, on the fifth of July, 1792. He received the rudiments of ignorance at Middlebury College. He studied, as they called it in that day, for the ministry, and was for a time under the tuition of a celebrated divine by the name of Josiah Hopkins. After having received a certificate to the effect that he understood the mysteries of orthodoxy, and was able to show that the infinite love of God was perfectly consistent with the damnation of the whole human race, he was ordained a 'New School' Presbyterian minister in 1823, and started in search of employment. He went from Vermont on foot through the great forest now known as the Adirondacks to St. Lawrence County, New York. Not finding any considerable number of sheep in want of a shepherd, he concluded to teach school. In a little log school-house, surrounded by about twenty children, he began to earn his bread.

" One Robert Livingston, of the town of Lisbon, as was his duty, visited the school for the purpose of finding out whether the young teacher was in all respects qualified to discharge the duties of his position. By some accident, Mr. Livingston took with him on that day, probably for company, his daughter, Mary.

" As this girl entered, the little school-house was filled with light—the poor constricted walls expanded, the ceiling lifted— the log-house became a palace inhabited by a king, a princess, and a lover. The eyes of Mary met the eyes of John Ingersoll. From each to each flew the shaft. Before a word was spoken the story was told and understood. The same story that has made the life of man worth living. The story that is just as enchanting in the huts of the poor as in the palaces of kings. Love, like death, makes all things even.

" In a few months, months filled with light and joy, they were married, joined in wedlock in the old town of Lisbon on the St. Lawrence River in September, 1821.

" John, my father, was filled with the idea that it was his duty to save his fellow men from the wrath of a God of infinite love. He was a believer in all the consolations of Christianity, including the dogma of eternal torment. In his day this dogma was in full force. Men believed in fire and sulphur, in devils and fiends. Ministers were engaged in warning the world—in crying ' Fire ! ' to the careless and sinful. My father carried the sorrows of the world. The frightful doctrine of eternal punishment furrowed his face and made his eyes familiar with tears. This horror darkened his life. He was loving and generous in his nature, but his theology filled his sky with cloud and storm." Robert's paternal grandfather, Ebenezer Ingersoll, " an old soldier of the Revolution, had sense enough and courage enough to be a Universalist," declaring " if any were spared, all would be "; but his grandmother, Margaret Whitcomb Ingersoll, " was a devotee." John Ingersoll " was the youngest of twelve children, and the favourite of his mother." Accordingly, " through her influence he became thoroughly religious."

The home of John and Mary Ingersoll was as rich in love and affection as it was poor in worldly goods. It was graced by a rare quality of refinement and culture, as both parents were persons of intellectual substance and background, the father steeped in orthodox theology and the mother deeply interested in social problems. Mary Ingersoll possessed the moral courage of her convictions, and was one of the first, if not the first, of her sex, in the State of New York, to prepare and circulate a petition calling for the abolition of Negro slavery in the District of Columbia. She was also an indefatigable worker in the temperance movement. Robert's mother is said to have been strikingly beautiful, and to have had a delightful sense of humour, as well as a naturally sceptical and inquiring mind, even concerning orthodox religion. She is reported to have read *The Age of Reason*, by Thomas Paine, with keen appreciation and zest. However, despite her grave doubts as to the cardinal tenets of the Presbyterian creed, she selflessly fulfilled her arduous duties as a minister's wife, ministering to the physical and spiritual needs of her husband's congregations, and swiftly wearing out her own gentle young life in the process.

Mary Ingersoll was with her children for only a pitifully brief period of time, as she died on December 2, 1835, at Cazenovia, New York, when the eldest child was only thirteen. Ruth, born on July 5, 1822, was followed by John Livingston, who came on October 24, 1823, and the second daughter, Mary Jane, was born on June 14, 1826. Ebon Clark was born on December 12, 1831, when John Ingersoll was pastor of a Congregational Church at Marshall, Oneida Co., New York. In the short interval before Robert was born the family had moved to the little village of Dresden, in Yates County, New York. Here, Robert, the youngest of the five children, came into the world on August 11, 1833.

Although their mother was taken from her family so soon, the tenderness, sweetness, and strength of her personality made such a deep and permanent impression upon the children that Robert, who was only two at the time of her death, later wrote: " Nearly forty-eight years ago, under the snow, in the little town of Cazenovia, my poor mother was buried. I was but two years old. I remember her as she looked in death. That sweet, cold face has kept my heart warm through all the changing years."

From the time they lost their mother the two small boys, " Robin " and Clark, always devoted to one another, became

3

absolutely inseparable. They clung together in their first great sorrow, softening each other's sense of loneliness and anguish; and gradually they reawakened to the joy and adventure of living, as all healthy small boys inevitably will. Together they frolicked and played, worked at their studies, suffered the ordeals of church- and Sunday-school, the rigours and discomforts of poverty, and the endless peregrinations from parsonage to parsonage made necessary by their father's uncompromising and unpopular anti-slavery views. Together they became heretics and Agnostics; revelled in the wonders and beauties of nature, and above all, as the years passed by, in the intellectual delights and inspirations of Burns, Shelley and Shakespeare, Voltaire and Paine, and other great master minds of the ages.

Ruth Ann, the elder sister of Robert, adored the very ground he walked upon, and she was as good a heretic as he was himself. Ruth was an exceptional mathematician, and a woman of high intelligence, depth and warmth of nature. She married Dr. John Carter of Erie, Pennsylvania, whose daughter Mary by a previous marriage became the wife of Ebon Clark Ingersoll.

John Livingston was the only one of the five children to have the benefit of a full college education. He attended Oberlin College for three years. Later he studied medicine in Lee County, Illinois, and took courses at Rush Medical College in Chicago from 1846 to 1848. He then went to Prospect Hill (now Prospect), Waukesha County, Wisconsin, in 1849, where he practised medicine for fifty years; and married Teressa Chamberlain Cheney, of Prospect Hill, in 1851. They had seven children.

Mary Jane became almost a second mother to Robert and Clark after the death of Mrs. Ingersoll. The story is told in Edward Garstin's *Life of Robert G. Ingersoll* that at her death " she called her daughter Mary, then in her tenth year, to her bedside and made a dying request, ' Mary, always watch over your little brothers, Robert and Clark.' . . . This sister Mary was to them both, thereafter, a sister and a watchful, kind little mother. She darned their stockings, patched their little pants, and every night tucked them in . bed and kissed them . just as a mother does. . . . After he [Robert] became a strong young man, when boys care more for other fellows' sisters than

4

their own, one word from his sister Mary would bring him home, away from any company at any time, and from any place."

Mary Jane was married twice, first to Sylvester C. Frisby and later to E. John Black; she had two children by her first husband, and two by Mr. Black.

An extraordinarily tender and strong affection united the members of the Ingersoll family throughout all their lives. Four years before Robert died, he wrote to his brother, Dr. John Ingersoll, about their father, Ruth, Mary, and Ebon Clark, in these loving terms:

> I have just read your beautiful letter written on my birthday. It fills my eyes with tears to think of the dear ones "who are no more," who have fallen asleep. Dear, dear father, filled with love for his children, anxious every moment that they were out of his sight. How much he suffered, how hard his life was, and how much he loved. How I wish he could have lived for many happy years. . . . And dear Mary, all affection and impulse, generous as the very heart of love. And dear Ruth, self-poised, full of good sense, good judgment, and without a fault so far as I know. And Clark, I think of him every hour, and dream of him a hundred times a year. The world can never be the same to me again. . . .

While Mary Jane ministered to the physical needs of the younger children, Mr. Ingersoll took full charge of their education. He was at once an exceedingly stern and a deeply affectionate father. He firmly believed that it was his bounden duty to follow literally the Biblical injunction not to spare the rod; yet he overflowed with love for his children, and felt an ever-present and passionate anxiety for their welfare. When " Robin " was still at a very tender age his father would give him an inch of candle and admonish him to memorize a certain number of passages of Hebrew, Greek, or Latin by the time the candle burned down, on pain of being compelled to sit in total darkness for a while, " to expiate the sin of idleness."

Yet in spite of his severity he instilled in his children those high principles of character and conduct upon which his own spartan, selfless life was built. It was inevitable that the Bible should have been his one great textbook for the instruction and guidance of his children; and Robert soon came to know it from cover to cover. However, the boy's studies of the Bible, the innumerable Biblical commentators, and the other theological works in his father's library served only to add fuel to the flame of his revolt against Christian theology.

Precisely when this revolt began is not certain, although he declared in later years that he could not recall a time in all his life when he ever really accepted the teachings of orthodox religion. As far back as he could remember anything, he had rebelled consciously or unconsciously against the cruelties and absurdities of the Christian creed. All through his childhood Robert listened to evangelical sermons, to " hundreds of the most frightful and vivid descriptions of the tortures inflicted in hell—of the horrible state of the lost."

[The first sermon that made any deep impression upon him was one he heard at the age of seven. A " Free Will " Baptist preacher gave such a graphic and frightful description of hell that it left " a mark, like a scar," on his mind for ever [The text of the sermon was " The Rich Man and Lazarus," and the preacher did full justice to his subject, painting an unforgettable picture of the two men, in life and in death, against the background of hell and its eternal torments. The eloquence of this itinerant evangelist brought home to Robert the true meaning of the dogma of eternal punishment—awakened his imagination to " the height and depth of the Christian horror." [From that moment he told himself: " It is a lie, and I hate your religion."] From that moment for him, " the flames of hell were quenched," and he " passionately hated every orthodox creed." This " Free Will " sermon marked the turning-point in young Ingersoll's intellectual life. It made him into a convinced Agnostic and conscious rebel against his orthodox family background and tradition.]

However, it was not until many years later that Robert was able to emancipate himself physically, as well as mentally, from the thraldom of his orthodox home and church community. Throughout his childhood he submitted to a discipline which was irksome enough on ordinary weekdays and all but intolerable on Sundays. " When I was a boy," said he, " Sunday was considered altogether too holy to be happy in. Sunday used to commence then when the sun went down on Saturday night. . . . A darkness fell upon the house ten thousand times deeper than that of night. Nobody said a pleasant word; nobody laughed; nobody smiled. . . On Sunday morning

. . . we went to church. The minister was in a pulpit about twenty feet high with a little sounding-board above him, and he commenced at firstly and went on and on and on to about twenty-thirdly. Then he made a few remarks by way of application; and then took a general view of the subject; and in about two hours reached the last chapter in *Revelation*.

" In those days, no matter how cold the weather was, there was no fire in the church. It was thought to be a kind of sin to be comfortable while you were thanking God. The first church that had a stove in it in New England divided on that account," Ingersoll declared. " After the sermon, we had an inter-mission," he continued. " Then came the catechism on the chief end of man. We sat in a row with our feet coming to about six inches of the floor. The minister asked us if we knew that we all deserved to go to hell, and we all answered ' yes.' Then we were asked if we would be willing to go to hell, if it was God's will, and every little liar shouted ' yes.' Then the same sermon was preached once more, commencing at the other end and going back. After that, we started for home, sad and solemn, overpowered with the wisdom displayed in the scheme of the atonement. When we got home, if we had been good boys . . sometimes they would take us out to the graveyard to cheer us up a little. It did cheer me. When I looked at the sunken tombs, and the leaning stones, and read the half-effaced inscriptions . . . it was a great comfort. The reflection came to my mind that the observance of the Sab-bath could not last always   "

For many long years, despite Robert's recalcitrance and irreverence regarding orthodox religion, the Rev. John Inger-soll patiently endeavoured to lead his erring son into the true faith. The two had endless discussions concerning belief in God, the immortality of the soul, the divinity of Christ, the inspiration of the Bible, and all the other great theological and philosophical questions which have tried men's souls throughout the ages.

Although always intense and often painful, these conversations were amiable and tolerant in temper; and little by little they achieved an unexpected and astonishing result: they pro-foundly modified and liberalized the orthodox faith of the father, while they only strengthened and fortified the unbelief of the son. There was an intrepid rectitude in the spirit of John Ingersoll which caused him to respect and accept the truth, as he saw it, at any cost to himself. In the final computation, the cost was great indeed: the almost complete repudiation of the beliefs of a lifetime, and the turn, at the end of his days, to new and untested spiritual pathways. The delicacy and pathos of his father's dilemma in later life was fully appreciated by Robert, who used all the tender affection and imaginative understanding of his nature to transmute the potential tragedy into rewarding serenity and peace of mind. The quiet climax of this personal drama came at the death-bed of John Ingersoll, when the brave old spiritual warrior requested Robert to read, not from the Bible, but from Plato on *The Death of Socrates*.

The childhood of Robert Ingersoll was one long migration from community to community, from one dull, doleful village to another even more dull and doleful, with revival meetings about the only source of what passed for amusement and recreation. The clergyman's constant changes of pulpit were owing to his fierce and fearless sermon-tirades against chattel slavery, which caused him to become anathema to the majority of his congregations. These early years were rootless, drab, and difficult years, ridden with poverty and privation and unending struggle for the means of bare subsistence, as may be readily understood from the fact that Mr. Ingersoll's salary varied between two and four hundred dollars a year. Robert Ingersoll never liked to be reminded of this period in his life, and never referred to it, if he could avoid doing so, in later and happier years.

However, Robert's healthy and joyful nature always came to his rescue, and enabled him to survive all the agonizing ordeals which he experienced. Brimful of innocent mirth and fun, life ran and rippled through his veins as sap through trees in spring, and shone as vernal sun in leaves and streams. He had a most infectious laugh and winning smile, and there was a quickening, brightening quality about him, like rainbows after storms. Furthermore, there were not lacking little compensations for the heart of boyhood in occasional visiting circuses, and in all sorts of mischievous pranks, like the setting off of firecrackers, making of bonfires, and playing of leap-frog in forbidden places, the clandestine ringing of church-bells, and the picking and appropriating of apples overhanging open thoroughfares.

8

From April 2, 1834, to February 4, 1835, John Ingersoll was minister of the Rev. Charles G. Finney's Broadway Tabernacle, in New York City. From there he went to the Congregational Free Church at Cazenovia, New York, where he remained until March, 1836, when he moved to Hampton, New York, staying there exactly two years. The year 1838 saw him at Belleville, New York, and in April, 1839, he went to Oberlin, Ohio, where the elder Ingersoll children studied at Oberlin College. In May, 1841, the family moved to Ashtabula.

Once when the Ingersolls were living in Ashtabula, Ohio, a cow became the chief actor in a highly exciting little tragicomedy in which " Robin " was intimately involved. The house occupied by the Ingersolls boasted a lawn and vegetable-garden that Robert and Clark were commissioned to keep in proper order. The boys were given special instructions to protect the lawn and garden from the incursions of neighbouring livestock, for it seems that Mr. Robertson, a substantial pillar of Mr. Ingersoll's church, who lived next door, owned a cow which was adventurously inclined. Accordingly, in due course the cow appeared in the minister's garden, gaily bedecked with a coronal of vegetables and flowers.

As luck would have it, " Robin " was alone on the job that day; and his frantic efforts to eject the cow through the gate of the fence resulted only in the incorrigible beast cavorting off in another direction. The youthful hero, however, would not easily admit defeat, and by dint of forcible persuasion finally succeeded in driving the cow to the extreme rear of the plot where she suddenly slipped, slid over an eighty-foot embankment, and vanished from sight. " Robin," his heart in his mouth, peered tremulously over the precipice to behold the poor creature rolling over and over down the embankment towards the Ashtabula River. He was never to forget his emotions at the awful sight of that dizzily rotating and supposedly doomed cow, nor his unutterable sense of relief when, upon rushing breathlessly to the foot of the embankment, he actually beheld the animal standing upon her own four feet, absolutely ·intact and unperturbed, " her handsome eyes seeming to shine with the soft light of forgiveness! "

It was in Ashtabula, also, that Robert first became known as ("Honest Bob.") Mr. Robertson (he of the cow episode), who gave him Sunday-school lessons, said of him: "Whatever prank Bob might be up to, there was never any meanness in it." Mr. Samuel W. Wetmore, a schoolmate of Bob's in the same town, writing in 1899, said: "More than fifty years ago I learned to love him for his honesty, truthfulness, integrity, sincerity, and noble nature. Life seemed to burst out on the face of that boy with all the effulgence that intelligence and goodness could portray in a noble character."

On one occasion Bob was scheduled to "speak a piece," which he had learned in school, at an entertainment in the Baptist Church. The piece was "I Remember, I Remember," by Thomas Hood. But alas, poor "Robin" could remember not so much as a single line or word after making his bow to the assembled company! Accordingly, he betook himself back to his seat, which he had no sooner reached than the poem rushed back into his mind. He forthwith returned to the stage, but, horror heaped upon horror, he forgot it all over again! Whereupon, marching off the platform, he exclaimed with infinite ingenuousness and assurance, "Clark knows it!" Then, suddenly the words flashed upon him once more, and this time he delivered the recitation without mishap; although then and there he vowed solemnly to himself never to recite anything in public again, and he never did. Thus began one of the greatest oratorical careers of all time!

The Ingersoll family lived in Ashtabula only a little more than a year (1841-42). From there they moved to North Madison, Ohio, where Mr. Ingersoll became pastor of the First Congregational Church, known as the "Bell Church," because it was the first church in the township of Madison to boast a bell. This small town differed in few respects from the many other small towns where the family had lived, save that it seemed to Robert and Clark somewhat drearier and a little less promising.

However, they remained in North Madison only two years, living then in Aurora and Amboy, Illinois, until July, 1848, when Mr. Ingersoll became the minister of the Congregational Church at Waukesha, Wisconsin. During their stay in Waukesha the two younger boys attended the Waukesha Academy and, later, Carrol College. They lived in this Wisconsin town until January, 1849, when they moved to

Milwaukee. In this more enterprising environment Mr. Ingersoll, Clark, and Robert ventured into the grocery business for a short time.

We next hear of Robert and his father establishing themselves at Greenville, Bond County, Illinois, in 1851, where life was enlivened by the reverberations of the fiery denunciations of slavery on the part of Owen Lovejoy, at Princeton, a nearby town. This great reformer and Abolitionist was courageously and eloquently upheld by John Ingersoll in his pulpit in Greenville. Sunday after Sunday he poured forth the vials of his righteous wrath upon the infamous institution, and, on this question, Bob and Clark were of one mind with their father, feeling a mighty pride in his moral and libertarian exhortations.

Bob was by now a youth of seventeen or eighteen, tall, well proportioned, alert and eager of mind, generous and warm of heart, enormously magnetic of personality. He overflowed with goodwill and friendliness towards all the world. He never seemed to be in a hurry, and did not give any evidence of being particularly ambitious, except to be happy and to make everybody around him happy. He appeared to prefer the society of his elders to that of the young people of his own age, although he was always the life of any party, and the most enthralling of storytellers.

While in Greenville, Bob attended the " Academy " conducted by Mr. Socrates Smith in the basement of Rev. Mr. Ingersoll's church, and was generally conceded to be the " star pupil " of this modest institution of learning. Indeed, so excessively easy did Robert find the acquisition of knowledge that he is said to have spent a quite shameless amount of time in the questionable pastime of flicking unnumbered paper wads at his more diligent if less nimble-witted fellow scholars. He would then add insult to injury by out-doing them all in his mastery of the studies and the quality of his recitations.

Since boyhood Bob had written occasional verses, but his first published poem appeared in the Greenville *Journal* for June, 1852. It discoursed rapturously about " dark-haired Indian girls, reclining on the breast of . . the glorious world . . . in morning dew and sunlight dressed . . ." and continued on this airy, delicate theme through some eight or ten stanzas of exuberant and smoothly flowing lines.

After his gifted pupil's appearance in the press Mr. Socrates Smith's pedagogic dignity felt somewhat at a disadvantage in the former's presence, so he urgently besought Mr. Ingersoll to remove Robert from the Academy on the ground that the youth was as fully qualified to dispense knowledge as he was himself. Accordingly, on September 16 Robert was writing his brother John from Mount Vernon, Jefferson County, Illinois, to say that he had come to that town a few days previously; that he intended staying there " this fall and winter," and that he was going to teach school. " I can get a very large school and I shall stay if I get a certificate. I am to be examined this afternoon. . I have to be examined by the Commissioner of the County, so that the scholars can have the benefit of the public money," he wrote. " This is a very pretty town of about six or eight hundred inhabitants, and it is finely located, and I think that I shall like to live here." He concluded with a postscript, after passing the examination: " There were two examiners, both of whom considered themselves particularly smart . . . one of them . . . is the present schoolmaster at this place. He asked me all the questions he could think of. I laughed at him and answered them all and asked him if he had any more to ask. He said no and gave me a certificate, and then I came away. The present school is out next Friday and I shall commence in about two weeks. . . ."

Robert's method of teaching was unorthodox, but highly effective. He instilled a love and zest for learning in the minds of his small pupils. The curriculum was unusual in many respects and remarkably comprehensive. Study was made a really exciting and romantic affair, and the youthful teacher's stories and illustrations of his points and facts captivated the children's imagination. During 1852 or 1853 Robert presided over another school, in Metropolis, Massac County, Illinois, where he once again made his pupils deeply enamoured of their studies, and achieved astonishing results with them in a very brief period of time. But unfortunately, due to a poor year of farming and the consequent failure of crops, the parent-farmers found themselves in the position of being unable to meet the expenses of their children's tuition; whereupon Robert, with characteristic benevolence, promptly receipted their bills in full.

While teaching, Bob was " boarding round " with various farm families of the districts. His reputation for wit and a well-informed and brilliant mind was growing rapidly, as was his influence in the tiny school and in the community. Suddenly, his sky was darkened by the visitation of a large band of Baptist revivalists. These individuals also " boarded round," and in the course of events some of their number put up at the house where Bob was staying. The preachers were wont to discuss religion at table, and although the young school-teacher generally refused to be drawn into these discussions, he was finally inveigled into giving his opinion of baptism. " With soap," he replied, " baptism is a good thing." The brethren were immoderately shocked, horrified. They spread the daring witticism swiftly on its way until the whole town became aroused in pious wrath. Whereupon, the school board waited upon the luckless Bob to notify him of his dismissal, without so much as a single dollar in salary.

The following day Robert started off on foot to join his father, his sister Mary, and Clark, at Marion, in Williamson County. He took this mode of travel from sheer necessity, as after paying his bill at the farmhouse where he had lodged he found himself without a penny.

In the autumn of 1853 Robert was teaching school in a little town called Waverly, in Tennessee, where he remained until the following spring. The Rev. Mr. Ingersoll says in a letter to his son, John, dated December 19, 1853 ". . . I returned home from my Southern Journey one week ago. . . . I left dear Robert in Waverly, Tennessee, in which place he is now teaching with much promise. . . ."

The following letter is one of the earliest known to the editor to have been written by Robert Ingersoll. The inferiority of this letter, both in style and content, to the letters written only a few years later is noteworthy.

> Waverly Humphry's Co., Tennessee
> Dec. 29, 1853

My very dear Bro. [John],

I wrote you not long ago (some three weeks) but have recd no answer as yet. Why don't you answer me? I wish you would. I am willing to write you as often as you answer me, but there is not much satisfaction when the writing is all on one side. I recd a letter from Father today & one from Clark [Robert's beloved brother].

All well. I know nothing about Ruth [his elder sister]. She never answers me. I believe I shall write her again today for all. I am doing very well in my school & shall I think be able to clear one hundred & fifty dollars or so. It is rather lonesome here all alone and in a slave state at that where the very air seems to be chained. Nothing but nigers [sic] nigers all the time. But I stand it as best I can. I have attended one negro sale where a woman and two little children were sold and parted. (She was the mother of both the children) and one was about two & the other three years old, & yet the Law of the state on that subject is " That no child shall be sold or separated from its mother till it shall have attained the age of eight years." But the Law is of no force for who will prosecute the breakers of the Law. It is an indictable offence & might only be taken notice of by a Grand Jury, & it is for the interest of Grand Jurors (Being all slave holders) to say nothing about it so as to sell themselves & let others sell children from their mothers. Well that's enough Law for one letter. They are now playing " Uncle Tom's Cabin " in New Orleans, St. Louis, Memphis, & Nashville & it meets with great applause & I hope it will do some good in making the condition of the slave better than it now is for the Lord knows it is bad enough. Yet tis better than it was 20 years ago. People here ask me " once and a while " if I think slavery wrong & I tell them I do & that I believe it is wrong enough to damn the whole of them, & they take it in good part. Last night I made a few lines which I send to you they are more lines without end or aim & dont criticize them too hard & I will send you some more next letter.

Your aff. Bro., Robert

It was probably soon after Robert's return north from Tennessee that he began the study of law, in Marion, Williamson County, Illinois, in the offices of the Hon. Willis Allen and his son, William Joshua Allen, who were practising in partnership. The elder Allen was a member of the United States Congress for two terms, and was a lawyer and jurist of marked ability and many years' experience, and undoubtedly Robert acquired much valuable legal knowledge from this connection. Marion was then, as it is today, the shire-town of Williamson County, where the Circuit Court convened. As assistant to the clerk of the Circuit and County Court, Robert earned his living, and contributed to the support of his father and sister Mary.

On November 5, 1854, more than a month before Robert and Clark were formally admitted to the Bar, the latter wrote to Dr. John Ingersoll: " For the last three months Roby and I have been applying ourselves to the study of the law . . . and we were admitted to the Bar ' ex gratia ' in one month after we commenced studying. We have had several cases . already, and what is better than all, have been successful in every case. . . ." The Ingersoll brothers were formally accepted into the ranks of the legal fraternity at Mount Vernon, Illinois, on December 20, 1854. Robert was twenty-one years of age. The requirements for admission were very simple indeed. The applicant was required to furnish a certificate of good moral character from the court of some county; to submit to a perfunctory examination in open court; to provide liquid refreshments for the officers of the court; and lastly, to take the oath of office as a full-fledged attorney.

Robert devoted a great part of his time to the further study of the law in the office of Judge William G. Bowman, a man of outstanding intellectual as well as legal attainments, and a Rationalist in religion. He possessed an unusually fine and extensive library of legal and general literature, of which Robert availed himself to the utmost. In this exciting library, almost every evening until long past midnight, the young man read the works of the great poets, philosophers, historians, and scientists. It was here that he laid the foundation of his creative intellectual life, an intellectual life which continued in undiminished vitality and lustre until the day of his death.

Here he read Plato on Socrates, immortal seeker of the good life. " Epicurus and Lucretius, who made human happiness the aim and end of life; Zeno, the founder of the Stoic philosophy; Democritus, father of the atomic theory "; Cicero's incomparable orations; Seneca's noble concepts of justice; and Marcus Aurelius's memorable essays on moderation and the golden mean. Here he became acquainted with the exalted ethics of Buddha, Confucius, and Lao-tze, and the great Indian mystics. He read Voltaire, whom he thought " did more to free the human mind than any other of the sons of men "; he studied Galileo, Descartes, and Newton; and learned of the epochal discoveries of Copernicus and Kepler, and other great scientists. He read the famous Encyclopædists, Diderot and d'Alembert, who codified human knowledge, Locke, *On the Human Understanding* ; Paine's *Rights of Man,* and *Age of Reason* ; Humboldt, the supreme Monist; Spinoza, the Pantheist; Hume, the unmasker of miracles; Mill, the Utilitarian;

15

Darwin, Huxley, Haeckel and Spencer, Buckle, Lecky, Tyndall, Gibbon and Draper, Büchner, Helmholtz and d'Holbach. Ingersoll learned about " Bruno, the bravest, and Spinoza, the subtilist of men "; about the universal Goethe, the noble Schiller, and the colossal Kant; of Wieland, " the Voltaire of Germany," and Herder, " who wrote the outlines of a philosophical history of man "; of " Schleiermacher, the Pantheist," and " Schopenhauer, the European Buddhist." He became enraptured with the novels of Victor Hugo and Dickens; with the poems of George Eliot and Elizabeth Barrett Browning, and his supreme literary idols, Burns, Shelley, Byron, Keats, and, above all, Shakespeare.

In 1855 the Ingersoll brothers began the practice of law on their own account, in Shawneetown, Gallatin County, under the name of " E. C. and R. G. Ingersoll, Attorneys and Counsellors at Law." Together Robert and Clark set to work to build up a name and career for themselves. They toiled early and late, and with a mighty determination and ambition to accomplish their aims. However, the congenial promising partnership was suddenly interrupted when Clark moved to Springfield in 1856, to serve a term in the Illinois State Legislature; and inevitably during Clark's absence almost all the legal work of the firm devolved upon Robert. Despite this augmented load of responsibility, his business prospered increasingly, and soon the " Metropolis of Southern Illinois," as Shawneetown was then called, proved too small and circumscribed a place to encompass the growing ambitions of the enterprising young lawyers. Accordingly, in 1857, they resolved to abandon it in favour of the more alluring town of Peoria. Ebon Clark probably moved there directly after his marriage to Miss Mary Carter, in November, 1857, and Robert joined his brother and new sister-in-law early in the following February (1858).

Peoria, Illinois
26 Feb., '58

Dear Bro. [John],
    It is a long time since I have written to you, or since I have received anything. I do not know who is indebted. I came to this city about a week ago and found Clark in excellent spirits & health as also his wife, who by the way is all one could wish in every respect. I think Clark has displayed his usual good taste and has met with unusual good luck even for him in selecting

& obtaining so good a wife. I never saw any woman I think better of.

If ever I marry I hope I shall be as fortunate. My health has been (as they say west) good except that I have had the ague all winter though as soon as spring comes I shall get clear of that and probably take something worse.

Our prospects here are very bright indeed. Clark has already become acquainted with everybody and all like him, and we are getting a great deal of business considering the time Clark has been here.

We have a very nice office & lighted with gas. Gas you know is an excellent thing in law, in fact indispensable.

Clark and his wife board at a very nice place and live finely. I sleep in the office and board at the finest hotel in the city. So you see we are getting along first rate. Well dear bro how do you get along? Are people provokingly healthy? I know I have often thought people too honest and civil for one to do with. There has been fine sleighing here for the last three weeks, but now the snow has turned into mud, and as usual in such places there is any amount of preaching drinking praying & swearing. You must give my love to Teressa [John's wife] and to your sweet little Mary & either spank or kiss the baby for me. I rather you would kiss.

From Your aff. Bro. Robert

Peoria, Illinois
May 6th, 1858

Dear Brother [John],

I received your letter this morning, and was very glad indeed to hear from you once more. I have but little or rather no news to tell you. Clark and I are getting along finely. Last week & week before criminal court was in session. Clark & I had most of the business. I defended three men for robbery and had the good luck to clear them all. Everybody surely thought that they would take a little trip to Alton and seemed surprised that I cleared them. There is not a single lawyer in town that is a good speaker, and Clark and I have already the reputation of being the *only* criminal lawyers at the bar. I think we are going to make lots of money. Since I have been here we have taken in in cash about one hundred dollars per month and charged on good men about one hundred and fifty or two hundred more. We are defending a man here who has been indicted for perjury. He is well off & can afford to pay us. He has made us a deed to six city lots worth at least two hundred and fifty dollars apiece. So you see that is a tolerable large fee. I think we shall have no difficulty in clearing him, though it is rather a hard case. We will get all the criminal practice in fact we have it nearly all now. In a little while as soon as Clark gets to keeping house I want father to come and live with us. I think he would like this place very much. As you say father after being tossed about so much must want rest. Poor man

17

how he has laboured and toiled, and suffered for others and how little for himself.

There is little going on but religion. Nothing heard of but prayer meetings though I think they are dying out a little now. As soon as the times get good people will stop praying and go to preying. They have them here in nearly all the churches every day but I have not been to a single one yet and do not think I shall.

I had a letter from Mary [his younger sister] the other day, and learned for the first time she was a spiritualist. I heard a lady or rather a she-fool lecture on spiritualism this winter & I got enough. Of all the humbugs I think spiritualism is the softest and as you say I do not think Mary will be one long . . . God bless you all is the prayer of your brother,*

Rob G. Ingersoll

Ingersoll early took rank with the ablest and most noted men of his profession. Practice in those early days covered a wide field, involving both criminal and civil cases. It is said that in the whole course of his legal career he never took a case in which he was convinced that the accused was guilty of intentional murder, nor did he ever prosecute any one for a capital offence. The record has it that " he was pre-eminently successful, seldom losing a case "; and his biographer, Herman E. Kittredge, tells us that " within a few years from his arrival in Peoria, he was recognized not only as the leader of his profession there, but as the peer in every respect, and the superior in most respects, of any lawyer who ever belonged to the bar of Illinois."

Edward Sharkey, Ingersoll's nephew by marriage, tells the story that one day as Robert was entering the Peoria Court House, he saw a poor Negro prisoner being led out to jail. He inquired as to whether the Negro had a lawyer to defend him, and on being informed that he had not, Ingersoll offered him his services. After he had succeeded in securing the man's acquittal, he asked him privately if he had really stolen the horse or cow which he had been accused of doing. The Negro replied that at first he had been sure that he was guilty, but as the trial proceeded and he listened to his attorney's powerful arguments in his defence, he finally became convinced that he was innocent!

Ingersoll once successfully defended, on the ground of

* It is the Editor's firm belief that the references to God and prayer in the above letter, as well as similar references and expressions in later letters, were inspired by what one might call a kind of *spiritual courtesy* to his quite orthodox brother John.

insanity, a man charged with murder. This case produced an extraordinary and unique result. It seems that the man suffered from periodic spells of derangement, and that each time one of these spells came upon him he would promptly hunt up his lawyer and remain near him, following him about like a faithful dog, until he recovered his normal state of mind, when he would return voluntarily to his home; the explanation for his strange behaviour was that Ingersoll's personality soothed and comforted him as did no other influence in his life.

Young attorney Ingersoll won many a notable legal and forensic victory in the old Metamora Court House, the county seat of Woodford County. Like all the lawyers and judges in those middle years of the nineteenth century, Robert " rode circuit " on horseback, or drove by buggy, from county to county. The circuits at that time comprised a dozen or more counties; and few roads were laid out, none were paved, and streams were unbridged. Metamora was a village of five hundred inhabitants, in the very heart of the beautiful Illinois prairies. It boasted a picturesque, though primitive, little inn, known as the Old Travellers' Home. The charges of this hostelry were " modest . . . $2·50 per week for board and lodging, washing and mending included. . . ." It was of this place that Ingersoll spoke, when, in his description of the tapestry at Windsor Castle, he said that it reminded him of " a Metamora tablecloth the second week of court." It was in the Metamora Court House that Robert defended a man charged with murder.

It was a case of one farmer who had killed another by an accidental blow during a quarrel. The prosecutor addressed the jury, and then Ingersoll rose and pleaded, with all the moving eloquence of which he was capable, for his client's life and freedom. He painted a wonderfully pathetic picture of the accused man's wife and children waiting, in an agony of hope and fear, for his return to their loving arms. The twelve tough-skinned prairie farmers were gradually and unanimously reduced to tears. Defence attorney Ingersoll continued: " Will you send this man back to his wife, to his children, waiting for him, waiting at the door with hearts torn with   "
The foreman of the jury, extracting from his pocket a large

bandana, his eyes streaming with tears, unable to bear more, cried out, " Yes, Bob, we will! ", and then vanished forthwith beneath the enveloping handkerchief. Young Mr. Ingersoll of Peoria sat down. He did not finish his address; he did not need to do so. He had already triumphed. In a few moments the jury brought in a verdict of not guilty.

In the autumn of 1861 an incident occurred, one which was fraught with consequences of deeper and more far-reaching significance than anything that had ever happened in the life of Robert Ingersoll. Some pigs belonging to a farmer of Peoria County strayed from home and were impounded. The farmer, upon instituting a search for his pigs, found them in the local pound, whereupon he proceeded to demolish the boards about the enclosure in order to release the animals. At this crucial moment the pound-master came upon the scene, chock-full of ire and brandishing a pick-handle. Fiery words followed. Then the owner of the pigs resumed the task of destroying the fence, at which point the pound-master grew still more threatening with the pick-handle. The farmer, now crazed with rage, drew a revolver from his pocket and fired several shots at his antagonist. Then, making an opening in the enclosure, the farmer collected his pigs and returned home, leaving the prostrate pound-master to his fate. An indictment for murder followed, and Robert was retained as counsel for the defendant.

As feeling in the community was at fever heat against his client, Ingersoll asked for a change of venue; and consequently, court was transferred to Groveland, in Tazewell County, a few miles from Peoria.

While in Groveland, Young Robert Ingersoll received a cordial invitation to dine at the home of Mr. and Mrs. Benjamin Weld Parker, the leading family of the town. He had met Mr. Parker on several previous occasions. The entire Parker household, being good heretics and " infidels " on their own account, had been intensely interested in Robert ever since he had made his first anti-theological speech, entitled *Progress*, at Pekin, Illinois, about a year before. Accordingly, they were much gratified to be given an opportunity to offer their hospitality to the young Agnostic lawyer. And Ingersoll, on his side, was happy to accept their invitation, as the Parker home was famous for its epicurean as well as intellectual delights, and had long been celebrated as the meeting-place of various distinguished statesmen, lawyers, and men of affairs of Illinois and the West.

At dinner the young man from Peoria sat next to a young woman of whose name he was not aware, but whose serene and sweet beauty of countenance captivated his senses. He forgot to eat, forgot to converse, or even to think with any coherence. An ecstatic spell suffused him, like the breaking of dawn, or the blossoming of spring. As young Ingersoll took leave of his genial host he somewhat shyly inquired as to the identity of the young lady at whose right hand he had had the honour of being seated at dinner, and was informed that her name was Eva Amelia Parker [born on May 4, 1841, at Groveland, Illinois], and that she was none other than his host's own daughter!

The very next day found Robert again at the Parkers', ostensibly to pay his party call. However, what excuse he had for calling the day after that, and for many days subsequently, is not on record. As was to be expected, the friendship between the two young people fast flowered into love. In January, Robert proposed to Eva and was accepted with extraordinary promptitude, and on February 13, 1862, they were married in the Parker home in Groveland. The Rev. Samuel Worthington performed the ceremony, chiefly, it is said, because he seemed to be the only immediately available person and was a warm friend of the family, his daughter being Eva Parker's most intimate friend at the time.

The marriage of Robert Ingersoll was the second and last great turning-point in his life. The first had been his conscious conversion to Agnosticism. When Robert fell in love with Eva Parker he became as one transfigured. Up to that time he had been a young man of unusual and splendid promise, but had lacked the stability and poise which from now on was to become so essential a part of him. At this point the swift, impulsive river flowed into the placid sea—the flashing meteor surrendered to the gentle sun.

The full influence of Eva upon Robert can never be adequately estimated. However, one thing is absolutely certain, Eva was everything, possessed every attribute that Robert required and wanted in a wife; every quality needed to help build, strengthen, enrich, and ennoble his character and personality.   She was the ballast for his sail, the compass on his ship of life.

Robert Ingersoll enjoyed the incomparable blessing of a supremely happy home from the day of his marriage until the day of his death.   For thirty-eight years husband and wife were intellectual and spiritual comrades as well as romantic lovers, sharing each other's beliefs, thoughts, and emotions, consecrated to the same ideals and purposes.   Robert inscribed his first published volume of lectures to " My Wife, a Woman Without Superstition."

If Robert had enjoyed life in his state of single blessedness, he loved it immeasurably more after marriage—felt, indeed, that real life began for him only when he took " the one woman of all the world " to his heart for evermore.

Robert Ingersoll had joined for service [in the American Civil War] in the Union Army on September 16, 1861; and with Colonel Basil D. Meek had been instrumental in raising three cavalry regiments of volunteers, and in equipping and commanding one.   Robert began recruiting in October, and by the end of the month had received his commission as Colonel of the Eleventh Illinois Cavalry Regiment from Governor Richard Yates.

Nine days after he married Eva Parker he was ordered to depart for St. Louis, Missouri.   But there were compensating circumstances, as his bride was permitted to accompany him.

The young couple remained in St. Louis for several weeks while the Colonel awaited further orders.   When Robert left there, Eva went home to Groveland for a brief visit, soon afterwards rejoining her husband at Jackson, Tennessee. From that time on the brave young wife was never far from the scene of action during the whole period of Colonel Ingersoll's war service.

Benton Barracks, St. Louis
Mch 9th, 1862

My dear Brother [John],
      Yesterday with my regiment I arrived at this place and we are all now comfortably quartered at what is called the Camp of Instruction.   There are now there about ten or twelve thousand soldiers.   I presume that we will be armed paid and moved this week.   There seems to be great activity in military circles just at this time.   Everything seems to be on the alert.   Away they go—

￸regt after regt, Battery after Battery—Infantry Cavalry & Artillery all commingled, going down the great river, covered now with transports and those terrible floating forts called Gunboats. I believe that in a few days the Mississippi will again be open to the commerce of the grand West. The greatest enthusiasm prevails in the army. The splendid victories of Roanoke, Somerset, Fort Henry, and then Fort Donelson crowning all as with a glory, have made the Army of the West invincible. I was in this city—in fact in the office of Genl Halleck—when the news [came]. The whole town was instantly in commotion. Procession after procession formed & marched through the streets decorated with thousands of flags, and old grey-haired men joined with children in singing at the tops of their voices our most shining & glorious National airs. The South find that Western men are heroes. I also had the pleasure of seeing at the levee in this city a few days after ten thousand eight hundred & sixty-five rebel prisoners taken at Fort Donelson. My regt crossed the river yesterday in six transports. When we started the boys gave three cheers for glorious Illinois and our band played " Sweet Home " and as the sounds floated away over the countless waves, I thought, " How many of us will recross—how many again meet father, mother, brother, sister, child, wife. How many will return to their own firesides, how many be maimed, killed, how long left on the field of battle to suffer & to die? " And then raising my eyes to the [sic] where the great clouds floated over us I asked for the blessing & protection of my Father's God.

I suppose you know that I was married on the 13th of last month. My wife is now at Peoria, but will be here this week. She is a good sweet natured woman, one that loves me and one that I love. That is enough. Do not fail to give my love to your wife & kiss your sweet children for me. I think of you daily and my heart goes out towards you and yours. Direct to this place.

Your Bro. Robert

[The following paragraphs were scrawled across the top and sides of the letter.]

The regt & myself with them marched through the country 200 miles. I have not slept in a house for 14 nights. Tent life is comfortable but not desirable.

I send a little notice of the regt published in the Missouri Republican.

The weather is terrible here, and the rain is now falling in torrents and the thunder nearly deafens one.

St. Louis, Mch 20th, 1862

Dear Brother [John],

Yesterday your kind letter arrived, I am grateful to you for the confidence you express in me. You may rest assured that I shall do what I consider to be my *duty* towards my country & myself.

The regt is now almost armed—with the exception of about 200 revolvers—entirely so. Every moment we expect the order to move. And every man in the regt is impatient to receive it. Since the evacuation of New Madrid & the taking of "Island No. 111," they almost fear that the war will be over before our regt gets into the field. For my own part the sooner the war closes the better I shall be pleased. Whether we will be paid before we are ordered away is a question. All the officers are out or nearly out of money and unless we are paid we will go away a regt of Don Quixotes.

Yesterday I rode out several miles in the country. The fields are all green again & the trees are budding & some are already in leaf. The weather is really delightful.

I visited the graves of soldiers who died in the hospitals here. In one graveyard I counted over 1500 graves. I think the army surgeons as a general thing are quacks. I think that the soldiers are not very well cared for. Where there are so many I suppose it is impossible that they should have the best of care. The soldiers in hospital are more to be pitied than all others. Of all things I am going to avoid Hospitals. They are far more dangerous than shot & shell. I shall write you every few days. You shall know all that happens to me whether good or bad. As soon as we absolutely get in the field I shall take great pleasure in writing you explicit letters in regard to the movements of the army—the country—the people & everything that I think will interest you. Give my love to yours.

Your aff. Bro. Robert

On March 26, 1862, the Eleventh Illinois Cavalry embarked for Pittsburg Landing, near Shiloh, where General Halleck took command of the armies of the West. On April 6 and 7 Ingersoll and his men were in the thick of the battle of Shiloh, which afforded the young commander his first experience under fire, and where he "won great admiration for his soldierly conduct and courage." On April 11 he wrote to Clark giving a most graphic and stirring account of the battle:

Seat of War
April 11, 1862

Dear Bro. [Clark],

A few days ago I promised to write you a description of the Great Battle.

We advanced towards where the battle seemed raging, about one mile, and formed in line of battle on the edge of an open field.

The shot and shell were tearing through the woods at this point in the most fearful manner. Trees as large as my body were shattered in pieces and great limbs came crashing around where we were formed. . . . The Rebels were driving our forces. We had been taken by surprise. The cavalry could be of no use unless the enemy were routed, so we were ordered to keep falling back, but always to be near enough our line of battle to be of use if the enemy should retreat. And so all day long we slowly retreated and anxiously watched the greatest battle ever fought on this continent.

The enemy were at least twenty-five thousand strong, about the same number of effective men that we had, though this is necessarily guesswork. The line of battle extended six or seven miles and formed a crescent opposite the centre of which, about three miles, was Pittsburg Landing. The roar of the guns was almost deafening. No thunder that I ever heard was at all comparable to this. Hundreds of cannon and in the neighbourhood of two hundred thousand muskets were discharged simultaneously and incessantly. There was no lull, no pause. They did not even wait a moment as great storms do to gather fresh strength, but the Rebels rushed on with the fury of hell and our soldiers disputed every bloody inch with more courage and more dauntless desperate heroism than I ever before imagined possessed by men. But after all we steadily fell back and the enemy as steadily advanced for twelve dreadful bloody hours.

All day long we had heard that [Brigadier General] Buell was coming, all day our soldiers had been supported by this belief. All day long thousands of eyes had anxiously looked for the promised coming. All day long they had expected to see over the river emerging from the great woods the sacred flag. And at last it was seen.. At last Buell did come—along the river, along the Point and along the bleeding, wavering lines ran the cry, " Buell has come! " And high over the volleys of musketry, over the roar and boom of the guns, rose the cheers of a hundred thousand tired and desperate men.

Buell's forces were quickly crossed. They manned our guns and rushed to the support of our lines. And in a few moments the terrible advance of the enemy was stayed, and along the whole of the lines firing ceased, and as though by common consent, both armies lay down upon the terrible bloody field surrounded by thousands of dead and wounded and slept upon their arms.

That night the Rebels occupied our tents and we lay upon our arms. The rain fell all night, slowly and sadly, as though the heavens were weeping for the dead. All night long I stood with my blanket around me, drearily by the side of a dead tree watching the shells of the gunboat. Every fifteen minutes would come a flash like heat lightning—then the boom—then the bluish line bending over the distant wood—then the roar of the bursting, and then last of all the double echo gradually dying over the far hills. During the whole night with perfect regularity the shells were thrown, and as we afterwards ascertained, doing terrible execution. Through the night our men had not been idle. The remainder of Buell's forces had crossed, Genl. Wallace marched up the river with six thousand men and marched all night.

The enemy supposed we were thoroughly beaten so that they were ordered to destroy nothing as they were to take all themselves. (Beauregard had in fact telegraphed to Richmond a shout of victory.) They also thought that our forces were crossing the river under the protection of our gunboats. On Monday morning a little after daylight the battle was renewed, but, thank God, we commenced the attack. For two hours the battle raged almost as terribly as on Sunday and then, this was the most glorious moment of my life, the enemy commenced falling back. Our attack was sustained admirably the whole length of the lines but we gained slowly. Hundreds of wounded were continually coming to the boats. Some supported by their comrades and some more dreadfully wounded were carried in those heart-sickening cots. At four o'clock cheer after cheer went up from our forces. The enemy had not only fallen back, had not only retreated, but were fleeing in the wildest confusion. The day was ours. The great Battle for the Union had been fought. The greatest, the bloodiest in American history, and had been won by the gallant sons of the Grand West.

Your aff. bro. Robert

N.B. Do not let any of this get in the papers in any form.

N.B. Owing to the fact that the battle was fought in the woods, the cavalry could be little used. During Monday, however, out of the stragglers that had left their regts. we formed two regiments and sent them to the lines and the effect really stopped three stampedes. Our boys were good pluck with the exception of a few privates that ran at the first fire, almost, and did not get back for three days. I am satisfied with what the regt. did and the manner in which they behaved. We lost four killed, one 1st Lieut., twenty wounded and missing and had sixty-seven horses killed or wounded so as to be worthless.

I think the loss of our army on Sunday and Monday was not less than 20,000 killed and wounded. The Rebels' loss probably about the same.

Seat of War. Ten miles from Corinth
May 5th, 1862

Dear Bro. [Ebon Clark],

I wrote you yesterday and also the day before. We were expecting a battle last night. Just at dark I read what is called the " order of battle " stating the position to be occupied by the different divisions.—Nothing however happened. Last night as usual it rained constantly from twilight last evening until broad day. Our teams with our baggage did not overtake us till this morning so that we had to sleep out doors and on the ground. You never saw it rain harder than last night. I had a poncho over me and one blanket under and was as wet as wet could be all night long. But what is rather strange I take no cold, though when I first get up I feel rather rheumatic. The health of the regiment is improving, though in the two Bat. under me over one hundred are now in hospital, we had as high as one hundred and sixty a few days ago. . . .

We are now encamped at a little miserable town called Monterey. Three or four days ago this town was occupied by a large force of the enemy, but they were driven out by Pope's Division. The natives in this part of the country have suffered a great deal for the actual necessaries of life. Corn is worth one dollar and a half a bushel and salt has been sold as high as thirty dollars per sack. Coffee cannot be obtained at any price, the people say they have had none for about five months. What few farms are in this vicinity have been entirely stripped by the Southern Army before we came. A rail on a farm in this country would be a curiosity—the farmers have planted nothing but a few onions. I have seen only about an acre of corn and forty or fifty acres of wheat and oats. They say that if they planted the soldiers would destroy. I asked several of them what they expected to do. One old butter-nut cuss said he "reckoned the Lord would take care of" him. I thought he expected the Lord to turn his attention to very small things. All the people I have seen are of the very meanest description. Lower if possible than their negroes.—They look and the country looks like Southern Illinois and its people. The country is certainly not worth fighting for.—Not worth one life, and the prospect of a union with such ignorant dogs is disgusting rather than pleasing. I hope and pray that the war may be closed, and quickly.

War is horrid beyond the conception of man. It is enough to break the heart to go through the hospitals. Old grey-haired veterans with lips whitening under the kiss of Death—hundreds of mere boys with thoughts of home—of sister and brother meeting the dark angel alone, nothing but pain, misery, neglect, and death. Every day I hear some band playing a funeral march—in a little while a few muskets are discharged, and I know some officer sleeps in the earth.—To see death around you, everywhere nothing but death—to think of the ones far away expecting the dead to return —hoping for one more embrace—listening for footsteps that never will be heard on earth—for voices that have grown still and for ever —it makes one tired—tired—of war.

It is now about five o'clock, and it is again clouding up—the rain will come again all the blessed night long.—The roads are already so bad that another flood could make them no worse. From here to Pittsburg Landing, some twelve or fourteen miles, the road is perfectly blockaded with artillery—baggage mules— women—niggers and sutlers: Every wagon is in the mud to the hubs, and there is cursing and swearing enough on that road every fifteen minutes to send a world to Hell. . . .

I presume I could obtain a pass for you, but a visit here would be terribly unsatisfactory when I would have to part with you again. You would see nothing but camp after camp—cannon after cannon, sore-backed mules, ragged breeches, faded caps and manure, and get nothing but a bad cold, sleeping on the ground, and the diarrhoea by drinking the water.

Your aff. Brother, Robert

Engagements took place at Bolivar, Tennessee, on August 30, and at Davis Bridge on the Hatchie River, Tennessee, on September 25, the latter encounter resulting in heavy losses to the young Colonel's regiment. In the battle of Corinth, on October 3 and 4, Ingersoll and his command won new laurels for their notable bravery and military prowess. Shortly thereafter Colonel Ingersoll took his men into winter quarters, marching to Jackson, Tennessee, where he joined the command of Brigadier General Jeremy C. Sullivan, and on December 2, 1862, was appointed Chief of Cavalry on that General's staff.

On December 16 Ingersoll left Jackson for Lexington, Tennessee, with two hundred men of his own regiment and two guns of the 14th Indiana Battery. At the latter place he was joined by 272 men of the 2nd West Tennessee and 200 men from the 5th Ohio; so that his whole force consisted of about 700 men and two guns, of which number something less than a third were seasoned troops.

General Forrest [a famous Confederate cavalry leader] soon approached with at least 5,000 men, more than half of whom were veterans of almost every battle that had occurred in the West. On the 18th, at dawn, Ingersoll fell back, placed his two guns in the Lexington road and awaited the onslaught of Forrest's greatly superior forces. As they appeared in great numbers, Colonel Ingersoll dismounted, and, seeking to rally his fast-diminishing command, he indulged in some jocular, witty remarks. However, emitting the famous Rebel yell, the Confederate ranks bore down upon the depleted lines of blue, and since the former outnumbered the latter by the very least four to one, the conflict was necessarily of short duration. Forrest's force has been variously estimated at 5,000 and 20,000 men with eight guns; yet, despite this great disparity, Ingersoll and his command thrice repulsed the enemy, although many of the raw recruits became demoralized and refused to be rallied. The intrepid Colonel with a dozen men fought until they actually emerged beyond the enemy's rear; however, retreat or escape was impossible. Upon being surrounded on all sides the Colonel shouted, " Stop firing! I'll acknowledge your damned old Confederacy! " and surrendered his sword to Major G. V. Rambaud.

When General Forrest rode up he waved his hand in the

direction of the fleeing cavalry and asked, "Who's in command of those troops?" Ingersoll coolly replied, "I don't know." Then Forrest inquired who had been in command, to which Colonel Ingersoll imperturbably rejoined, "If you'll keep the secret, I'll tell you. I was." The sangfroid displayed by Ingersoll on this crucial occasion won the genuine admiration of Nathan Bedford Forrest; and the two men were fast friends from that moment until the General's death.

Major Rambaud escorted Colonel Ingersoll to the general store in Lexington; and for many hours thereafter Ingersoll regaled his erstwhile captors with brilliant and heart-moving talk about liberty and justice until his audience dissolved in tears, and General Forrest, who had been listening on the outskirts of the crowd, suddenly burst into its midst exclaiming, " Here, Ingersoll, stop that speech, and I'll exchange you for a government mule." And when the young Colonel of the Union forces was paroled, his horse was returned to him by the Rebel General with the remark that he (Ingersoll) was the man who had saved his life by a joke.

Jackson, Tenn.
December 27, 1862

Brig. Gen. Jer. C. Sullivan,
Commanding District of Jackson.

I have the honour to report that in accordance with orders received from you I proceeded towards the Tennessee River on the evening of the 16th instant with one section of Captain Kidd's Fourteenth Indiana Battery, under Lieutenant McGuire, and 200 of the Eleventh Illinois Cavalry, under Lieutenant-Colonel Meek.

We arrived at Lexington, 28 miles east of this place, on the morning of the 17th, where I was joined by Colonel Hawkins, of the Second West Tennessee, with 272 men. At noon we marched to Beech Creek, about 5 miles east of Lexington. Three days before, Captain O'Hara had been sent to Tennessee River with 68 men.

Halting at Beech Creek I sent Captain Burbridge forward with one company to gather information, and, if possible, find Captain O'Hara. After proceeding about 5 miles Captain Burbridge joined Captain O'Hara, who reported the enemy at least 1,000 strong a few miles in front. In a short time the enemy's pickets came in sight.

On receiving this information I ordered Captain Burbridge to fall slowly back, using every endeavour to find out the strength of the enemy. The enemy appearing in large force, Captain Burbridge fell back and crossed Beech Creek. It was now dark.

Ordering Lieutenant Fox, of the Second West Tennessee, to destroy the bridge and picket the road from the bridge, I fell back to within half a mile of Lexington. Here I was joined by 200 of the Fifth Ohio, under command of Adjutant Harrison. They were raw recruits, never having been under fire and never drilled.

At this place are two roads, the right-hand road called the old Stage road and the left the Lower road. Upon the old Stage road the bridge had been destroyed. Lieutenant Fox, as I afterwards learned, failed to destroy the Lower bridge.

About daylight of the 18th, Major Funke, of the Eleventh Illinois, with the first battalion, advanced on the old Stage road, as I expected the enemy on this road. Col. Hawkins, with two companies of his regiment, was sent on the Lower road to defend that crossing. Major Funke had advanced about 4 miles when he came on the advanced pickets of the enemy and immediately commenced skirmishing. He drove in their pickets, when he came upon a full regiment. He then fell slowly back, fighting all the way, his men in fine order, and holding at bay a much superior force for several hours.

In the mean time my two guns were placed in position commanding the crossing of the creek. Major Funke retreated across the creek, closely pursued by the enemy. As soon as the enemy's advance appeared Lieutenant McGuire opened with his guns, when they retreated hastily and in confusion. They attempted to place a gun in position, but it had no sooner made its appearance than it was dismounted by a well-directed shot from our guns. Learning that the enemy were in great force on the Lower road, although there had been little firing in that direction, I ordered the guns to fall back with all possible dispatch, leaving Major Kerr and Captain Woods, of the Eleventh, and Lieutenant Overturf, of the Fifth Ohio, to protect the crossing.

When I gained my new position on the Lower road I found that the enemy were pouring in on all directions. I then ordered the force at the crossing to join me at the guns, first, however, sending Captain Hays, of the Second West Tennessee, to hold the point. I understand he did not fire a single gun. The force on the Lower road (the Second West Tennessee) came back in confusion and on the full run, pursued by the enemy. It was impossible to stop them.

Captain Burbridge, of the Eleventh Illinois Cavalry, who was in the rear of the guns, was ordered to advance, and, as soon as our men were out of the way, charge the enemy. This order was obeyed in splendid style, Captain Burbridge driving the enemy back; they made another attack on the guns, which was again handsomely repulsed. Before I ordered the guns to be brought back I was informed that one regiment had been sent to my right and another to my left with intent to get between me and Jackson. I endeavoured to bring a company of the Second West Tennessee to the right of the guns, but found it impossible. They were not very well equipped and had never before been under fire. They were rallied three times, but did not succeed in making a stand. Had they held the right for only a minute or two the guns could have been brought off. All connected with the artillery fought splendidly; men could not have acted better. Lieutenant McGuire proved himself a brave and gallant officer. Twice the enemy were repulsed, but coming in overpowering numbers the third attempt proved successful; the guns were taken, with every man but one, and he did not leave his post until the gun was taken. From all information I have received I believe the enemy were at least 5,000 strong, with eight pieces of artillery (12-pounders), under command of Brigadier-General Forrest, Confederate Army.

A moment after the guns were taken, I was taken prisoner, and the command devolved upon Colonel Meek, Eleventh Illinois Cavalry, Colonel Hawkins being missing. The enemy took 124 prisoners. As far as I can learn, the Eleventh Illinois lost in killed First Lieutenant Slater, Second Lieutenant [Bernard] Wagner, and 7 men; in wounded, 9, and in prisoners, 51. Some of the prisoners were taken in the retreat. The Fifth Ohio lost in prisoners Adjutant Harrison and 51 men, and the Second West Tennessee about 15 taken prisoners.

The Fourteenth Indiana Battery had 2 men killed, and 2 wounded and 29 prisoners, with Lieutenant McGuire, Major Kerr, Captain Sheppard, and Lieutenant Cornell, of the Eleventh, among the prisoners.

I have the honour to remain,
Your obedient servant, Robert G. Ingersoll,
Colonel Eleventh Illinois Cavalry

Peoria, Mch 16th, 1863

Dear Bro. [John],
Today I recd your last letter. I will explain how I came to be captured. General Forrest crossed the Tenn River & menaced Jackson. We had only thirteen hundred men at Jackson. Forrest was within 30 miles. The rail road had been cut in several places so that we could not get reinforcements in less than two days. I was sent out with six hundred & fifty men & two pieces artillery only 160 of my men had ever heard a gun fired in earnest. The rest had not even been drilled. My orders were, " Engage with the enemy whatever his force may be. Keep him back if possible long enough for Jackson to be reinforced." Under such orders I started. I found the enemy after marching all night about six miles beyond Lexington a place 25 miles east of Jackson.

I skirmished with them nearly all that day. The next night I fell back five miles & we all slept that night with our eyes open. The next morning at day light we commenced again. I was defending two bridges. I sent a lot of Union Tenn. Troops to defend one bridge; I was at the other. The Tennesseans surr[endered] without making any resistance worth speaking of. I was then flanked. I had with my two pieces only about seventy men that stood fire.

We repulsed them three times, over thirty of my seventy men were killed or wounded—16 were killed on the spot. The fourth time the enemy run [sic] over us—actually took the rammers out of the men's hands. I was the last to leave the guns. Away I went over a field, and away they "went" after me. They shot at me it seemed hundreds of times. My men had no idea but that I must be killed. I came to a high fence. I made my horse jump. It was too much for him. He jumped the fence clear & fine, but when he came down on the other side his knees gave way & he fell flat—off I went, & surr. "Sesesh" bagged the aforesaid. They kept me four days—paroled me. I went back to Jackson my wife being there. Genl Sullivan comdg that place complimented me highly & said that I had saved Jackson. The re-inforcements got there. Forrest tried to take Jackson & got whipped. Now you know all about it. I am going to St. Louis to day. Have not yet been exchanged. Love to all.

Your aff. Bro., Robt

Three days after his capture, Colonel Ingersoll was sent to St. Louis, where he was placed in charge of a camp of other paroled prisoners. There, after many weary months of waiting to be exchanged and returned to active duty, he resigned his commission, and was honourably discharged on June 30, 1863.

Robert Ingersoll was of too compassionate and imaginative a nature to make a perfect soldier; and he frankly confessed that he "never saw his men in the fighting line without thinking of the widows and orphans they would make, and half hoping they would miss their aim." The chaplain of the 11th Illinois Cavalry Regiment said of Ingersoll: "During the time he was with us he was almost constantly by the sick and wounded, and was as kind to them as though they had been his own children. At the battle of Shiloh he gave his blankets to the wounded, then slept upon the ground uncovered, with the chilling rain pouring upon him the whole dreary night." With every drop of his blood Ingersoll hated war and all its monstrous and unmentionable cruelty.

Robert and Eva Ingersoll's first daughter was born on September 22, 1863, at Groveland, Illinois. She was named Eva Robert Ingersoll in honour of both parents. The fulfilment and flower of perfect love, it was small wonder that this child developed into a woman of ideal beauty, tenderness, and goodness.

Maud Robert, the second child, was born in Peoria, Illinois, on October 4, 1864. As her advent into this world was made on Election night, some of her father's politically minded friends proposed that she be called Molly Stark, for Stark County, Ill., where Ingersoll had been campaigning that very day. However, Maud Robert she became; as well as the third member of the " Holy Trinity " that Robert Ingersoll worshipped in the persons of his wife and two daughters. Maud, too, blossomed into a womanhood of surpassing loveliness and intellectual brilliancy; and was the almost constant companion of her father on his numerous lecture tours and travels for many happy, if mightily strenuous, years.

The large and lucrative law practice of Robert Ingersoll was interrupted by the outbreak of the Civil War; but upon his discharge from the service he immediately resumed active practice. He early became attorney for the Peoria and Rock Island Railroad, and at various times between 1874 and 1878 acted as legal adviser to a number of other railways. In 1865 he was admitted to practice in both the United States District and Circuit Courts, and in the course of his legal career he argued numerous cases before the courts of many States, as well as before the United States Supreme Court.

Peoria, Mch 17th, 1865

My dear Bro. [John],

This being Saint Patrick's day in the morning, and having a few leisure moments, I take my pen in hand etc. We are all well, never in better health any of us in the world. The little children are perfectly well, growing with all their might, and enjoying themselves " beyond " all telling.

I have been very busy for the last few months and travelling all over the Country. I get nearly sick of this kind of life and sometimes wish that I was living in some quiet neighbourhood on a small piece of land, with a horse & cow—a weekly newspaper, and " Weems " life of Washington.

If there is any life in the world that is absolutely devoid of everything like real happiness, I believe it is what is called a political life. A low dirty scramble, through misrepresentation slander falsehood and filth, and success brings nothing but annoyance & fear of defeat next time, and yet if one gets started in that kind of business it is very hard to get out. I find myself planning & scheming all the time, thinking what I will try for, and calculating the chances. I was at Springfield several weeks during the sitting of the Legislature & I suppose a more scaly set of one-horse thieves & low lived political tricksters never assembled on the earth. The thing called law I am daily losing respect for, and I think that Congress is but little better than our own legislature.

I have been reading this winter *Buckles History of Civilization in England* and I think it is the greatest work I ever read. He was a man of vast learning, and had the clearest and most logical head in the world. I think you would be delighted with him. Frank Gilbert our cousin you know is preaching here, and Simeon Gilbert I believe is going to settle at Quincy in this state. I mean young Simeon. He is also a preacher. There seems to be a theological streak running through their family and they are full of argument on whether this is a state of probation, and as to the measuring of a few passages in Revelations etc etc. Questions I think that they will fail to entirely settle. Hearing them talk takes me back to the times when ministers used to stop at our house & discuss with father on infant baptism and other equally important subjects. Why don't you write me once in a while? I believe you have not written me a word for months; but I suppose you are busy . Enclosed find ten dollars, I wish I had a thousand for you.

Your aff. Bro., Robert

Robert Ingersoll's reputation as a lawyer grew steadily and rapidly, to such a degree that, as one biographer has said, he " came to enjoy no leisure whatsoever, but so wide and far did he travel in his state that at least one of every three inhabitants came to look upon him as a personal friend and benefactor." He set himself what would have been a killing pace to a man of more ordinary physical and mental stamina.

His fame as a lawyer throughout Illinois and the West was by this time widespread and well-established, but the so-called Munn trial in 1876 was the first of his law cases to bring him nation-wide publicity. This case concerned a revenue officer charged with illicit dealings in whisky. Ingersoll was the attorney for the defendant, and succeeded in securing his client's acquittal. The Colonel's " Address to the Jury " is chiefly notable for its peroration, which constitutes a flamingly eloquent arraignment of alcohol [see page 275].

In the autumn of 1877 or early in 1878 Robert Ingersoll and his family moved to Washington, D.C. He and Ebon Clark resumed their active legal partnership in the national capital where Clark had been living since entering Congress in 1864. This partnership continued until Clark's untimely death in 1879.

The celebrated " Star Route " trials were the outstanding events in the legal career of Robert Ingersoll during his residence in Washington. The first trial began in the early part of 1882, and the second and last concluded in the middle of the following year. A former U.S. Senator, Stephen W. Dorsey, his brother, John W. Dorsey, an Assistant Postmaster-General, Joseph J. Brady, and four others were indicted for attempting to defraud the U.S. Government through certain contracts for transporting the mails over what were known as Star Routes. It was contended by the prosecution that the Government had been defrauded to the extent of nearly five million dollars. Ingersoll's address to the jury on the final day of the first trial took twelve solid hours. On this occasion the jury disagreed regarding his clients. The result of the second trial was acquittal for all the defendants, a verdict which represented a sensational personal triumph for Robert Ingersoll.

In an interview, many years later, the Colonel gives us a clear impression of the general situation with which he was confronted. The reporter asked him what he considered " the most unique case in which he was ever engaged," and the lawyer replied: " The Star Route trial. Every paper in the country, but one, was against the defence, and that one was a little sheet owned by one of the defendants. I received a note from a man living in a little town in Ohio criticizing me for defending the accused. In reply I wrote that I supposed he was a sensible man and that he, of course, knew what he was talking about when he said the accused were guilty; that the Government needed just such men as he, and that he should come to the trial at once and testify. The man wrote back: ' Dear Colonel: I am a —— fool.' "

Dr. Kittredge, Ingersoll's biographer, declares that: " It is no exaggeration to state that this verdict was the greatest personal victory ever won by an American lawyer. It was so regarded at the time. . . . Even the dignity of the Court was impotent to prevent an ovation to the great lawyer. And shortly afterwards, as he rode homeward with his family, through Pennsylvania Avenue, he was so frequently greeted by the people that he was finally obliged to sit with head uncovered, waving his hands to either side, much after the manner of a conquering hero. Telegrams of congratulation came from all parts of the country. Callers, in an almost unbroken procession, thronged his house during the day and concluded their

35

manifestations of gladness with a serenade in the evening when Ingersoll responded in a short speech."

Two years after Robert Ingersoll moved to New York City in the autumn of 1885, he was counsel for the Merchants' and Bankers' Telegraph Company against the Western Union Telegraph Company, and won a verdict for the former corporation to the amount of $1,500,000.

The famous Reynolds' " blasphemy " trial also occurred during the same year. This case involved Charles B. Reynolds, a Freethought lecturer, who was indicted for " blasphemy " by a grand jury in Morristown, New Jersey, after having been set upon some time previously by a fanatical mob in Boonton. Ingersoll took up the cudgels for Mr. Reynolds in one of the most stirring arguments on behalf of intellectual freedom and the rights of the individual conscience to which he ever gave utterance.

Pointing out the unprovability, even the impossibility, of theological blasphemy, he proceeded to furnish characteristically Ingersollian definitions of blasphemy: " To live on the unpaid labour of other men. . . . To enslave your fellow-man, to put chains upon his body. . . . To strike the weak and unprotected in order that you may gain the applause of the ignorant and superstitious mob. . . . To enslave the minds of men, to put manacles upon the brain, padlocks upon the lips. . . . To persecute the intelligent few, at the command of the ignorant many. . . . To pollute the souls of children with the dogma of eternal pain. . . . To violate your conscience. . . ." these things represented real blasphemy. Ingersoll argued that the statute against blasphemy was contrary to the constitution of New Jersey, which declares that, " The liberty of speech shall not be abridged." However, he further contended that, even granting that the statute is constitutional, it would still be necessary to prove that the defendant " made the statements attributed to him knowing that they were not true "; since the statute reads, " Whoever shall *wilfully* speak against . . ." Ingersoll insisted that if the jury believed that " he [Reynolds] was honest in what he said, then this statute does not touch him "; for, " even under this statute, a man may give his honest opinion. Certainly, there is no law that charges a man with ' wilfully ' being honest, ' wilfully ' telling his real opinion. . . "

The lawyer pleaded with the men of the jury to acquit Mr. Reynolds, for the sake of their state, their country, and " the great cause of Liberty."

However, since, in the eyes of the jury, the law was the law, a verdict of guilt was rendered; and a minimum fine imposed upon Reynolds, of twenty-five dollars, with costs, which was paid by the Colonel, whose services had also been given free of charge.

During Robert Ingersoll's legal career, covering a period of forty-four years, he was engaged in hundreds of cases, some of which involved large sums of money. From the middle 'eighties until well into the 'nineties, his yearly income often amounted to over $100,000. However, he was not primarily interested in winning a case for the fee which went with it, nor yet for the satisfaction to be found in victory. He was chiefly concerned with serving the ends of impartial justice; and, in so far as the law represented justice, and the preservation and promotion of liberty and equality, he accorded it his homage and respect. The fundamental principles of law and equity fascinated his mind; but for the befogging technicalities, sophistries, and perversions of law he felt nothing but impatience and disgust. His quick and clear perception of legal problems, no matter how intricate or involved, seemed little less than miraculous. " In the trial of a case before a jury," I. Newton Baker has written in his *Intimate View of Robert G. Ingersoll*, " Ingersoll was probably at his best in the examination of a witness. He was so patient, though persistent, in getting at the facts, so considerate, and so fair, that he often compelled the truth from hesitating and unwilling lips. . He did not abuse his privilege as a lawyer and treat a witness on the stand as if he were a criminal in the dock. . . Before a jury he was persuasive and convincing, not only by the power of his eloquence, but by the force of his cogent reasoning, and the skilful marshalling of evidence to sustain his case. He appealed to the reason and conscience of his jury, not to their prejudices or passions. He was truly entitled to the reputation he bore as one of the greatest jury lawyers of his time. Before court and counsel he was always the courteous gentleman. . He was always sure of his subject and object. . The fitting retort was always at the door of his lips waiting to leap into utterance.

" One instance will serve for many: In a Toledo, Ohio, terminal suit counsel for the other side interrupted Mr. Ingersoll in the midst of his argument by asking, ' Colonel, did you ever read the story of Ananias and Sapphira? ' ' Yes,' came the reply, quick as a flash, ' and while you were speaking this afternoon, I looked to see you drop dead every minute! ' The hit was so palpable, so perfect, that even the dignified Court [Judge] of a Federal District joined in the general convulsion and tilted so violently in his chair that he came perilously near toppling over. . . .

" He, Ingersoll, was in truth, with all his other claims to greatness, one of the really great lawyers of his day."

Law and politics, from the beginning of their careers, had been equal and inseparable interests of the two Ingersoll brothers. In 1860 Robert was a candidate for political office, running as a Douglas Democrat against Judge William B. Kellogg, the Republican nominee, from the Fourth Congressional District of Illinois. Judge Kellogg was Ingersoll's senior by many years; a veteran campaigner and politician; having been one of the organizers of the Republican party, and having already served two terms in Congress. Ingersoll was a young man of twenty-seven, had never been a candidate for office, and was without experience in the arena of debate. Yet, despite these many serious disadvantages, the young Peoria attorney undoubtedly emerged the intellectual and spiritual victor of the contest, although he lost the election to Judge Kellogg, who was swept into office on the tidal wave of Lincoln's popularity.

Colonel Clark E. Carr, a close friend and political colleague of Ingersoll in the early days, has glowingly described his impressions of the Ingersollian oratory and personality: " In the campaign [1860], there first appeared upon the hustings and before public assemblages in Illinois a man who became known as the greatest of American orators. . . . This wonderful man was none other than Robert G. Ingersoll, then the Democratic candidate for Congress in our district. Douglas man although he was, no one was so eloquent in denunciation of human slavery and of those who were plotting against the Union. . . . No man can estimate the power and influence of Ingersoll in arousing the American people to a sense of their solemn responsibilities when the war came upon them, or in awakening them to a sense of justice and a proper appreciation of the rights of men. One must have heard him before a great audience in the open air, as we in Illinois so often did, to appreciate his great power. Every emotion of his soul, every pulsation of his heart, was for his country and for liberty; and no other man has ever been able in so high a degree to inspire others with the sentiments that animated him."

The exact date when Ingersoll ceased to call himself a War Democrat and became a Republican is not definitely known; but that he joined the latter party not later than 1863 is certain. He had always hated slavery, as well as injustice in all its forms. However, for some reason which has never been adequately explained, he had more faith and confidence in Stephen A. Douglas than in Abraham Lincoln until the outbreak of the Civil War.

But by 1864 Colonel Ingersoll was working with tireless and titanic energy for the election of Lincoln and the entire Republican ticket, speaking in most of the towns, large and small, throughout Central Illinois, against a background of unbounded excitement and electric enthusiasm.

Although Governor Richard J. Oglesby appointed Ingersoll Attorney-General of Illinois—this was the only political position he ever held—for the two-year period from 1867 to 1869, before his term had ended the Colonel became a candidate for the gubernatorial nomination of his State, on the Republican ticket. Ingersoll was the first choice of three-fourths of the delegates to the Republican State Convention of May 6, 1868. However, as his heterodox religious opinions had already become well known throughout Illinois, and as the John M. Palmer backers were capitalizing this fact to the utmost, it was felt needful to secure from Ingersoll some pledge to remain silent concerning the subject of religion. But when the matter was put before him he flatly refused to make any pledge or promise whatever. The consequences of this uncompromising moral position, together with General Palmer's breach of his own pledge not to accept the nomination, were the failure of Colonel Ingersoll to win the coveted political prize, and the victory of General Palmer.

The defeat marked the abrupt and dramatic termination of

Ingersoll's personal political career. In that Republican Convention of 1868 he made his final choice, between political ambition and intellectual integrity. Never, throughout the subsequent course of his life, did he swerve from the position there taken. From that time onward, he gave undivided allegiance to his cherished Republican principles and to his adored country, absolutely without thought of self, and without hope or expectation of personal recognition or reward.

The Colonel strove as valiantly for the success of Grant in 1868 as if he had not been disappointed in his own ambitions that very year; and it need scarcely be added that he worked for his brother Clark's re-election to Congress with all the energy and ability at his command, and rejoiced extravagantly at his ultimate triumph at the polls. Two years later, he once again supported Clark's candidacy, doing everything within his power on the latter's behalf, but this election resulted in the defeat of Clark and in his permanent retirement from public office.

The Colonel took no active part in politics during the ensuing six years until 1876, when he nominated James G. Blaine at the National Republican Convention at Cincinnati.

Notwithstanding the fact that Rutherford B. Hayes won the nomination for President, Ingersoll took a leading part in the campaign which followed, doing as much as any other individual to accomplish a Republican victory.

It was shortly after the inauguration of President Hayes that many of Ingersoll's friends, including the entire Congressional representation from Illinois, called upon Hayes with the request that he appoint the Colonel American minister to Germany. However, without allowing the Chief Executive sufficient time to make a decision in the matter, Ingersoll went to see William M. Evarts, the Secretary of State, and declared that under no circumstances would he consider accepting this proposed appointment, adding that there was no office in the gift of the administration that he would accept.

Ingersoll was a zealous supporter of James A. Garfield in the campaign of 1880. The two men had been good friends for many years. "The marvellously eloquent and powerful speeches made by Ingersoll . . . will long be remembered and admired. He almost persuaded the country that Garfield was a god incarnate, and the enthusiastic admiration which he evoked for the hero of his glowing oratory contributed mightily to Garfield's election," says a contemporary newspaper whose comment is typical of most of the Republican press of the day.

Washington, D. C.
July 5, '81

Dear Brother [John],

Of course nothing is thought or talked of here but the condition of the President [Garfield].

I was with the President on Friday evening July 1st from eight to ten and had an engagement to meet him the next morning. I was not up in time and met him going to the depot as I drove to the White House. I went home and in fifteen minutes or less a man came running to my house & said " The President has been shot." I went immediately to the depot. The President had been carried upstairs. I was admitted to the room, and found him stretched on the floor, surrounded by doctors. He recognized me and I had considerable talk with him. I thought he would certainly die. He had the look of death and I had no hope and never have had until this morning. I suppose now that there is a chance. Of course you have read all about the affair in the papers. I get news from the White House every few minutes. We have been so stretched and strained on the rack of hope and fear that we are all worn out. Otherwise we are all in the best of health. All the stuff in the papers about Conspiracy is stuff and nothing else. All the charges .that Conkling and Arthur are responsible are too absurd to be talked about.

Guiteau, the murderer, wanted an office. The President was troubled by him—ordered him to keep away—told the servants not to admit him. Guiteau became malicious and shot the President. That is all there is about it. The crime has no political significance. It is humiliating to read the follics of the press & pulpit on this matter. Love to all.

Robert

The Colonel took no part in the Presidential contest between Cleveland and Harrison in 1892, although his preference was for the latter. But in the McKinley–Bryan campaign, four years later, he was more active than he had been since the election of 1876, since he liked McKinley the man and admired McKinley the statesman, whereas of Bryan he said that " his mind was full of vagaries, his brain an insane asylum without a keeper."

From about 1890 Ingersoll spent the leisure portions of his summers at " Walston," the beautiful country estate of his son-in-law, Walston Hill Brown. During the last years he continued to lecture all over the country, and always returned to his headquarters at " Walston," for rest and relaxation with his family.

The first warning that he must spare his failing strength came in November, 1896, when he suffered a stroke during a lecture at Janesville, Wisconsin. He concluded the address, however, and even continued to speak for several days. At the urgent request of his family he consulted Dr. Frank Billings, who advised him to take a complete rest for at least two months. It was not until early the following year that he resumed his speaking engagements, which he continued in lightened form for more than two years.

Colonel Ingersoll had been told by his physicians that he had angina pectoris and that he might die at any moment. He exacted from them the promise that they would tell no one, so that his family might not learn the tragic secret.

On the night of July 20, 1899, Ingersoll suffered an attack of acute indigestion, although he got up for breakfast the following morning, and sat on " Walston's " wide verandah, talking and reading with the family, as usual. About half past ten he decided to lie down and rest for a while. Later, he said, he would come back and play pool with Walston.

Mrs. Ingersoll went upstairs with her husband to their bedroom and stayed by his side as he slept. About a quarter past twelve he arose and sat down in his favourite chair by the window to put on his shoes. Miss Sue Sharkey, a beloved member of the household, came into the room, followed by Mrs. Clinton P. Farrell, the Colonel's sister-in-law. Mrs. Ingersoll said, " Do not dress, Papa, until after luncheon—I will eat upstairs with you." He answered, " Oh, no, I do not want to trouble you." Mrs. Farrell then exclaimed, " How absurd, after the hundreds of times you have eaten upstairs with her ! " Ingersoll looked up laughingly at Mrs. Farrell as she turned to go out of the room. Then Mrs. Ingersoll said, " Why, Papa, your tongue is coated—I must give you some medicine." He looked at her with a smile on his face, and said, " I am better now," and then closed his eyes in the peaceful sleep of death.

On Tuesday, July 25, at four o'clock, the funeral services were held in the room in which he died. They were private, and of the most extreme simplicity. In the presence of the family and thirty or forty friends, Professor John Clark Ridpath read *The Declaration of the Free* ; *My Religion, or The Creed of Science* was read by Major Orlando Jay Smith; and *A Tribute to Ebon C. Ingersoll*, by Dr. John Lovejoy Elliott. On Thursday, July 27, cremation took place, and the family then returned to " Walston " with an urn containing the ashes of the adored husband and father. The urn, resting on a base of porphyry, is of handsome bronze, ovoid in form, and adorned with branches of cypress and laurel done in delicate bas-relief. The inscription reads:

> *L'Urne garde*
> *La Poussière,*
> *Le Cœur*
> *Le Souvenir*

(" The urn holds the dust, the heart the memory ") and on the back: " Robert G. Ingersoll."

The ashes of Colonel and Mrs. Ingersoll now rest under a massive granite monument in Arlington Cemetery, in the National Capital of the U.S.A.

The death of Robert Ingersoll caused deep and widespread sorrow and regret throughout America and in all parts of the world. Many persons who had never known him except by reputation felt a profound sense of personal loss and grief; and the effect upon his family and friends was overwhelming. Telegrams, cablegrams, letters, and telephone calls poured in upon Mrs. Ingersoll and her daughters like an avalanche, from people in all walks of life, expressing their affection and admiration for the Colonel. Newspapers all over the U.S.A., as well as in Canada, Mexico, Europe, Asia, and Africa, published long accounts of his death, biographical sketches, anecdotes, editorials, and excerpts from his writings. Innumerable sermons were preached about him, the majority of which voiced admiration for the man, if not for his views on religion. The popular and scholarly magazines and journals vied with each other in printing glowing eulogies, both in verse and prose. Memorial meetings were held in many places in the country; also in Canada and England. Numbers of societies were organized in his name, and plans for the erection of monuments to him were initiated in several cities.

The citizens of Peoria started a subscription for this purpose two days after Ingersoll's death. In their invitation to the public to subscribe to the monument fund the sponsors included these lines: " The late Colonel Robert G. Ingersoll was a conspicuous figure in the history of the present century. Of heroic character, indomitable perseverance, and fearlessness he was at once the gentlest, most affectionable, lovable, and the strongest character of his day." The Peoria Monument Association was formed at the great Memorial meeting held in the Tabernacle in that city on July 23, 1899. It was addressed by many of his oldest and dearest friends, who stated in a touching resolution that ". . . he was greater than a saint, greater that a mere hero—he was a thoroughly honest man. . . ."

On July 26 the surviving members of Ingersoll's own Eleventh Illinois Cavalry Regiment poured out their love for their former Commander in the following resolution which I quote in part:

Robert G. Ingersoll is dead. The brave soldier, the unswerving patriot, the true friend . . . sleeps his last sleep. . . .

No words of ours, though written in flame, no chaplet that our hands can weave . . . will add anything to his fame. . . .

We know him as the general public did not. We knew him in the military camp where he reigned an uncrowned king, ruling with that bright sceptre of human benevolence which death alone could wrest from his hand. We had the honour to obey, as we could, his calm but resolute commands at Shiloh, at Corinth, and at Lexington, knowing as we did, that he would never command a man to go where he would not dare to lead the way.

Hence we recognize only a small circle around his recent heaven and home who could know more of his manliness and worth than we do. And to such we say: Look up, if you can, through natural tears; try to be as brave as he was, and try to remember—in the midst of a grief which his greatest wish for life would have been to help you to bear—that he had no fear of death nor of anything beyond.

And we, the survivors, comrades of the Eleventh Illinois Cavalry, extend to his widow and children our condolence in this hour of their sad bereavement.

One of the most impressive of all the memorial meetings took place in Studebaker Hall, Chicago, on August 6. It was presided over by Mr. Thomas Cratty of Peoria, and among a long list of speakers was Clarence Darrow, who concluded his tribute thus: " Robert G. Ingersoll was a great man, a wonderful intellect, a great soul of matchless courage, one of the great men of the earth—and yet we have no right to bow down to his memory simply because he was great. . . . Great orators, great lawyers, often use their gifts for a most unholy cause. . . We meet to pay a tribute of love and respect to Robert G. Ingersoll   because he used his matchless powers for the good of man."

On the same date as the Chicago meeting, Governor Charles S. Thomas, of Colorado, addressed a meeting of thousands of Denver citizens. The Governor declared that "the character of Ingersoll was as nearly perfect as it is possible for the character of mortal man to be. . . . He had the earnestness of a Luther, the genius for humour and wit and satire of a Voltaire, a wide amplitude of imagination, and a greatness of heart and brain that placed him upon an equal footing with the greatest thinkers of antiquity. . . . He stands at the close of his career, the first great reformer of the age."

Ernst Haeckel, whom Ingersoll called "the Darwin of Germany," reciprocated by terming Ingersoll "the valorous champion in the struggle of truth." Björnson, who translated the Colonel's works into Norwegian, wrote: "I envy the land that brings forth such glorious fruit as an Ingersoll." Swinburne declared that up to July 21, 1899, he had just one reason for wishing to visit America, and that was "to make the acquaintance of Robert Ingersoll."

Almost all of the appraisals of Ingersoll, at the time of his death, had one peculiarly striking and significant aspect in common. That was the evidence they offered of the totally changed attitude on the part of the vast majority of Americans towards the man and his life work. From a feared and execrated exponent of Agnosticism and general godlessness Ingersoll had come at last to be universally respected and beloved for his integrity, purity, and nobility of character and purpose. This man who had fought all his life for the emancipation of men from the trammels of tradition had, at his death, become a rare sort of tradition himself; a symbol of intellectual freedom, independence, honesty, and courage.

The tradition he embodied represents the current trend of enlightened thought, as relevant now as in his day. In our modern democratic world, as in Ingersoll's vision, liberty is exalted above all other spiritual values. Ingersoll's quality of greatness was timeless, and so remains ever timely and contemporary. He was the supreme evangel of the free mind, but was perhaps no less pre-eminent in his passionate and noble conception and practice of social justice and equality for men and women of all races, creeds, colours, and classes; in his theories of rational, secular education of the head, heart, and hand; in his implacable hatred of prejudice, superstition, tyranny, and cruelty in every form.

However, he shared the uncritical faith of the nineteenth century in science as the essential basis for human well-being and progress. In his identification of science with truth he saw no conflict between science and ethics. He never dreamed that this marvellous new instrument of knowledge would be divorced from moral responsibility, to threaten man with destruction at his own hands. He recognized only the conflict between science and orthodox religion; and he was confident that science would triumph, and eliminate the last barrier to the achievement of the good and just society.

Robert G. Ingersoll is significant for us today because he was incurably and incredibly innocent and pure in heart, and as idealistic as if he had just emerged out of the dawn of the world; and because idealism and realism must become practically synonymous in terms of human behaviour; because he preserved the spirit of youth to the end of his life—the spirit of eager, honest, and fearless inquiry, and the unshakable conviction that man should pursue this inquiry in the light of his reason, wherever it might lead him; and because, above all, his mind and heart were focused at the centre of moral truth.

PART TWO

Ingersoll—the Orator

ROBERT INGERSOLL BECAME an orator and lecturer for the purpose of spreading his own gospel of Humanism, the gospel of liberty, justice, and happiness for man, woman, and child, the gospel of the dignity and sanctity of the individual and of the right of each individual to think for himself and to express his honest thought. He regarded himself as the spokesman of all who dared not speak for themselves.

For more than thirty years he put his incomparable oratorical genius at the service of his fellowmen, in the fields of law, politics, religion, and intellectual culture. He sought "to shed light in the dark places, which so sadly needed light," as Luther Burbank said of him; sought to awaken in men a love of truth and beauty, a horror of falsehood and superstition; and a belief in themselves as the makers of their own destinies.

He wanted to make his beloved country "intellectually free." He felt that he might as well try to do this as to wait for someone else to perform what was, in any case, an absolutely essential, indispensable mission. He discovered that though America was called free, it was actually far from free. It was proudly boasted that in the U.S.A. Church and State were divorced, and yet in fact the Church was supported by the State in many respects, and that in many places persons who did not believe in the orthodox religious creeds were not permitted to testify in court or to hold public office. "This is the way I came to make speeches," he said, with characteristic forthrightness and simplicity. "It was an action in favour of liberty. I have said things because I wanted to say them, and because I thought they ought to be said."

Few persons will now deny that Ingersoll succeeded to an amazing degree in accomplishing his self-appointed mission. For he became the supreme liberating force of his time in

47

America, as well as one of the greatest intellectually emancipating influences of all time. It is a noteworthy fact that Ingersoll actually grew more, rather than less, radical with the passing years.

The way Ingersoll said what he had to say was unforgettable and unsurpassed, because at heart he was a prophet, selflessly consecrated to his conception of truth; and accordingly, his words were the spontaneous, natural utterance of his thoughts, and, at the same time, the products of refined and subtle art.

" Robert G. Ingersoll did for the English language what Isocrates did for the Greek: he was the first among English-speaking orators to perfect the prose rhythms of our native speech. His ear for musical ' time ' is so nearly that of a poet, that many of his most eloquent passages have only to be divided and capitalized properly to become blank verse, governed by recurrent vowels, as are the hexameters of Homer, the pentameters of the Greek tragedians, or the odes of Pindar.

" He was typically American in his entire freedom from any approach to social aloofness. He was popular as an orator, primarily, because he felt the unity of his own mind . . . with the average mind of the average American community. His greatest strength lies   . in a compelling power of musical expression, voicing his own emotions, and appealing to the related emotions of his hearers through their sense of the harmonies of language. In the ability to do this, he has not been equalled by any other American orator." Thus wrote David J. Brewer, an Associate Justice of the U.S. Supreme Court, and a distinguished author.

Ingersoll maintained that oratory, in the deepest and broadest sense, is the same the world over; and this was his definition and ideal of the orator, a definition which perfectly describes himself: " The man who thinks on his feet, who has the pose of passion, the face that thought illumines, a voice in harmony with the ideals expressed, who has logic like a column, and poetry like a vine, who transfigures the common, dresses the ideals of the people in purple and fine linen, who has the art of finding the best and noblest in his hearers, and who in a thousand ways creates the climate in which the best grows and flourishes and bursts into blossom—that man is an orator. . . ."

New York
Nov. 23rd, 1886

L. H. Dyce, Esq.,
Portland, Me.

My dear Sir:

Oratory is something that cannot be taught. Neither can it be learned. If one is not naturally an orator, he can never become so artificially. You might as well be taught to be a poet. A great many things an orator can be taught *not* to do; but what he really does that stamps him as an orator, must be perfectly natural. He must become the instrumentality of a thought, or of a passion, and to that degree that he forgets himself. His motions, his attitudes, his gestures, must all come from the inside—that is to say, be an outward manifestation of an inward thought—the effect of a certain passion or feeling upon the body. Whenever he begins to learn from the outside, so that he thinks of the motion he makes, the naturalness is gone, and the orator does not exist—you have then only an elocutionist; and there is as much difference between an elocutionist and an orator, as there is between a spring and a pump.

Yours very truly, R. G. Ingersoll

Mrs. H. H. Mills,   New York, Feby 18th, 1887
Washington, D. C.

My dear Mrs. Mills:

Gesture should be the natural effect of the effort to express a thought. Certain ideas, certain feelings, naturally give to the body a certain poise—to the arms a certain position—and where the body has not been prejudiced by habits, I believe it will respond naturally and spontaneously to the thought.

Gesture should have its origin inside. Of course peculiarities can be corrected—and awkward movement can be avoided by study and by practice—but true gestures, appropriate and graceful, must be unconsciously made. Certain thoughts naturally affect the muscles, which relax or shorten. Certain thoughts affect the blood—the stream is hastened or delayed. Gesture should be in perfect harmony with these results.

Hoping that you will never have to make any gestures in self-defence,

Very truly yours, R. G. Ingersoll

Ingersoll "had that indefinable something called presence," writes Herman E. Kittredge, his earliest biographer. "Tall, commanding, erect—simple in speech, graceful in compliment, titanic in denunciation, rich in illustration, prodigal of comparison and metaphor—and his sentences, measured and rhythmical, fell like music on the enraptured throng."

49

Heredity played little part in the making of Ingersoll the orator, with the single important exception of the inheritance from his father, Rev. John Ingersoll, who achieved a great reputation as an orator. From his father, Robert received many intellectual and spiritual gifts: inviolable integrity of character; profound sincerity; passionate dedication to principle; and complete courage of conviction, coupled with the rare ability to clothe conviction in appropriate and beautiful garments of expression.

Robert Ingersoll doubtless learned much, garnered many fruitful suggestions and inspirations from the great orators, poets, and creative thinkers of all lands and times. He must have revelled in the magic rhythms of Isocrates whose sense of verbal music was almost as faultless as his own. Demosthenes was one of his greatest oratorical "creditors"; and Cicero he placed "at the head of all the ancients." Pericles, in his view, was one of the world's ablest orators. He regarded Danton as an authentic, if fanatical, oratorical genius. The lords of speech who aroused his deepest enthusiasm were the orators of ancient Greece and Rome to whom I have already alluded, together with a few outstanding Englishmen and Americans. He knew of no English orator equal to Webster or Thomas Corwin or Henry Ward Beecher. However, he thought that perhaps the "finest paragraph ever uttered in Great Britain" was delivered by John Philpot Curran, the great Irish patriot and statesman, in his oration entitled "England and English Liberties." He placed Thomas Corwin "at the top of the natural orators .

he was an actor. His body talked; his meaning was in his eyes and lips, as well as in his words." Governor Oliver P. Morton of Indiana "had the greatest power of statement of any man" that Ingersoll ever heard. "All the argument was in his statement; the facts were perfectly grouped; the conclusion was a necessity." He was a great admirer of Theodore Parker as a thinker and lecturer. In Ingersoll's opinion, Lincoln failed to measure up to the highest standards of oratory because "his presence was not good; his voice was poor, his gestures awkward." However, the Colonel appreciated fully the lucidity and logic of his thought, and the marvellous beauty of his language; and considered the Gettysburg Address an almost perfect speech, marred only by too many repetitions of the word "here."

All these and many more influenced, and contributed to the making of Ingersoll the orator. However, his oratorical genius was inborn, and could no more be separated from the man as a whole than trees can be separated from their trunks, or autumn from its harvests. . It was the natural and inevitable out-flowering of his thought and feeling—accordant and integrated with his entire organism—his, physical, intellectual, and spiritual being.

Ingersoll often delivered a lecture several times before writing it down. At other times he would dictate his speech and then deliver it from manuscript; or jot down brief outlines of his subjects, under headings and sub-headings; and not infrequently he spoke without any notes whatever. The method he employed at any particular time was determined by how he happened to feel at the time. He believed that not only methods of work, but " attitude, gesture, voice, emphasis, should all be in accord with and spring from feeling, from the inside."

From the beginning, Ingersoll's audiences were large and enthusiastic, and comprised a very high proportion of intelligent and cultivated persons; and with the passage of time their size and responsiveness increased, and their always superior quality improved. More women attended his lectures than turned out to hear any other speaker, and all lecture-managers agreed that Ingersoll possessed a far greater drawing-power than any other speaker of his day.

An interesting illustration of Ingersoll's attitude in fixing a price for his lectures is furnished by the following quotation from *Reminiscences of Robert G. Ingersoll*, collected by Edward Garstin Smith in an Appendix to his biography of Ingersoll. This excerpt from Mr. Smith's book is entitled " Ingersoll's Sense of Justice."

Dr. George Harvey, of Claremont, N. H., tells me an interesting episode in connection with Colonel Ingersoll's lecture at that town a number of years ago. Several bright young men who had heard Colonel Ingersoll speak, had so interested others who had not heard him that they concluded they would try and get him to come there to deliver a lecture.

Correspondence, explaining the situation and dwelling on the fact that it was a decidedly puritanical community, solicited as low a figure as the Colonel would accept for a lecture. His answer came, $300 and expenses. It was accepted. The boys billed the whole surrounding country and did all they could to "whoop her up."

One characteristic letter they received illustrates the gloomy atmosphere to which these boys invited the great Agnostic. They received a letter from the Congressman of that district saying, " I gladly enclose twenty-five dollars, but will not be able to be present at the lecture. If I were in Boston I would buy a front seat; but here at home I would not dare to, because it would defeat me at the polls."

The attendance at the lecture was very slender. Next morning the boys called on the Colonel at his hotel and made a settlement, handing him $300, as agreed. The Colonel took the money, put it in his pocket, and then said, " Now, boys, honour bright, tell me how much money was in the house last night after paying expenses." They (the boys) protested, saying that made no difference, that they had agreed to certain terms and had kept their word. Ingersoll said, " But you must tell me; I shall be very much displeased with you if you don't." They finally yielded to Colonel Ingersoll's wishes, and told him that after paying incidental expenses there were just twenty-eight dollars left. Colonel Ingersoll then took the roll out of his pocket, counted out twenty-eight dollars, and handed back $272, saying that he would never be on good terms with himself again, if he let a dozen bright, clever boys dip into their own pockets to pay him for a lecture that ought to have been paid by a proper attendance. He said that he had spent a delightful day, and thanked the boys for their kindness.

POLITICAL ORATOR

[In the American edition of this book there is included here a lengthy section on Colonel Ingersoll as a political orator. It is omitted from this edition, as many of the allusions would be lost on the English reader, and, moreover, Ingersoll's fame rests not on his political activities—great and influential as they were in his day—but on his speeches on matters of a much more universal and enduring importance.]

ORATOR OF PATRIOTISM

Robert Ingersoll was a supreme patriot. He declared that " he loves his country best who strives to make it best." He differentiated between politicians and statesmen in this wise: " the politician wants his country to do something for him; while the statesman wants to do something for his country." Ingersoll practised his patriotic ideal of statesmanship as consistently and selflessly as any American who has ever lived. He served his beloved country over a period of more than thirty years without thought of personal gain or material reward. Although he was internationally minded, feeling that no nation has a monopoly of virtue or greatness, still he did believe that America is the best of all countries; and he cherished a glorious " Vision of the Future," of his country and of the future of the whole world :

" I see our country filled with happy homes, with firesides of content; the foremost land of all the earth. I see a world where thrones have crumbled, and where kings are dust. The aristocracy of idleness has perished from the earth. I see a world without a slave; man at last is free. Nature's forces have by Science been enslaved. .

" I see a world at peace; adorned with every form of art; with music's myriad voices thrilled; while lips are rich with words of love and truth; a world in which no exile sighs, no prisoner mourns; a world on which the gibbet's shadow does not fall; a world where labour reaps its full reward, where work and worth go hand in hand

" I see a world without disease of flesh or brain—shapely and fair—the married harmony of form and function;—and, as I look, life lengthens, joy deepens, love canopies the earth; and over all, in the great dome, shines the eternal star of human hope."

The dominant purpose of Robert Ingersoll's whole life was to further the cause of intellectual freedom—to liberate the mind and spirit of man. And, in view of the fact that he regarded the orthodox church and theological superstition as the two greatest obstacles to intellectual liberty, it was natural and inevitable that his lectures upon the subject of religion should be chiefly concerned with fearless and merciless arraignments of the church and the Bible.

Early in his Agnostic career Ingersoll began to receive many letters from religious fanatics threatening his life. On several occasions he appeared before his audiences with a letter in his pocket assuring him that he would not live to complete his lecture. One man actually admitted that he had once attended a lecture with the firm intention of shooting Ingersoll, but that when he saw the cherubic, smiling face, and heard the golden voice of the man he meant to kill, he could not bring himself to do the dreadful deed.

ORATOR ON RELIGION

As a confirmed, consistent, and outspoken Agnostic, Ingersoll's paramount mission in life was the liberation of the human mind from superstition in general and the dogmas of hell and eternal damnation in particular, to the end of the greatest possible happiness for men, women, and children in this world, rather than in some hypothetical future existence. To the fulfilment of this mission he dedicated his career of Agnostic-orator and lecturer, covering a period of over forty years.

During the course of his long anti-theological crusade Ingersoll lectured in almost every town and city large enough to have an auditorium or a theatre, in nearly every state of the U.S.A. as well as in many parts of Canada. In most of these places he lectured many times, and in some of the larger centres once or twice or three times each year. He had nearly thirty different lectures in his rationalistic repertory. Accordingly he could arrange his subjects to suit his itineraries, never repeating the same lecture in the same town, except at long intervals, unless specially requested to do so.

Young Robert Ingersoll delivered his maiden speech at a church picnic on the outskirts of Shawneetown, Illinois, in 1856, at the age of twenty-three, on the subject of Thomas Paine; and he continued to lecture on religious topics until 1899, the year of his death.

He had not been scheduled to speak at the Shawneetown picnic. A local divine of considerable reputation had been secured to address the farming population of Gallatin County. However, the said distinguished divine disappointed the picnickers at the last moment, and accordingly, young " Bob " Ingersoll was called upon to substitute for him. The gentlemen in charge of arrangements had suggested to Ingersoll that he say a few words " of devotional import "; but when the budding orator rose to his feet he completely forgot their prudent counsel, only remembering that he had long since promised himself never to make a speech without mentioning the name of his hero, Paine. Therefore, Paine was the theme of his address. It is said that Robert made a deep impression upon his rural audience, although the individuals who had invited him to speak were not a little perturbed by the nature of his discourse. This maiden speech was entirely extemporaneous, but in later years Ingersoll expanded and developed into an eloquent and stirring lecture his ideas concerning the great patriot hero of two revolutions.

The Colonel's style of thought and expression in the antitheological lectures was an extraordinary blend of insouciance and audacity. He said the most " subversive " things in the gentlest and sweetest way. He had an unmistakable genius for terse, epigrammatic phrasing. Into a few simple paragraphs he could pack the pith and sapience of a whole philosophy of life; or demolish age-old traditions and beliefs in a shining, shattering sentence. There was a certain naïve, though superb, intellectual unction in his iconoclasm. He was boundlessly fertile in these pat, felicitous, and, indeed, revolutionary phrases: " Man must learn to rely upon himself. Reading Bibles will not protect him from the blasts of winter, but houses, fire, and clothing will. To prevent famine, one plough is worth a million sermons, and even patent medicines will cure more diseases than all the prayers uttered since the beginning of the world." " What right have we to expect that an infinitely wise, good, and powerful being will ever do better than he has done, and is doing? . . . Can the conduct of infinite wisdom, power, and love ever change? Is the Infinite capable of any improvement whatever? "

The first lecture in which Ingersoll gave expression to his agnosticism was entitled Progress, and was delivered at Pekin, Illinois, in 1860. It voiced in vigorous terms the budding Agnostic's abhorrence of superstition, and concluded with an eloquent peroration about the forward march of " the sublime army of progress."

It was the lecture called *The Gods* which made Ingersoll famous overnight as an Agnostic. This brilliant and audacious oration created a sensation, and was widely discussed by Press and pulpit. The bold paraphrase of Alexander Pope, " an honest God is the noblest work of man," is perhaps the most celebrated line in all of Ingersoll's lectures.

The Colonel did not mean this to be taken literally, for he did not believe that an honest God is the noblest work of man. On the contrary, in his opinion, god-manufacturing was one of the least important and useful of human occupations. What

E
55

he did mean was that man has always made his God or gods in his own image; that the conception of God had developed as man himself has developed; and that in order to have an honest God there must first be honest men.

It was a paragraph from *The Gods* which inspired Georg Brandes, the great Danish critic, to exclaim that " In Ingersoll, common sense rose to genius." This was the paragraph: " No one has ever been persecuted by the church for believing God bad, while hundreds of millions have been destroyed for thinking him good. The orthodox church never will forgive the Universalist for saying, ' God is love '; and it has always been considered as one of the very highest evidences of true and undefiled religion to insist that all men, women, and children deserve eternal damnation."

" Give me the storm and tempest of thought and action, rather than the dead calm of ignorance and faith. Banish me from Eden, if you will; but first let me eat of the fruit of the tree of knowledge! " Ingersoll cried.

He was once taken to task by a pious friend for having said that the world was woefully imperfect. " Be kind enough," demanded the pious gentleman, " to name even one improvement that you would make, if you had the power." " Well," replied Ingersoll, " I would make good health catching instead of disease."

In *The Gods*, as in the later lectures on *Ghosts*, *Superstition*, and *The Devil*, Ingersoll sought to show that the concept of the One God of the Jews and Christians, as of the many gods of the pagans and primitive peoples, originated in the ignorant and fearful imagination of man; and that the Devil as well as a multitude of lesser demons and evil spirits had a similar origin. He declared that the idea of God evolved as man has risen in the scale of civilization; that the caveman's god was a simple savage, like himself, but gradually, in the course of countless centuries, God grew into an ever higher and nobler being, until, with the Unitarians and Universalists, he became " a perfect gentleman."

However, Ingersoll assailed the God-idea as manifested in the Church and the Bible as the basic and primary cause of man's inhumanity to man—of the tyranny and injustice characterizing the history of mankind.

56

In such lectures as *About the Holy Bible* (which Maud Ingersoll said that in some respects was her father's favourite among all his works on `religion), *Some Mistakes of Moses*, *Orthodoxy*, and *Foundations of Faith*, Ingersoll tried and condemned revealed religion as set forth in the Bible.

He declared that our beliefs, religious or otherwise, are chiefly determined by the place and period in which we happen to be born—by heredity, environment, education, and many other preconditioning factors. If we had been inhabitants of some primitive part of the world we would probably have believed in other " sacred scriptures "; " we might have believed in a God with three heads, instead of three Gods with one head, as we do now," argued Ingersoll the incorrigible.

Ingersoll denied that the Bible is the inspired word of God, maintaining that it was the product of the fallible brains of many men labouring upon it over a long period of time. These Biblical writers often contradicted each other, and occasionally themselves; and their works are a mingling of the good, the true, and the beautiful, and of the base, the obscene, the false, and the infamous, he asserted; however, it has been the insistence upon certain theological beliefs and dogmas being necessary to salvation that has made the Bible such a terrible barrier to intellectual freedom and advancement. The doctrine of salvation by faith and faith alone, and of damnation through mere lack of faith, was utterly abhorrent to Ingersoll's mind and heart, and accordingly, he continuously marshalled all his magnificent intellectual and oratorical resources against it.

He demanded to know why God should have created human beings in the first place when he must have known that he would eventually be obliged to destroy all except eight of them as unfit for survival, if the Biblical account is to be credited. However, he contended that if God created us he will not destroy us, because " infinite wisdom never made a poor investment. Upon all the works of an infinite God, a dividend must finally be declared."

Ingersoll believed that supernatural religion will disappear from the world and be superseded by reason—by " the religion of mutual love and assistance—the great religion of reciprocity." He believed this in his inmost soul; and yet, in his less optimistic moods, he felt that " most people never renounce the supernatural; they merely transfer their allegiance from one God to another. When they abandon Jehovah, they proceed to worship a sort of personification of ' the power not ourselves that makes for righteousness.' " But the Colonel had no more faith in the existence of such a power than he had in the existence of Jehovah, contending that " the accumulated experience of the world "—of humanity as a whole—is the only power that works for righteousness.

Ingersoll hated the orthodox church, whose function it has always been to inculcate and enforce the theological precepts and doctrines propounded in the Bible.

In his lectures of *The Liberty of Man, Woman, and Child, Voltaire, Heretics and Heresies,* and *The Great Infidels,* he gives a graphic and colourful account of the part played by the orthodox Christian church in human affairs when it was in a position of supreme authority, and tells how for long centuries it enslaved the minds of men. " I have made up my mind to say my say. I shall do it kindly, distinctly; but I am going to do it. I know there are thousands of men who substantially agree with me but who are not in a condition to express their thoughts. They are poor, and they are in business; and they know that should they tell their honest thoughts, persons would refuse to patronize them, to trade with them; they wish to get bread for their little children; they wish to take care of their wives. . Every such person is a certificate of the meanness of the community in which he resides. And yet I do not blame these people for not expressing their thoughts. I say to them: ' Keep your ideas to yourselves; feed and clothe the ones you love; I will do your talking for you. The Church cannot touch, cannot crush, cannot starve, cannot stop or stay me; I will express your thoughts ' "—thus rang out the Ingersollian trumpet-blast to an incredulous, conformist, timorous world—a world that the Agnostic-orator half-scandalized and half-disarmed in one and the same breath.

The Liberty of Man, Woman, and Child is Ingersoll's intellectual declaration of independence. With a few vivid, sweeping strokes of his oratorical brush Ingersoll paints for us in this lecture an impressive picture of the intellectual development of man from the lowest savage to Shakespeare—from the tomtom to the violin—from the " crooked stick " to the modern implements of agriculture, industry, and science; from the cruelty and bestiality of the caveman to the conscience and creative intelligence of a Lincoln. Theology alone remained static; it alone failed to evolve and progress; and Ingersoll maintained that man should have the same right to improve upon primitive theology that he had to advance along other lines. However, he cheerfully conceded that if the church and the clergy had not made very real progress he would not be permitted to express his honest thought.

The *Soliloquy at the Tomb of Napoleon* (see page 112), which forms a part of this lecture, is one of Ingersoll's most famous and brilliantly effective word paintings and oratorical flights; it is outstanding for splendour of rhetoric, poignant drama of contrast, profundity of pathos, and, above all, for wisdom of the heart.

The Liberty of Man, Woman, and Child is also a romantic pæan of praise of the domestic virtues—an annunciation in terms of love for wife, and child, and home, of a new set of beatitudes by a peculiarily religious irreligionist.

Mrs. Elizabeth Cady Stanton, one of the great women leaders of America, paid to Ingersoll's oratory the following tribute:
" . The greatest triumph of oratory I had ever witnessed was the first time he delivered his matchless speech, *The Liberty of Man, Woman, and Child*. . . . I have heard the greatest orators of this century in England and America O'Connell in his palmiest days, on the Home Rule question; Gladstone and John Bright in the House of Commons; Spurgeon, James, and Stopford Brooke, in their respective pulpits; our own Wendell Phillips, Henry Ward Beecher, and Webster and Clay, on great occasions . . . but none of them ever equalled Robert G. Ingersoll in his highest flights."

The Great Infidels examines the various legends concerning the dying moments of unbelievers, which were alleged to have been unspeakably horrible; and demonstrates the falsity of these theologically inspired popular assumptions. Said Ingersoll: " It would not do to have the common people understand that a man could deny the Bible, contend that Christ was only a man, and yet die as calmly as Calvin did after he murdered Servetus, or as King David did after advising one son to kill another."

One of the most imaginative and poetic of the addresses on

rationalist and religious themes is *Myth and Miracle*. " In all these myths and legends of the past we find philosophies and dreams and efforts, stained with tears, of great and tender souls who tried to pierce the mysteries of life and death . . . and who vainly sought with bits of shattered glass to make a mirror that would in very truth reflect the face and form of Nature's perfect self. . These myths, though false in fact, are beautiful and true in thought, and have for many ages and in countless ways enriched the heart, and kindled thought." Ingersoll held that " there is a great difference between a myth and a miracle"; that " a myth is the idealization of a fact" and " a miracle is a counterfeit of a fact. . . . There is the same difference between a myth and a miracle that there is between fiction and falsehood—between poetry and perjury. . . ."

In Ingersoll's opinion, " the first religion was probably Sun-worship. Nothing could have been more natural. Light was life and warmth and love. . . . The sun was the ' All-Seeing ' —the ' Sky Father.' Darkness was grief and death, and in the shadows crawled the serpents of despair and fear. Apollo was the sun . . . Agni, the generous, who loved the lowliest and visited the humblest, was the sun." Hercules, Jonah, Samson, Osiris, Bacchus, Mithra, Hermes, Quetzalcoatl, Prometheus, Perseus, and Horus were all sun-gods. " All these gods had gods for fathers and their mothers were virgins. The births of nearly all were announced by stars. When they were born there was celestial music. . . . Tyrants sought to kill all of these gods when they were babes. . . . All were born on the 25th of December. Nearly all were worshipped by ' wise men.' All of them fasted for forty days. All met with a violent death. All rose from the dead. "

Ingersoll went on to say that " the history of these gods is the history of our Christ "; and that " Christ was a sun-god." " In the religion of our day there is nothing original. All of its doctrines, its symbols, and ceremonies are but the survivals of creeds that perished long ago," he maintained.

The irrepressible conflict between the supernatural and the natural—the religious and the secular or Humanist philosophies of life—is the principal theme of such lectures as *Some Reasons Why*; *Which Way?*; and *What is Religion?* Ingersoll contrasts the ethical teachings of the Bible with those of the great pagan philosophers, like Socrates, Epictetus, Zeno, and Marcus Aurelius, as well as with the teachings of the sacred books of the Hindus, the Chinese, and the Persians, to the disadvantage of the Christian Bible.

Why I Am an Agnostic (1896) marked the crown and culmination of Ingersoll's anti-theological lecture career; it might almost be described as his intellectual autobiography in miniature. It relates the story of his orthodox background and upbringing, how he emancipated himself by means of study, reflection, and the education which life itself affords, from the trammels and tyranny of supernatural religion; and the philosophic conclusions at which he arrived. He determined to " leave the forts and barricades of fear; to stand erect, and face the future with a smile."

What is Religion ? (given before the American Free Religious Association at Boston on April 2, 1899) represents the full flowering of Ingersoll's intellectual maturity, combining the serenity and poise of age with the idealism and radicalism of youth. The final paragraph of this lecture radiates a sort of rapturous morality and exaltation of spirit: " Then to rouse yourself to do all useful things, to reach with thought and deed the ideal in your brain; to give your fancies wing, that they, like chemist bees, may find art's nectar in the weeds of common things; to look with trained and steady eyes for facts; to find the subtle threads that join the distant with the now; to increase knowledge, to take burdens from the weak, to develop the brain, to defend the right, to make a palace for the soul. This is real religion. This is real worship."

The lectures on Humboldt, Thomas Paine, and Voltaire indict the Bible and the Church in equal measure; however, they are mostly concerned with the magnificent and immortal contributions made by these three intellectual giants to the cause of religious freedom and enlightenment. Ingersoll said that " Humboldt was to science what Shakespeare was to the drama. . . . He demonstrated beyond all contradiction that the universe is governed by law "; and that " all facts are simply the different aspects of one general fact."

In Ingersoll's opinion, Thomas Paine was one of the greatest of all benefactors of the human race. He strove tirelessly and heroically to emancipate mankind from its enslavement to

Creed, Church, and State—to superstition and tyranny. The Colonel declared that "Paine had the generosity, the exalted patriotism, the goodness to say, 'the world is my country, to do good my religion.' There is in all the utterances of the world, no grander, no sublimer sentiment," Ingersoll felt. "Voltaire was the greatest man of his century, and did more to free the human race than any other of the sons of men," in Ingersoll's view. Voltaire shot the arrows of ridicule at all "holy superstition," and all "sacred mistakes." However, he never scoffed at truth, knowing that "he who attempts to ridicule the truth, ridicules himself."

ORATOR IN EULOGY

Robert Ingersoll's famous tributes to his departed loved ones and friends reveal and emphasize certain distinctive qualities of his oratory as do none of his other speeches or lectures, for into these eulogies he poured the overflowing fountains of his generous and tender heart and the wealth of his poetic imagination. They contain pure lyric beauty and verbal magic, although they are all conceived from a surprisingly simple and unified pattern: first, the character of his subject is portrayed— his ethical philosophy and conduct of life; and then the character and the life are related to their place in nature, and to the supreme, insoluble mysteries of life and death.

The following lines are typical of Ingersoll's manner of eulogy: "Her heart was open as the gates of day. She shed kindness as the sun sheds light. If all her deeds were flowers, the air would be faint with perfume. If all her charities could change to melodies, a symphony would fill the sky. . . ."

And here are a few illustrations of Ingersoll's way of philosophizing upon the human heart, and the eternal enigma of life and death.

He assures us that "good deeds are never childless"; and that "a noble life is never lost"; although "the mystery of life and death we cannot comprehend; . . . the chaos called the world has never been explained. The golden bridge of life from gloom emerges, and on shadow rests." He says that "Immortality is a word that Hope through all the ages has been whispering to Love." Ingersoll liked to recall the wise thought of Epicurus: "Why should I fear death? If I am, death is

62

not. If death is, I am not. Why should I fear that which cannot exist when I do?" In Ingersoll's opinion, "the idea of immortality, that like a sea has ebbed and flowed in the human heart, with its countless waves of hope and fear beating against the shores and rocks of time and fate, was not born of any religion or of any creed. It was born of the human affections, and it will continue to ebb and flow beneath the tides and waves of doubt and darkness as long as Love kisses the lips of Death. It is the rainbow—Hope shining upon the tears of grief." Ingersoll declared that "we do not know which is the greater blessing—life or death. We cannot say that death is not a good. We do not know whether the grave is the end of this life or the door of another, or whether the night here is not somewhere else a dawn. Neither can we tell which is the more fortunate—the child dying in its mother's arms . . . or he who journeys all the length of life's uneven road, painfully taking the last slow steps with staff and crutch." At any rate, he emphasized that we have this supreme consolation: "The dead do not suffer. If they live again, their lives will surely be as good as ours. We are all children of the same mother, and the same fate awaits us all." Ingersoll pointed out that he and his fellow Agnostics have their religion, and it is this: "Help for the living—Hope for the dead."

Among the more memorable and celebrated of the eulogies delivered by Ingersoll are: those to his brother, Ebon Clark, which is universally acknowledged to be a masterpiece of oratory in the purest classic tradition; to his father-in-law, Mr. Benjamin Weld Parker; to the Hon. Roscoe Conkling; to the Rev. Henry Ward Beecher; the oration *At a Child's Grave*; and his eulogy of Walt Whitman. However, some of the less well-known tributes are fully equal both in form and content to the more famous ones cited above.

The literary lectures of Robert Ingersoll reveal the style and quality of his oratory at its highest and best. Other scholars and students of Shakespeare and Lincoln, Burns and Whitman, may have had many of his ideas, and have formed opinions and judgments very similar to his own; however, it was the orator and poet in Ingersoll that gave him his unique power to express those ideas and judgments with such incomparable eloquence and beauty.

The lecture on *Shakespeare* is generally considered to be the greatest and most beautiful of his works from the point of view of pure literature, *The Man of Imagination*, which forms the peroration of the lecture, probably being Ingersoll's supreme oratorical and poetic achievement (see page 165).

On the seventy-first birthday of his beloved friend and literary idol, Walt Whitman, Ingersoll journeyed to Philadelphia to attend a dinner in the poet's honour; and it is recorded that he captivated the latter by an extemporaneous discussion for fifty-five minutes or more, which Whitman described as " the greatest oratory that he had ever heard." Five months later Ingersoll delivered the lecture known as *A Testimonial to Walt Whitman* in Horticultural Hall, Philadelphia, from which nearly nine hundred dollars was realized for the poet's benefit.

Ingersoll was entirely unprepared when he was bidden to Camden on March 30, 1891, to place a last offering of love upon the dead poet's tomb.

The lecture on *Abraham Lincoln* is second only to *Shakespeare* in literary and philosophic distinction and beauty. ". . . On the twenty-second day of September, 1862, the most glorious date in the history of the Republic," says Ingersoll, " the Proclamation of Emancipation was issued. Lincoln had reached the generalization of all argument upon the question of slavery and freedom—a generalization that never has been, and probably never will be, excelled: ' In giving freedom to the slave, we assure freedom to the free.' " And Ingersoll goes on to say that " liberty can be retained . . . only by giving it to others. The spendthrift saves, the miser is prodigal. In the realm of Freedom, waste is husbandry."

And here is his psychologically profound and subtle characterization of the Great Emancipator: "Abraham Lincoln—strange mingling of mirth and tears, of the tragic and grotesque, of cap and crown, of Socrates and Democritus, of Æsop and Marcus Aurelius, of all that is gentle and just, humorous and honest, merciful, wise, laughable, lovable and divine, and all consecrated to the use of man; while through all, and over all, were an overwhelming sense of obligation, of chivalric loyalty to truth, and upon all, the shadow of the tragic end. . . . Lincoln was an immense personality—firm but not obstinate. . . .

64

He was severe with himself, and for that reason lenient with others. He appeared to apologize for being kinder than his fellows; he did merciful things as stealthily as others commit crimes. . . . He knew no fear except the fear of doing wrong. . . . Lincoln was the grandest figure of the fiercest civil war. He is the gentlest memory of our world."

The lecture on *Robert Burns* was originally written in 1878, although it was not published until after Ingersoll's death. This study is a spontaneous outpouring of his love for the " ploughman-poet "; and it is also an interpretation of the genius of Burns, of deep poetic insight, critical analysis, and understanding.

To conclude this section, it should be made clear that Robert G. Ingersoll's oratory figured just as significantly in his legal, as in his rationalistic, anti-theological, political, and cultural activities.

The Hon. Albert J. Beveridge, distinguished jurist, statesman, and biographer of Lincoln, has this to say concerning the many-sidedness of Ingersoll's oratorical genius: " This wonderful man was one of the greatest masters of the noble art of public speaking which America or the world has ever produced. His gifts and reputation as an orator, however, were so commanding that they took public attention from his remarkable power as a lawyer. Colonel Ingersoll was in mind, learning, and aptitude one of the foremost leaders of his profession. As an advocate he was, during his life, unrivalled in this or any other country. He was as fearless as Lord Erskine or Sir James Mackintosh; he was more eloquent, and as heroically devoted to liberty as either. Colonel Ingersoll will for ever stand as one of those historic figures who from Socrates to Milton, from Milton to Erskine, from Erskine to Lincoln, fearlessly battled for human rights."

Mr. Charles Edward Russell, publicist, author, and reformer, gave his devoted friendship and intellectual admiration to Ingersoll. Here is his appreciation of the religious and intellectual revolution achieved by the Agnostic:

He (Ingersoll) found the intellectual world wandering in a medieval midnight and brought to it the dawn. . . . All the sullen squadrons of bigotry were massed against him. He faced them almost alone. To stand resolute against an overwhelming psychology, and to stand thus only for faith in the righteousness of a cause, is the supreme test of character and courage. Ten thousand pulpits thundered and bellowed against this man as the arch enemy of society, of civilization, of all virtue.

And now . . . a momentous change has come over the world of thought. The right of the individual to form his free and un-fettered decisions in regard to religion . . . is acknowledged by all men of intellectual development above that of the caves. The very influences that denounced him then, (now) accept the funda-mentals of his faith. Men are no longer afraid or ashamed to say " I do not know." Even the church that sought to pillory this apostle of freedom as the perilous foe of mankind, has now been brought, protesting and resisting, to acknowledge that great was the emancipation he wrought.

He has taken his place with all of the great souls that have braved the current of unthinking opinion and stood forth for light and the great advance; with . . . Voltaire and Humboldt, with the Gracchi and Rienzi, with Bruno and Huss. . . . Because of him, millions of men and women today that knew him not, have less of fear and more of serenity, less of the tyranny of dogmatism, and more of the priceless liberty of thought and speech, less of grief and more of joy, less of darkness and more of light. . . .

For the modern reader Ingersoll the Orator is a man of his day. His oratory was redolent not alone of his ardent, opti-mistic personality, but of the prevailing atmosphere and spirit of the century in which he lived. Yet he was also more than an orator of his day, because his quality and mode of thought and manner of expression were timeless—relevant to all times—relevant for our day. His exalted idealism, wealth of imagina-tion, gorgeous imagery, subtle and profound understanding, sense of comedy, pathos, and humour, infinite compassion, and, above all, the magical beauty of his oratorical and literary style, derived directly from Shakespeare. His elaborate and efflorescent language was, indeed, Ingersoll's heritage from Shakespeare, and its opulence distinguishes it sharply from the more austere oratorical tradition and style of Churchill and Roosevelt.

PART THREE

Ingersoll—the Agnostic

ROBERT G. INGERSOLL WAS both an Agnostic and an Atheist. No God is visible on the broad horizon of his intellect. He accepted nothing as true that could not be tested by means of experience, observation, and reason. Like Socrates, he "thrust the spear of question through the shield and heart of falsehood"; unlike Plato or Berkeley, he did not believe that the abstract idea is the only abiding reality, for this world and the things of this world were very real to him. Ingersoll did not believe in divine revelation, but he did believe in the secular revelations of reason, observation, and experience —"the Holy Trinity of Science." He put his faith in the study and ascertainment of, and obedience to, the laws of nature, rather than in the commandments of Jehovah.

Ingersoll thrilled to the "sublime truth" enunciated by Alexander von Humboldt that "the universe is governed by law"; that "all facts are simply the different aspects of one general fact." The method of science is the sole means of ascertaining truth, according to Ingersoll, whose philosophical and religious thinking centred in man rather than in God. He contended that nothing exists apart from or beyond the boundaries of the natural; hence the supernatural does not and cannot exist. God, Christ, the Bible, and the Church were all conceived by the mind of man.

He felt that Darwin's theory of men as evolved apes is far more rational, and hopeful for ultimate human redemption, than is the biblical doctrine of men as fallen angels. He asserted that he would rather belong to "a race that started from the skull-less vertebrates in the Laurentian seas . . . that came up by degrees through millions of ages through all the animal world and finally produced the gentleman in the dug-out; and then from this man, getting a little grander, and each one below calling every one above him a heretic—rather come from a race that started from that skull-less vertebrate, and came up and up and up and finally produced Shakespeare . . . a race that has before it an infinite future, with the angel of progress leaning from the far horizon, beckoning men forward, upward and onward for ever . . . than to have sprung from a perfect pair upon which the Lord has lost money every moment from that day to this."

In Ingersoll's view the scientific discoveries of Darwin should uproot from " every thoughtful mind the last vestige of orthodox Christianity," based as it is on blind, unreasoning faith in a supernatural God.

His study of and faith in the findings of science convinced Ingersoll that the universe is governed by law, but he did not feel that this fact justified the assumption of design or purpose in the order of nature. He did not concur in the view of St. Paul and the orthodox Christian Church that " all things work together for good "; he did not believe that " all is for the best in the best of all possible worlds "; nor did he follow the line of the professional philosophers in their erudite arguments for design, for a Master Mind directing phenomena towards some supreme, unseen goal. He asserted that religionists and religious-minded persons " see design everywhere. They say that the universe has been created, and that the adaptation of means to ends is perfectly apparent. They point us to the sunshine, to the flowers . . . and to all there is of beauty and of use in the world. Did it ever occur to them that a cancer is as beautiful in its development as is the reddest rose? That what they are pleased to call the adaptation of means to ends is as apparent in the cancer as in the April rain? "

Accordingly, Ingersoll continues, " what right have we to expect that a perfectly wise, good, and powerful being will ever do better than he has done, and is doing? The world is filled with imperfections. If it was made by an infinite being, what reason have we for saying that he will render it nearer perfect than it now is? If the Infinite Father allows a majority of his children to live in ignorance and wretchedness now, what evidence is there that he will ever improve their condition? Will God have more power? Will he become more merciful? Will his love for his poor creatures increase? Can the conduct of infinite wisdom, power, and love ever change? Is the Infinite capable of any improvement whatever? "

Ingersoll's fundamental intellectual honesty forced him to insist that the existence of evil deprives the theory of design of validity. Unless one can identify or harmonize evil with good, he argued, one is compelled to concede that nature is devoid of rational plan or purpose; that she is completely neutral toward and heedless of man's aims, hopes, and welfare; that " she produces man without purpose, and obliterates him without regret." Ingersoll maintained that man, so far as we know, represents the highest intelligence that exists in the universe; and that it is " only through man that nature takes cognizance of the good, the true, and the beautiful." He held with Protagoras that " man is the measure of all things "; the product of an unending chain of efficient causes; the result of innumerable and immemorial co-mingled elements of heredity, environment, and education.

Ironically enough, at this point the Agnostic converges upon the Christian in his thinking, as both accept the basic doctrine of determinism or predestination. Indeed, the Agnostic was a more thoroughgoing determinist than the Christian, in so far as he disbelieved in free moral agency; whereas the Christian has always made the attempt to reconcile the irreconcilable doctrines of predestination and free moral agency. Ingersoll, for his part, was fairly consistent in his " scientific determinism," upholding the position that " men do as they must."

At the same time, Ingersoll was the very prototype of the individualist in his quality and attitude of mind and in his way of life. He did not believe at all in the freedom of man in his relation to the order of the universe—to the laws of nature—but he believed passionately and above all else in the principle and ideal of individual liberty; believed that man should act *as if* he possessed absolute freedom of will.

The fact that Ingersoll took the philosophical position that all knowledge derives from experience, scientific experiment, and observation, guided by human reason, made belief in orthodox theology impossible for him; for neither intellectual theory nor scientific practice is capable of proving the existence of God. He declared that " an honest God is the noblest work of man," because he held that all gods have been created by man; that as man evolves intellectually and ethically his ideas of God likewise develop. For example, he contrasted

the wrathful Jehovah of the ancient Jews with the benign,
" gentlemanly God " of the modern Unitarians or Universalists.

The majority of gods have belonged to the masculine gender
for the obvious reason that men for the most part have ruled
over women because of their superior physical strength. " The
Negroes worshipped deities with black skins; the Mongolians'
gods had a yellow complexion; and the Jews imagined Jehovah
with a long beard, an oval face, and aquiline nose. Zeus was a
perfect Greek, and Jove looked as though he were a member of
the Roman Senate. The gods of Egypt had the patient face
and placid look of the loving people who made them. . . ."

Man has never been at a loss for gods. " He has worshipped
almost everything, including the vilest and most disgusting
beasts . fire, air, earth, water, light, stars, and for hundreds
of ages prostrated himself before enormous snakes. The
savage Todas worship a cowbell. The Kotas worship two
silver plates which they regard as husband and wife; and
another tribe manufactured a god out of a king of hearts.
Some nations have borrowed their gods; of this number, we
are compelled to say, is our own. The Jews having ceased to
exist as a nation, and having no further use for a god, our
ancestors appropriated him and adopted their (the Jews') devil
at the same time."

Ingersoll contended that the long Dark Ages bore unassailable witness to the devastating effect of theological superstition
upon the human spirit. In those ages men were enslaved to
figments and phantoms of their own imaginings, and freedom,
justice, common sense, and even sanity gave place to tyranny,
oppression, ignorance, hypocrisy, and blind faith. " Let the
ghosts go," he cried. " We will worship them no more. Let
them cover their eyeless sockets with their fleshless hands, and
fade for ever from the imaginations of men."

He assailed with relentless shafts of wit, scorn, and logic the
orthodox Christian God. If God is omnipotent, all-loving,
wise, good, and forgiving, as he is portrayed by the Christians,
why is it necessary for man to fear him, Ingersoll inquired?
Surely man need have no fear of a being of infinite love and
compassion. Yet we are commanded to propitiate him with
blind and abject faith.

How can an omnipotent God be angered or in any way

affected by the ideas and actions of men? It is utterly lacking in good sense to fear a God whom one cannot injure, Ingersoll argued; one cannot injure God, because he is conditionless. One cannot increase or decrease the happiness of any being without changing that being's condition; and since God is conditionless, one can neither harm nor benefit him.

Ingersoll said that civilized men have come to believe it their moral duty to accord complete religious liberty to all; and assuredly we must take it for granted that God, if he exists, is at least as just and tolerant as the best of men.

Two central dogmas of Christianity which Ingersoll felt to be utterly incompatible with the concept of a merciful God, and which he held in particular abhorrence, were the dogmas of salvation by faith and eternal damnation.

He early resolved never to deliver a lecture without attacking the latter doctrine. It filled his tender heart with horror; and he dedicated himself to do his heroic best to destroy this evil superstition. In his opinion this world will never be civilized as long as there are criminals and prisons in our midst, and yet, if we are to credit the Christian religion, " God is to have an eternal penitentiary; he is to be an everlasting jailer . . . a warden of an eternal dungeon; and he is to keep prisoners there for ever, not for the purpose of reforming them—because they are never going to get better—but for the purpose of purposeless punishment." Poor human souls, perhaps victims of poverty, toil, and nameless suffering, are to be for ever tortured and held responsible through all eternity for something they failed to believe on earth.

" No man can think of a greater horror; no man can dream of a greater absurdity! " cried Ingersoll. " If this frightful creed were true, many of the best and noblest of the human race would be among the damned." With every fibre of his being he repudiated the doctrine of eternal damnation, and with equal passion of soul affirmed that " there is no world—there can be no world—in which every human being will not have the eternal opportunity of doing right."

As to the dogma of salvation by faith, Ingersoll pointed out that according to the gospels of Matthew, Mark, and Luke, salvation did not depend upon any theological belief whatever, but rather upon being merciful to the merciful; forgiving others

F

their trespasses; judging not lest you be judged; returning good for evil—in other words, salvation depends upon good works, not upon theological faith. He realized that there is a single isolated passage in Mark which would seem to belie the all-sufficiency of good works: " And he, Christ, said unto them [his disciples] : ' Go ye into all the world and preach the gospel to every creature. He that believeth and is baptized shall be saved; but he that believeth not shall be damned.' "

However, Ingersoll believed this passage to be an interpolation. Is it possible, he asked, that the three disciples should have forgotten such a supremely important statement? Is it credible that John alone should have remembered to mention it? " If Christ did indeed make this pronouncement, they were the most momentous words that ever issued from the divine lips." Therefore, Ingersoll felt that the only conceivable explanation is that Christ never uttered these words.

He held that in the doctrine of the Trinity orthodox Christianity attained the apogee of absurdity and inconsistency. " Is it possible for a human being who has been born but once, to comprehend . . . the existence of three beings, each of whom is equal to the three? Think of one of these beings as the father of one, and think of that one as half-human, and all God, and think of the third as having proceeded from the other two, and then think of all three as one. Think that after the Father begot the Son, the Father was still alone, and after the Holy Ghost proceeded from the Father and the Son, the Father was still alone—because there never was and never will be but one God. At this point, absurdity having reached its limit, nothing more can be said except: ' Let us pray! ' "

Ingersoll insisted that he neither affirmed nor denied the existence of a God. He was what the modern dictionaries term a negative Atheist—that is, he did not positively deny that a God exists; he simply maintained that no one knows nor can know anything certain about origin and destiny; and he was absolutely without belief in a God. " The Agnostic is an Atheist; the Atheist, an Agnostic. The Agnostic says I do not know, but I do not believe there is any God. The Atheist says the same. The orthodox Christian says he knows there is a God; but we know that he does not know; he simply believes; he cannot know. And the Atheist cannot know that God does not exist."

However, Ingersoll was indeed a dogmatic Atheist concerning an anthropomorphic or personal God.

He was equally atheistic in his denial of the inspiration of the Bible. He declared that if the Bible were in truth the word of God, it would necessarily have to be absolutely accurate and flawless in its philosophy, history, economics, ethics—in letter and in spirit. It would have to be the greatest, noblest, most beautiful and perfect of all books—superior not only to any one book, but to all other books of the world combined. However, he felt that the Bible is false in its astronomy, geology, history, philosophy, and religion; and that in all matters of fact it has ceased to be regarded as a standard by intelligent persons.

Ingersoll contended that if the Bible were inspired by God, it would have to be in every sense of the word a guide and model for all mankind, absolutely consistent and true. Nevertheless, much of the Bible in his opinion is valueless, or worse, as there are many obscene and immoral passages in Genesis and other Old Testament books which " no minister in the United States would read to his congregation, for any reward whatever. There are narratives utterly unfit to be told." He found no inspiration in Genesis, Exodus, Leviticus, Numbers, Deuteronomy, Joshua, Judges, Samuel, Kings, Chronicles, Ezra, or Nehemiah. Even Isaiah was not of deep significance to him; and Jeremiah and Lamentations, which he considered long, unbroken wails of pessimism and despair, struck no responsive chord in his mind or heart.

The Song of Solomon, Ingersoll regarded as " the best book in the Old Testament; it is a drama of love—of human love." He asserted that " Ecclesiastes was written by an unbeliever, a philosopher, an Agnostic," and that " it is the most thoughtful book in the Bible." In the Book of Job he found " some elevated sentiments, some sublime and foolish thoughts, something of the wonder and sublimity of nature, the joys and sorrows of life." He admired some of the Psalms greatly; many seemed to him merely indifferent, and a few horrifying. He felt that " in the literature of the world there is nothing more heartless, more infamous, than the 109th Psalm."

Ingersoll maintained that the Bible is not reliable concerning its claims as to its authorship. The Pentateuch, although it is attributed to Moses, was nevertheless not written until long after the death of Moses; and the true authors of the New Testament, upon which the structure of Christianity has been erected, are lost in oblivion. " Christ never wrote a solitary word of the New Testament. . . . There is an account that he once stooped and wrote something in the sand, but that has not been preserved. He never told anybody to write a word. . . . And it has always seemed to me that a being coming from another world with a message of infinite importance to mankind, should at least have verified that message by his own signature," Ingersoll argued.

However, he concluded, if the " Bible is true, it does not need to be inspired. If it is true, it makes no difference whether it was written by a man or a god. . . . The multiplication table is just as useful, just as true as though God had arranged the figures himself."

But the Bible, Ingersoll insisted, is not true or consistent. There are two separate and incompatible accounts of the creation in Genesis, and Moses, its supposed author, " although he was inspired and obtained his information directly from God, did not know as much about our solar system as the Chinese did a thousand years before he was born."

The story of the Flood and Noah's Ark seemed pure fantasy to him. He wanted to know how all the birds, beasts, reptiles, insects, and animalculæ managed to get into the ark, along with the eight persons; and how they were all fed and watered. He asked how all the different creatures found their way to the ark, before the flood, and their way home, after its subsidence.

" Some of the creeping things must have started for the ark just as soon as they were made, and kept up a steady jog for sixteen hundred years. . . . Polar bears must have gone several thousand miles, and so sudden a change in climate must have been exceedingly trying upon their health. . . . Two sloths had to make the journey from South America. These creatures cannot travel to exceed three rods a day. At this rate, they would make a mile in about a hundred days. They must have gone about six thousand five hundred miles to reach the ark. Supposing them to have travelled by a reasonably direct route, in order to complete the journey before Noah hauled in the plank, they must have started several years before the world was created. We must also consider that these sloths had to board themselves on the way, and that most of their time had to be taken up getting food and water. It is exceedingly doubtful whether a sloth could travel six thousand miles and board himself in less than three thousand years."

Ingersoll was entirely sceptical of the truth of all the miracles described in the Bible. He asked if it was possible to conceive of actions more childish, senseless, and cruel than the miracles alleged to have been wrought by the Almighty for the purpose of prevailing upon Pharaoh to liberate the children of Israel. Ingersoll felt that it was far more reasonable to believe that the Hebrew tribes, in their ignorance and superstitious imagination, falsely ascribed these acts to their God, than that God himself could be guilty of such infamies. The Agnostic asserted that the God of the Pentateuch is a thoroughly despicable, ignoble being, without a redeeming quality.

The divine birth of Christ is in contradiction to all human history, on the testimony of which it must be conceded that Jesus was the son of Joseph and Mary. The bodily resurrection and ascension of Christ is unacceptable to the modern mind. The idea that the God-man who was master of death, could be crucified, is an insult to the intelligence which cannot be given credence.

In a word, the Bible is so unreliable, inaccurate, inconsistent, and out of harmony with established scientific facts as well as moral ideals and truths, that it can only be accounted the production of many exceedingly fallible persons—a collection of tradition, legend, superstition, and a certain amount of more or less authentic history.

For the man, Jesus, Ingersoll had " infinite respect." He believed that " He was a reformer in his day; and . . . an infidel in his time. He was regarded as a blasphemer, and his life was destroyed by hypocrites, who have, in all ages, done what they could to trample freedom and manhood out of the human mind."

Once Jesus has been divested of the myths and miracles which surround him, he takes his appropriate place with the other great teachers of mankind. He was " a man who hated oppression; who despised and denounced superstition and hypocrisy; who attacked the heartless church of his time; who excited the hatred of bigots and priests, and who, rather than be false to his conception of truth, met and bravely suffered even death."

But towards the theological Christ, Ingersoll entertained an altogether different attitude, having no belief or faith whatever in the " Lord Jesus Christ." " If Christ said and did what the writers of the gospels say he said and did, then Christ was mistaken. If he was mistaken, certainly he was not inspired."

Ingersoll pointed out the glaring discrepancies between the various statements attributed to Christ; as well as what he considered the often highly doubtful and unrealistic, and, in a few instances, even evil character of these alleged teachings. His " *Resist not evil*," and " If smitten on one cheek turn the other " . . . " takes from goodness, from virtue, from the truth, the right of self-defence. Vice becomes the master of the world, and the good become the victims of the infamous."

Ingersoll did not believe it possible to " *Love your Enemies*." " Did any human being ever love his enemies? . . . Did Christ love his, when he denounced them as ' whited sepulchres,' ' hypocrites,' and ' vipers '? " " Is there the least sense in the belief, ' Take no thought for the morrow ' with its idea ' That God would take care of us as he did of sparrows and lilies '? " Or " is it sane to say ' If thy right eye offend thee, pluck it out. If thy right hand offend thee, cut it off '? " " If Christ actually said, ' Think not I am come to send peace on earth. I came not to send peace, but a sword. For I am come to set a man at variance against his father, and the daughter against her mother '—how much better it would have been had he remained away," Ingersoll declared.

In the saying: " ' And every one that hath forsaken houses, or brethren, or sistern, or father, or mother, or wife, or children, or lands, for my name's sake, shall receive an hundred fold, and shall inherit everlasting life,' Christ offered the bribe of eternal joy to those who would desert their fathers, their mothers, their wives and children. Are we to win the happiness of heaven by deserting the ones we love? Is a home to be ruined here, for the sake of a mansion there? "

How, Ingersoll asked, can the Christ of these pronouncements be held up as the perfect example to all mankind—

when he said nothing in favour of education, was entirely ignorant of science, and apparently had no practical plans for improving the condition of humanity in this world?

" Christ cared nothing for any . . . art. He said nothing about the duties of nation to nation . . . nothing about intellectual liberty, or freedom of speech . . . nothing about the sacredness of home   . not a word in favour of marriage, in honour of maternity. He never married. He wandered homeless from place to place, with a few disciples   . . and they seem to have lived on alms. All human ties were held in contempt; this world was sacrificed for the next; all human effort was discouraged. God would support and protect his children. At last, in the dusk of death, Christ, finding that he was mistaken, cried out ' My God! My God! Why hast thou forsaken me?' "

" For many centuries the great Peasant of Palestine has been worshipped as God; his name has carried consolation to the sick and the dying; it has dispelled the darkness of death, and filled the dungeon with light. . . . The outcasts, the deserted, the fallen, felt that Christ was their friend; felt he knew their sorrows and pitied their sufferings. . . . In his name have been preached charity, forgiveness, and love. He it was who, according to the faith, brought immortality to life, and many millions have entered the valley of the shadow with their hands in his. All this is true, and if it were all, how beautiful, how touching, how glorious it would be," exclaimed Ingersoll. " But it is not all. There is another side," the Agnostic pointed out.

" In his name, also, millions and millions of men and women have been imprisoned, tortured, and killed.   In his name, the thinkers, the investigators, have been branded as criminals, and his followers have shed the blood of the wisest and the best. In his name, the progress of many nations was stayed for a thousand years. In his gospel was found the dogma of eternal pain, and his words added an infinite horror to death. His gospel filled the world with hatred and revenge; made intellectual honesty a crime; made happiness here the road to hell . . . canonized credulity, crowned bigotry, and destroyed the liberty of man."

And it was largely because he revealed this other side of the biblical portrait of Jesus Christ that the orthodox Christians could never forgive Ingersoll.*

Ingersoll held that throughout history the Christian Church has been a withering blight upon original, independent thought. Because the Church could not meet the challenge of science, could not answer its arguments or disprove its findings, science was anathematized and, whenever possible, suppressed. Intellectual development was heresy. Ingersoll called heresy " a cradle—orthodoxy, a coffin." He exposed to ridicule and scorn any God who would prohibit honest investigation of the laws and facts of nature, and of truth as revealed by reason and free inquiry. " Is it possible that God delights in threatening and terrifying men? " he asked. " What glory, what honour and renown a God must win on such a field! The ocean, raving at a drop; a star, envious of a candle; the sun, jealous of a firefly! "

He maintained that it is to the worldly, the practical men, that we are indebted for all intellectual progress and enlightenment. But he did not mean worldly in the narrow, purely conventional sense; rather in the sense of those who have created and increased the physical and mental wealth and well-being of mankind.

It was not until he looked upon the torture-chambers of the Inquisition that Ingersoll came to a complete realization of the outrages which had been perpetrated upon humanity by the Christian Church when it enjoyed supreme authority. Church and State, " like two vultures," had ruled and oppressed the ignorant multitudes, and had endeavoured through appeal to fear, coercion, and torture to destroy for ever the free human spirit.

" I saw the thumb-screw—two little pieces of iron, armed on the inner surface with protuberances, to prevent their slipping; through each end a screw uniting the two pieces. And when some man denied the efficacy of baptism, or maybe said ' I do not believe that a fish ever swallowed a man to keep him from drowning,' then they put his thumb between these two pieces

* " During three succeeding periods, Ingersoll held as many different views of the Christ of the New Testament: first, that he was a man; second, that he was either a myth or a man; third, that he was a myth. The views held during the first two periods were, of course, modified by more comprehensive research and thought."—Ingersoll: A Biographical Appreciation, by Herman E. Kittredge.

of iron, and in the name of love and universal forgiveness, began to screw these pieces together. As these screws came closer and closer together, most men would shout, ' Stop! I will recant! ' Thus hypocrites by the millions can be made. You can make a man say that he has changed his mind; but he remains of the same opinion still. Put fetters all over him; crush his feet in iron boots; stretch him to the last gasp upon the holy rack; burn him, if you please, but his ashes will be of the same opinion still," Ingersoll declared.

But the power of orthodoxy can no longer bar the pathway of marching thought, for science has at last triumphed over its ancient adversary, Ingersoll fondly believed. "A few years ago, Science endeavoured to show that it was not inconsistent with the Bible; now Religion is endeavouring to prove that the Bible is not inconsistent with science." The Agnostic held one faith to be indispensable to human advancement, and that is *faith in man* and his unmeasured potentialities. "Theology is a superstition—Humanity, a religion," he affirmed.

Ingersoll was accused by the religionists of deliberately seeking to destroy the hope of a future life. He refuted this charge with the assertion that he would not " destroy one star of human hope."

Upon the question of immortality he was agnostic—he did not know " whether death is a wall or a door; the beginning or end of a day; the spreading of pinions to soar; or the folding for ever of wings; the rise or the set of a sun; or an endless life that will bring the rapture of love to everyone." He said that whether or not we are immortal is a fact in nature, and our desires and hopes have no relevancy to that fact whatever. He insisted that " the idea of immortality was not born of any religion," that " it was born of human affection," of the imperishable universal desire to be reunited with the loved and lost.

However, even if " death does end all, next to eternal joy, next to being for ever with those we love, is to be wrapped in the dreamless drapery of eternal peace. Next to eternal life is eternal sleep."

Ingersoll never claimed to have found the final or absolute truth. He merely expressed what appeared to him to be true. Like the true agnostic he was, he possessed the grace of mental modesty. All that he asked was liberty of thought and speech for everyone; that all men give to all others every right they claim for themselves.

As a Secularist and Humanist, Ingersoll was concerned with man and his welfare rather than with God and his worship. He believed that " the chief end of man " is not " to glorify God and enjoy him for ever," but to better the condition, improve the character and conduct, and increase the happiness of humanity here on this planet.

The consecrated purpose of his life was to do what he could to make the world truly free and unafraid, and to bring about a state of affairs in which every man will feel at liberty to investigate every book and creed and idea for himself. It is safe to say that no young acolyte ever entered upon his religious offices with purer or more self-effacing ardour than Ingersoll embarked upon his religious life of irreligion. However, there was one vital difference between acolyte and agnostic, inasmuch as one recognized authority for truth, and the other, truth for authority.

" He sounded forth the trumpet that shall never call retreat " —the battle cry of the Intellectual Rebel of all time : " I want no heaven for which I must give up my reason; no happiness in exchange for my liberty; and no immortality that demands the surrender of my individuality. Better rot in the windowless tomb, to which there is no door but the red mouth of the pallid worm, than wear the jewelled collar even of a god ! "

In reply to a statement in *The New York Observer*, a religious weekly, that Thomas Paine had recanted his freethought philosophy on his death-bed, Ingersoll published *A Vindication of Thomas Paine*, in which he offered *The Observer* a thousand-dollar reward if it could prove its assertion. However, the newspaper was never able to prove its charges against Paine, and Colonel Ingersoll even forced the editor, Rev. Irenæus Prine, to admit that the author of the *Age of Reason* never recanted.

1877

To *The New York Observer*.

Dear Sir:

. . . There is one thing I have noticed during this controversy regarding Thomas Paine. In no instance that I now call to mind, has any Christian writer spoken respectfully of Mr. Paine. All have taken particular pains to call him " Tom " Paine. Is it not a little strange that religion should make men so coarse and vulgar? I have often wondered what these same gentlemen would say if I should speak of the men eminent in the annals of Christianity in the same way. What would they say if I should write about " Dick " Whately, " Bill " Paley, and " Jack " Calvin? They would say of me then, just what I think of them now. Even if we have religion, do not let us try to get along without good manners. Rudeness is exceedingly unbecoming even in a saint. Persons who forgive their enemies, ought, to say the least, to treat with politeness those who have never injured them . . .

Very truly yours, R. G. Ingersoll

Moncure D. Conway, a distinguished American clergyman of liberal views, and biographer of Thomas Paine, was born in Stafford County, Virginia, on March 17, 1832. He was minister of the South Place Chapel, in London, from 1863 to 1897. He was the author, among other books, of *Testimonies Concerning Slavery, Christianity, Demonology and Devil Lore, Thomas Carlyle*, and *The Life of Thomas Paine*, in two volumes. He died in Paris, on November 15, 1907. On October 22, 1908, an annual series of lectures was established in London as a memorial to Mr. Conway.

" In his crusade against slavery, Conway was the militant humanitarian. . . . Throughout his life he befriended the downtrodden, whether the downtrodden one was a slave, or some Atheist or Agnostic attacked for his opinions. Into this also entered a moral courage which never wavered, even when the fight was hottest. He was the opponent of war as the enemy of mankind. And it should be added that his humanitarianism increased rather than diminished after he gave up the belief in theism. Conway was a genius for the humanizing of knowledge." (S. D. Wakefield, in *Truth Seeker*, March 19, 1927.)

Washington, D. C.
Dec. 5, 1877

Moncure D. Conway, Esq.

My dear Sir:

Yours of Nov. 12 was received today. I am a thousand times obliged to you for your flattering words and charming invitation.

You have probably seen by the dispatches that I have declined the mission [i.e., to go as U.S. ambassador to Berlin]. The religious press raised a most lugubrious howl of pious anguish. Hypocrites of the secular papers joined with the true believers in denouncing the appt. It was laughable to see the panic occasioned by so small a matter. I was anxious to see what would be said. Upon the whole the comments of the leading papers were very gratifying indeed. Not so much because they were full of kindness to me, but for the reason that they took the ground that religion was purely a personal matter with which the public had no right to meddle, one way or the other.

I have taken the liberty to send you a book, also a pamphlet in vindication of Thomas Paine.

Next year, in the autumn, I shall be in London and hope to make your acquaintance. I cannot express to you how much I was gratified and flattered by your note. I have read with the greatest pleasure many articles from your pen. Will you be kind enough to present Mrs. Conway with my highest regards.

I remain, Gratefully yours, R. G. Ingersoll

Washington, D. C.
February 6th, 1878

A. B. Harrower, Esq.

Dear Sir:

I have many objections to the philosophy of Christ. I do not believe in returning good for evil. I believe in returning justice for evil. I do not believe that I can put a man under a moral obligation to do me a favour by doing him a wrong. The doctrine of non-resistance is to me absurd. The right should be defended and the wrong resisted. Goodness should have the right to protect itself. Neither do I believe in decrying this world.

We should not say " Thou fool " to the man who works for those he loves. Poverty is not a virtue, nor is wealth a crime.

Christ is not my ideal.—Above any one man is humanity. With me, happiness is the end. I believe in the religion of this world.

Yours truly, R. G. Ingersoll

New York
February 25th, 1878

My sweet Wife:

I date this the 25th because it is a few minutes after twelve o'clock. Had a fine meeting tonight. I spoke two hours and a half.—The world is getting free. I thank God every day that he does *not* exist.

Mrs. Van Cott the woman preacher in an interview published in the papers this morning said she regarded me as a " poor barking dog." I wrote her a letter today as follows.

February 24th, 1878

Mrs. Van Cott.

My dear Madam:

Were you constrained by the love of Christ to say of a man who never injured you that he was " a poor barking dog "? Did you make this remark as a Christian or as a lady?

Did you say these bitter words to show in some slight degree the refining influence upon woman of the religion you preach? What would you think of me if I should retort, using your language, changing only the sex of the last word.

I have the honour to remain,

Yours truly, R. G. Ingersoll

A reporter happened to come in, and in the interview I gave him a copy of the letter. I think Mrs. Van Cott will wish she had let me alone. Ruth came at 1.30. She sends her love to all. I love you. I adore you. Kisses and love.

Robert

[So far as is known, the lady in question was never heard from again!]

Washington, D. C.
April 10th, 1878

Mr. Matt H. Carpenter.

My dear Sir:

The lecture delivered by me upon " Hell " has never been correctly published. Portions were taken by reporters and published in papers and pamphlets. They were filled with mistakes. In a little while I am going to publish what I did say upon that subject and will be pleased to send you a copy.

If, however, you wish to substantiate the pleasing dogma of eternal torment, in order that no argument may be lacking to prove the mercy of God I will give you an outline of my lecture. I did say among other things:

1. All religions have been made by man.
2. All books have been written by man.
3. Man gets all his ideas from his surroundings—from all that has been experienced by his ancestors and by himself.
4. Man knows nothing of origin and destiny. Nothing of a future state of torment.
5. The idea of hell was born of ignorance, hatred, barbarism, and malice.
6. Finite man cannot commit an infinite sin.
7. Finite beings cannot commit *any* against an infinite being. We can sin only against those we can *injure*. We cannot injure the infinite.
8. Hell is simply the consummation of revenge.

9. No good man can be perfectly happy while he knows that even one being is in torment. No good god can be perfectly happy while misery inflicted by him exists.

10. Apart from revenge, there can be no explanation of eternal torment.

11. The doctrine of " Hell " is an infamous lie. It has been an unmixed curse, filling the heart with hatred, and covering the world with blood. Whoever says he believes this doctrine ought to feel his cheeks redden with shame. It is a dogma unworthy of men—it would taint the reputation of a hyena, and smirch the fair name of an anaconda.

Yours truly, R. G. Ingersoll

Mrs. Annie Besant, a celebrated Freethinker and Agnostic who later became a leading Theosophist, was arrested in 1877 with Mr. Charles Bradlaugh, English Atheist, for publishing *Fruits of Philosophy*. Although the indictment was withdrawn the next year and was never renewed, a petition in chancery was presented to deprive Mrs. Besant of her child on the ground of Atheistic and Malthusian views. The petition was granted.

Washington, D. C.
June 10th, 1878

Mrs. Annie Besant.

My dear Madam:

I read a few moments ago an account of the proceedings in court when your child was torn from your arms by a robed brute acting as an English judge.

Such decisions bring a nation into contempt. There is no language strong enough to express my hatred for Sir George Jessel and my sympathy for you. A country in which such a decision can be allowed to stand is not civilized. Sir George Jessel will stand in the pillory of History as a cruel, cringing, and subservient tool of Christian hypocrisy.

Every good man—every virtuous woman, every loving mother should point the finger of scorn at such a beast. He is as contemptible and heartless as the God he pretends to worship. Is it possible that Christianity must be defended and preserved in this way? Must its infamous doctrines be sustained by the agonies and tears of mothers? Nearly all the cruelties have been inflicted in the name of God. All religions have been selfish and heartless and there never will be real liberty upon earth until the heavens are reaved of the Infinite Monster who threatens to inflict eternal torments upon mankind.

From the bottom of my heart I sympathize with you in your great and overwhelming grief. You have been true to yourself and your country has been false to you.

Your rights were submitted to that meanest and most despicable of beings—an unjust judge—and they have been trampled into the bloody dust of superstition. Every civilized American will despise this judge and give to you the tribute of respect and admiration.

I have the honour to remain your friend,

R. G. Ingersoll

Ingersoll felt that the " scheme of Redemption," or the Atonement, was " a complete subversion of all ideas of justice and morality." He maintained that the innocent cannot justly suffer for the guilty—" A God could not accept his own sufferings in justification of the guilty." He illustrated his point in legal terms: " A man has committed murder, has been tried, convicted, and condemned to death. Another man goes to the governor and says that he is willing to die in place of the murderer. The governor says: ' All right, I accept your offer, a murder has been committed, somebody must be hung and your death will satisfy the law.' But that is not the law. The law says, not that somebody shall be hanged, but that the murderer shall suffer death. Even if the governor should die in the place of the criminal, it would be no better. ·There would be two murders instead of one, two innocent men killed, one by the first murderer and one by the State, and the real murderer would be free." This is what Christians call " satisfying the law."

Washington, D. C.
July 31, 1879

Jos. E. Gould, Esq.,
154 John St., Toronto, Canada.
My dear Sir:

I received the pamphlets, and read a portion of each. To me, the doctrines of Substitution and Redemption are simply absurdities. The idea that an Infinite God would be foolish enough to make folks that he would afterwards have to die to redeem, seems to me utterly destitute of common sense. Nothing is more absurd than this, except the doctrine of substitution. I cannot see why an innocent man should be punished in place of the guilty one.

These ideas are born of the superstition, ignorance, and barbarism of the past, and seem to me hardly worthy of being gravely discussed in the enlightened present.

I want no innocent man to suffer for me. Neither do I wish to go to Heaven by virtue of the agony of an innocent God or an innocent son of a God. Man must save himself. He neither needs, nor can he have any other saviours.

I am much obliged to you, however, for the pamphlets, and should not have written so freely had you been the author.

Yours truly, R. G. Ingersoll

August 4, 1879

G. Mewhirk, Esq.

My dear Sir:

I am glad that you agree with me on the Jewish question. I take it that what Christians have always done because they had the power, is the natural outgrowth of Christianity. In every country where Christians have had the power, until they were somewhat civilized by commercial polity, the Jews have been persecuted, and so I look upon persecution as the natural result of Christianity; and allow me to ask here, why a Christian should have any hesitancy in burning a man a few minutes for heresy, when he worships a God who will burn the same man for ever.

Yours truly, R. G. Ingersoll

August 5th, 1879

J. E. Remsburg,
Atchison, Kansas.

My dear Sir:

I read your article upon Thomas Paine with interest.

My idea has always been, that no matter who wrote the Declaration of Independence, the principal ideas were furnished by Thomas Paine. Most of the expressions are his, and so I rather incline to your view of the matter.

Hoping sometime to make your acquaintance and thank you in person for the extremely kind and complimentary things you have said of me,

I remain, Your friend, R. G. Ingersoll

Washington, D. C.
March 27, 1880

To the Editor of *The Chicago Times*:

Today Messrs. Wright, Dickey, O'Connor, and March, of the select Committee on the Causes of the Present Depression of Labour, presented the majority a special report upon Chinese immigration.

These gentlemen are in great fear for the future of our most holy and perfectly authenticated religion, and have, like faithful watchmen, from the walls and towers of Zion, hastened to give the alarm. They have informed Congress that " Joss has his temple of worship in the Chinese quarters, in San Francisco." Within the walls of a dilapidated structure is exposed to the view of the faithful the god of the Chinaman, and here are his altars of worship. Here he tears up his pieces of paper; here he offers up his prayers; here he receives his religious consolations; and here is his road to the celestial land; that "Joss is located in a long, narrow room in a building in a back alley, upon a kind of altar"; that "he is a wooden image, looking as much like an alligator as a human being"; that "the Chinese think there is such a place as heaven"; that "all classes of Chinamen worship idols"; that "the temple is open every day at all hours"; that "the Chinese have no Sunday"; that this heathen god has "huge jaws, a big red tongue, large white teeth, a half-dozen arms, and big, fiery eyeballs. About him are placed offerings of meat, and other eatables —a sacrificial offering."

The world is also informed by these gentlemen that "idolatry of the Chinese produces a demoralizing effect upon our American youth by bringing sacred things into disrespect, and making religion a theme of disgust and contempt."

In San Francisco there are some three hundred thousand people. Is it possible that a few Chinese can bring our "holy religion" into disgust and contempt? In that city there are fifty times as many churches as joss-houses. Scores of sermons are uttered every week; religious books and papers are plentiful as leaves in autumn, and somewhat drier; thousands of bibles are within the reach of all. And there, too, is the example of a Christian city.

Why should we send missionaries to China, if we cannot convert the heathen when they come here? When missionaries go to a foreign land, the poor, benighted people have to take their word for the blessings showered upon a Christian people; but when the heathen come here they can see for themselves. What was simply a story becomes a demonstrated fact. They come in contact with people who love their enemies. They see that in a Christian land men tell the truth; that they will not take advantage of strangers; that they are just and patient, kind and tender; that they never resort to force; that they have no prejudice on account of colour, race, or religion; that they look upon mankind as brethren; that they speak of God as a universal father and are willing to work, and even to suffer, for the good not only of their own countrymen, but of the heathen as well. All this the Chinese see and know, and why they still cling to the religion of their country, is to me a matter of amazement.

We all know that the disciples of Jesus do unto others as they would that others should do unto them, and that those of Confucius do not unto others anything that they would not that others should do unto them. Surely such people ought to live together in perfect peace.

Rising with the subject, growing heated with a kind of holy indignation, these Christian representatives of a Christian people most solemnly declare that: "Any one who is really endowed with a correct knowledge of our religious system, which acknowledges the existence of a living God and an accountability to him, and a future state of reward and punishment, who feels that he has an apology for this abominable pagan worship, is not a fit person to be ranked as a good citizen of the American union. It is absurd to make an apology for its toleration. It must be abolished, and the sooner the decree goes forth by the power of this government, the better it will be for the interests of this land."

I take this, the earliest opportunity, to inform these gentlemen composing a majority of the committee that we have in the United States no " religious system "; that this is a secular government; that it has no religious creed; that it does not believe nor disbelieve in a future state of reward and punishment; that it neither affirms nor denies the existence of a " living God "; and that the only god, so far as this government is concerned, is the legally expressed will of the majority of the people. Under our flag the Chinese have the same right to worship a wooden god that you have to worship any other. The constitution protects equally the church of Jehovah and the house of Joss. Whatever their relative positions may be in heaven, they stand upon a perfect equality in the United States. This government is an infidel government. We have a constitution with man put in and God left out; and it is the glory of this country that we have such a constitution.

Our religion can only be brought into contempt by the actions of those who profess to be governed by its teachings. This report will do more in that direction than millions of Chinese could do by burning pieces of paper before a wooden image. If you wish to impress the Chinese with the value of our religion, of what you are pleased to call the " American system," show them that Christians are better than heathens. Prove to them that what you are pleased to call the " living God," teaches higher and nobler things, a grander and purer code of morals than can be found upon pagan pages. Excel these wretches in industry, in honesty, in reverence for parents, in cleanliness, in frugality; and above all by advocating the absolute liberty of human thought.

Do not trample upon these people because they have a different conception of things about which even this committee knows nothing.

Congress has nothing to do with the religion of the people. Its members are not responsible to God for the opinions of their constituents, and it may tend to the happiness of the constituents for me to state that they are in no way responsible for the religion of the members. Religion is an individual, not a national, matter. And where the nation interferes with the right of conscience, the liberties of the people are devoured by the monster superstition.

If you wish to drive out the Chinese do not make a pretext of religion. Do not pretend that you are trying to do God a favour. Injustice in his name is doubly detestable. The assassin

88

cannot sanctify his dagger by falling on his knees, and it does not help a falsehood if it be uttered as a prayer. Religion used to intensify the hatred of men towards men under the pretence of pleasing God, has cursed the world.

A portion of this most remarkable report is intensely religious. There is in it almost the odour of sanctity; and when reading it, one is impressed with the living piety of its authors. But on the 25th page there are a few passages that must pain the hearts of true believers. Leaving their religious views, the members immediately betake themselves to philosophy and prediction. Listen:

" The Chinese race and the American citizen, whether native born or who is eligible to our naturalization laws and becomes a citizen, are in a state of antagonism. They cannot nor will not ever meet upon common ground and occupy together the same social level. This is impossible. The pagan and the Christian travel different paths. This one believes in a living God; that one, in the type of monsters and worship of wood and stone. Thus, in the religion of the two races of men they are as wide apart as the poles of the two hemispheres. They cannot now and never will approach the same religious altar. The Christian will not recede to barbarism, nor will the Chinese advance to the enlightened belt (whatever it is) of civilization . . . He cannot be converted to those modern ideas of religious worship which have been accepted by Europe and which crowns the American system."

Christians used to believe that through their religion all the nations of the earth were finally to be blest. In accordance with that belief missionaries have been sent to every land, and untold wealth has been expended for what has been called the spread of the gospel.

I am almost sure that I have read somewhere that " Christ died for all men," and that " God is no respecter of persons." It was once taught that it was the duty of Christians to tell to all people the " tidings of great joy." I have never believed these things myself, but have always contended that an honest merchant was the best missionary. Commerce makes friends, religion makes enemies; the one enriches, and the other impoverishes; the one thrives best where the truth is told, the other, where falsehoods are believed. For myself, I have but little confidence in any business, or enterprise, or investment that promises dividends only after the death of the stockholders.

But I am astonished that four Christian statesmen, four members of Congress in the last quarter of the nineteenth century, who seriously object to people on account of their religious convictions, should still assert that the very religion in which they believe—and the only religion established by the living God, head of the American law—is not adapted to the spiritual needs of one-third of the human race. It is amazing that these four gentlemen have, in the defence of the Christian religion, announced the discovery that it is wholly inadequate for the civilization of mankind that the light of the cross can never penetrate the darkness of China; " that all the labours of the missionary, the example of the good, the exalted character of our civilization, makes no impression upon the pagan life of the Chinese "; and that even the report of this committee will not tend to elevate, refine, and Christianize the yellow heathen of the Pacific coast. In the name of religion these gentlemen have denied its power and mocked at the enthusiasm of its founder. Worse than this, they have predicted for the Chinese a future of ignorance and idolatry in this world, and, if the " American system " of religion is true, hell-fire in the next.

For the benefit of these four philosophers and prophets, I will give a few extracts from the writings of Confucius, that will, in my judgment, compare favourably with the best passages of their report:

" My doctrine is that man must be true to the principles of his nature, and the benevolent exercise of them towards others."

" With coarse rice to eat, with water to drink, and with my bended arm for a pillow, I still have joy."

" Riches and honour acquired by injustice are to me but floating clouds."

" The man who, in view of gain, thinks of righteousness; who, in view of danger, forgets life, and who remembers an old agreement, however far back it extends, such a man may be reckoned a complete man."

" Recompense injury with justice, and kindness with kindness."

" There is one word which may serve as a rule of practice for all one's life; Reciprocity is that word."

When the ancestors of the four Christian Congressmen were barbarians, when they lived in caves, gnawed bones, and worshipped dried snakes, the infamous Chinese were reading these sublime sentences of Confucius. When the forefathers of these Christian statesmen were hunting toads to get the jewels out of their heads, to be used as charms, the wretched Chinese were calculating eclipses, and measuring the circumference of the earth. When the progenitors of these representatives of the " American system of religion " were burning women charged with nursing devils, the people " incapable of being influenced by the exalted character of our civilization," were building asylums for the insane.

Neither should it be forgotten that, for thousands of years, the Chinese honestly practised the great principle known as civil-service reform—a something that even the administration of Mr. Hayes has reached only through the proxy of promise.

If we wish to prevent the immigration of the Chinese, let us reform our treaties with the vast empire from whence they came. For thousands of years the Chinese secluded themselves from the rest of the world. They did not deem the Christian nations fit to associate with. We forced ourselves upon them. We called not with cards, but with cannon. The English battered down the doors in the names of opium and Christ. The infamy was regarded as another triumph for the gospel. At last, in self-defence the Chinese allowed Christians to touch their shores. Their wise men, their philosophers protested, and prophesied that time would show that the Christians could not be trusted. This report proves that the wise men were not only philosophers but prophets.

Treat China as you would England. Keep a treaty while it is in force. Change it if you will, according to the laws of nations, but, on no account excuse a breach of national faith by pretending that we are dishonest for God's sake.

Robert G. Ingersoll

The designation " Infidel " seems to have been in far more general favour among freethinkers and religious liberals back in the 'eighties and 'nineties of the last century than it is in our day. Robert Ingersoll often used the term to describe irreligionists in general and himself in particular; and " infidel " was habitually employed by Mrs. Ingersoll in private conversation in apparent preference to " Agnostic " or " Freethinker."

Washington, D. C.
November 8, 1880

Stephen S. Day, Esq.

Dear Sir:

I am an infidel because I hate tyranny, injustice, and slavery in all their forms. I am an infidel because I love liberty, justice, and intellectual light in all their forms. I am an infidel because I hate the infamous dogma of eternal punishment, because I hate the selfish heaven of the saved, and because I hate a God who would make a human being, knowing that that being would suffer forever.

I love all the good there is in the teachings of Christ, and I hate the dogmas of most of his followers. So you will see that I am an Infidel because I hate, and because I love. I love mankind, I worship liberty, and I hate all forms of superstition that enslave the mind and petrify the heart.

Yours truly, R. G. Ingersoll

Washington, D. C.
Jan. 3rd, 1882

To the Editor of the *Duluth Tribune*.

My dear Mr. Mitchell,

Much obliged to you for your letter of the 29th. The clippings you send me appeared in the papers two or three years ago. I had a correspondence with one of the ministers upon the subject, and convicted him of having told a falsehood. These ministers were really not worth noticing. I had delivered a lecture in Chicago that the clergy could not answer. Fifteen or twenty of them tried, and yet the people, speaking through the principal papers of the city, decided that the replies were entirely unsatisfactory. This aroused these particular preachers up to the lying point. As they could not answer my arguments, they did the next best thing—they attacked me. They could not lie so as to answer the points I had made, because, as a matter of fact, there is no logic in lies. As lies cannot hurt logic, they used them to destroy, not the logic, but the logician. I can always tell when my arrows have reached the heart of superstition. If the points I have made cannot be answered, then my character gets bad, as my arguments get good. I presume if I were to make a weak speech, my reputation would be excellent.

Of course my reputation has nothing to do with the question, one way or the other. Admitting that I am the worst man in the world, still there is some doubt about the general deluge. If it should be proved that I am the unfortunate possessor of all the vices, still some people might have their doubt about the whale's having swallowed Jonah. And should I be so unfortunate as to die in the penitentiary, even after that, some folks might say that the doctrine of the Trinity was mathematically absurd.

I have no time to answer all the attacks made upon me; and if I had, I might be engaged in better business. There is an old saying that he who takes medicine every time he feels unwell will soon ruin his constitution, and that he who defends his character from every attack will soon lose it. I have been charged with everything; but what has that to do with the existence of the supernatural? Suppose all these charges to be true, is the Bible then inspired; and is an eternity of pain the lot of nearly all the sons of men?

A very good story is told of Sydney Smith. He was conversing with a young man, who it seems used a great deal of profane language. After a while, Mr. Smith said to him, " Let us admit, for the purpose of this conversation, that everything in the universe has been thoroughly damned, and go on with the discussion." So I say to the ministers, " Let us go on with the discussion." No matter what I may have done, and no matter what I may do, gentlemen, be kind enough to answer what I say.

Most of these gentlemen claim that they love even their enemies. In order to get a little practice, so that to love enemies will at least be comparatively easy, would it not be well enough to commence by treating those decently who are *not* their enemies? I do not ask their friendship. I do not want their praise. I have only one request to make of the clergy of the whole world, and that is, that they will not tell falsehoods about me. There are two things I would like to have them stick to—one is, the *subject under discussion*, and the other is, the *truth*. Until I read some of the attacks that have been made upon me, I had no conception of the malignity of the modern churches. They do not seem to care for the consequences of their acts. They are willing to malign men, women, and children. They have no respect for the feelings of others. They are perfectly willing to wreck the life of any man who has the courage to express his honest thoughts. They would be delighted to see his wife in want, his children clad in rags. They would repeat with infinite unction the prayer recorded in the 109th Psalm. With folded hands and upturned eyes they would say to God: "Let his children be fatherless and his wife a widow. Let his children be continuously vagabonds, and beg. Let them seek their bread also out of the desolate places. Let there be none to extend mercy unto them, neither let there be any to favour his fatherless children."

Of course, there are *many* exceptions. There are good, honest, self-sacrificing men in the pulpits and the pews; but, judging from my experience, I would almost hate to say *how* few.

Yours truly, R. G. Ingersoll

George Jacob Holyoake and Robert Ingersoll were devoted and loving friends. The two corresponded over a period of years, although they had the opportunity to meet only during the visits that Mr. Holyoake made to the U.S.A. in the late 'seventies and early 'eighties, when he was a frequent and most welcome guest at the Ingersoll home. "I am charmed with you, and count it one of the happiest events of my life to have made your acquaintance. We talk of you every day," the Colonel wrote. "It seems a thousand years since we met. . . . Do you expect to visit America again? You would meet with a splendid reception now we know you. . . ." In another letter he said: "You are doing great good, and the great regret I have when thinking of you is that there are no others like you. I read your last article on Bradlaugh. You expressed my feelings to a hair." At last, in June, 1882, Ingersoll heard that he was coming with his daughter, and invited them to spend a week with him at Long Beach. "I anticipate one of the best visits of my life with you and yours," and Holyoake spent ten days with Ingersoll and his family at Long Beach. Ingersoll and Holyoake spoke the same language of the spirit, and the glowing friendship between them was cherished by both as among the deepest and richest satisfactions of their lives.

At an early age Mr. Holyoake reacted against his orthodox religious upbringing, and became an avowed Rationalist.

Although not an Atheist in the accepted sense, it is said that he was the last person to be imprisoned in England on the charge of Atheism (1841 or 1842). He established and edited many Rationalist and radical papers, and took a leading part in founding the Rationalist Press Association of London, of which he was the first Chairman.

Rationalism may be termed the intellectual attitude of which " Secularism " is the expression in action. Holyoake was the first to use the name " Secularist " as a designation for himself and his followers. He organized Secularist societies in London and the provinces, and for many years was President of the British Secular Union. He defined Secularism as " a code of duty pertaining to this life, founded on considerations purely human." Ingersoll described Secularism as " the religion of humanity " which " embraces the affairs of this world "; is " interested in everything that touches the welfare of a sentient being. . . . It is another name for common sense; that is to say, the adaptation of means to such ends as are desired and understood. . . . Secularism believes in building a home here, in this world. It trusts to individual effort, to energy, to intelligence, to observation and experience, rather than to the unknown and the supernatural. It desires to be happy on this side of the grave. . . ." Secularism was the nineteenth-century equivalent of twentieth-century Humanism.

Mr. Holyoake was a pioneer in the great Co-operative movement in England and on the Continent.

Charles Bradlaugh (1833–91), referred to in the letter below, was a great English Secularist and reformer. In 1866 he founded the National Secular Society. He campaigned for a seat in the House of Commons from Northampton, in 1868; however, he was not permitted to take his seat, to which he had been repeatedly re-elected, until 1886, because the House refused him permission to take the oath. He made three lecture tours in the United States (1873–74–75). He successfully sponsored the famous bill giving the right to affirm, instead of taking an oath, in 1888, and in the following year he introduced a bill to abolish the laws against blasphemy. Mr. Bradlaugh was an extraordinarily eloquent and effective orator, and exerted a powerful influence in the emancipation of English working-men.

Washington, D. C., March 31, 1882

My dear Holyoake:

I was greatly pleased to get your letter and thank you for all the kind things you say. I read your little article on the course of the newspaper and agree with every word you say. There is no argument in epithets. The idea of referring to the mother of Jesus as a harlot is low, vile, and disgusting. No paper can afford to print such stuff. Neither do I believe in calling a bishop a liar simply because he is a bishop. It is bad enough to call a man a bishop.

Your position on the oath business is just exactly right. Where nothing is said, where no point is made, it may be well enough for an " infidel " to take the ordinary oath, feeling that he is bound by every consideration to tell the truth. But where the point is raised, where it can be even suspected that you are willing to gain any advantage by taking an oath inconsistent with your belief, then of course there is but one way. You must refuse, no matter what the consequences may be.

I have been sworn in courts, and have always been sworn in the usual way. In the West there is no Bible kissing. You hold up your hand, the clerk in a mumbling way repeats some words— ending with " s'help you God "—I have always held up my hand with the rest. It seemed to me too small a matter to make any complaint about, as every one in the Court-room knew my real opinions. But if anyone had raised the point that I was an atheist, I should have said that I was, and that I did not intend to admit the existence of God by holding up my hand, and that in taking an oath I merely intended to make myself liable to the pains and penalties of perjury if I should swear falsely. If, then, the Court had held that I must take the oath in order to testify, I should have refused.

In this country, in nearly all the States, and maybe in all, witnesses are allowed to affirm, and in consequence few care whether they swear or affirm. Members of Congress, and in fact all Federal officers are allowed to swear or affirm, and it seems to me that all in England should have the same right. If it was claimed in this country that in taking the usual oath any theological dogma was admitted, under no circumstances would I be sworn. The truth is, that until Bradlaugh's case came up I never thought anything about it. If you and I were in China, and you were falsely charged with an offence, and the Court would not believe my testimony unless I would kill a chicken or break a saucer, I would kill the fowl and shatter the pottery. I would do this simply in order that the truth might be believed. I regard the entire oath business as perfectly absurd. It has no effect on honest men, and can be taken advantage of by rogues. Most jurors place all testimony on an equality, because the witnesses have been sworn. The oath is the best friend that falsehood has. It is the solemn mask of a lie. I would like to see all oaths abolished. The good and bad should not be put on a level in a court of justice. A brazen falsehood gilded with an oath passes for pure gold .

95

Washington, D. C.
April 22, 1882

Dr. T. L. Brown.

My dear Friend,

I received your *Funeral Sermon* and am exceedingly glad that you are still alive and well, and that it may be many long and happy years before the sermon is needed.

I see nothing in what you say calculated to injure the cause of mental freedom. I want you to say your say, and it makes no difference whether I agree or disagree with all your thoughts. As to whether we live again, I have no knowledge. I do not say that we will not, because I do not *know*. I do not say that we will, because I do not know. I am not trying to destroy a belief in Heaven. Hell is the place that I wish to have blotted from the map of the future.

I wish to get the demon of fear out of the human heart. I believe your address would be just a little better if it contained the admission that you do not know. I do not want to destroy a hope—nothing that sheds one ray of light on the weary pathway of a life. I want freedom, and I want all devils exorcised and all hells extinguished.

I must say that your address shows great courage—great confidence in your position, and that it is honest and manly in the highest degree.

Yours always, R. G. Ingersoll

Washington, D. C.
October 26th, '82

Jno. J. Cushing, Esq.,
Ashton, Spink Co., Dakota.

Dear Sir:

Your letter of the 19th just received. Of course, I never denied my daughters the privilege of attending Sunday-school. Neither of my children even desired to attend Sunday-school— never thought of such a thing—never mentioned such a wish. If they desired to attend Church or Sunday-school, I should not interpose the slightest objection. So much for your first question.

As for Thomas Paine—he died as he had lived—a consistent deist. He was a believer in God and hoped for immortality. As to the charge that he was a drunkard, he drank, I presume, about the same quantity absorbed by the average preacher of his day. At that time nearly all people drank some, and Thomas Paine was no exception. Of course, a glass in a Christian would be a barrel in a deist.

Neither has it ever been established that Thomas Paine was a cruel man in his family—on the contrary, he was an extremely kind man. He and his wife separated. She was asked the cause of the separation, and replied: "It was no fault of Mr. Paine." Mr.

Paine was asked the same question and replied: "It was not my wife's fault." These answers were extremely honourable to both. No one knows, to this day, the cause of the separation.

The Church could not answer the arguments of Thomas Paine, and defamed him for that reason.

Yours truly, R. G. Ingersoll

Washington, D. C.
October 31st, '82

D. Smith, Esq.,
Medford, N. J.

My dear Sir:

I received the "leaflets" you were kind enough to send.

I do not consider it a very important question whether Christ was the Son of God, or not. After all, what difference does it make? If he never existed, we are under the same obligation to do what we believe to be right; and believing that he was the Son of God, or disbelieving it, is of no earthly importance. If we are ever judged at all it will be by our actions, and not by our beliefs. If Christ was good enough to die for me, he certainly will not be bad enough to damn me for honestly failing to believe in his divinity. He will behave just as well in heaven as he did while on earth; and certainly I should have no fear of the fury of love and forgiveness! The only question is, am I honest? and at the day of judgment, if there is to be one, Christ will understand my case, if he is what you say he is. He will know that the evidence was insufficient to my mind, and as he made the mind, and furnished the evidence, if the evidence failed to convince—that is, to agree with the mind, or the mind, to comprehend the evidence, it is not the fault of the mind, but of Christ.

Hoping that some time you will have confidence enough in Jesus to believe that in all circumstances, he will do the fair thing,

I remain, Yours truly, R. G. Ingersoll

What might be called the quietly revolutionary quality of Ingersoll's mind—and the utter independence and courage of his thinking, are strikingly in evidence in the letter which follows.

November 3, 1882

Albert H. Walker, Esq.,
Hartford, Conn.

Dear Sir:

I shall read your book at the first opportunity. Of course I admit that Christ was right on several questions, and I also think he was wrong on some others. It is remarkable how little he had to say about the family—about the rights of wives and children—about the common duties without which society is an impossibility. Neither do I regard him as the highest example for anybody.

97

He discovered no new truth, moral or physical; he invented nothing of use; he seemed to know nothing of government. He said nothing against slavery, nothing in favour of education— seemed to know nothing of commerce, and had not the slightest information upon any scientific subject. Had he known the shape of the earth, his theory in regard to the winds would have been different. His idea seemed to be that as God took care of the birds, he would take care of his children, provided they would rely entirely upon him. He held this world in supreme contempt; and not only its pains but its pleasures. He taught the doctrine of forgiveness for this world, and reserved the luxury of revenge for heaven.

Men are but fragments—the complete circle of excellence has never been attained.

At the very best Christ was but a sentiment. I am very glad, however, that you agree with me in the sentiment that Christ was never ignorant enough, nor malicious enough, to have spoken the words attributed to him in the last chapter of Mark.

Very truly yours, R. G. Ingersoll

December 7th, '82

G. T. Lancaster, Esq.,
Lyons, Wayne Co., N. Y.

Dear Sir:
The charges you refer to concerning my family, are false.

1. We never lived in Baltimore.

2. My wife never joined any church.

3. I have two daughters, and no sons. Neither of my daughters ever joined any church, and never expressed a desire to do so— never thought of such a thing.

You were therefore perfectly right in denying the charges. I will state, in this connection, that I do not think there is the slightest danger of any of my family joining the Presbyterian, or any other church.

Very truly yours, R. G. Ingersoll

Washington, D. C.
December 30th, '82

N. Currier, Esq.,
Enfield, N. H.

Dear Sir:
I am greatly obliged to you for giving me an account of the tempest in the theological teapot in your town. If the clergy had the power, of course they would prevent the reading of all such books; and, if Christianity, as commonly understood, be true, such books ought not to be read. The Government should not allow them to be printed. If " salvation " depends upon " belief," nothing can be more important than " belief," and no act can be

more criminal than to try to undermine this "belief." The argument is this: God gives a large amount of brains to A, and a small amount to B. B is a Christian. A, by presenting arguments that B cannot answer, destroys the "belief" of B. As a consequence, B is "lost for ever." Now if God made them both, he certainly should have given B brains enough to be able to answer A's arguments, and escape the fearful doom. Again: If a giant should attack a feeble person, and throw him over a precipice, nobody would blame the feeble person, they would blame the giant. Now if a mental giant should overthrow the belief of an intellectual pigmy, certainly God should not punish the pigmy, he should either quit making pigmies, or punish giants for interfering with pigmies! During the [Civil] war I heard a story about a Methodist preacher who commenced his prayer with the invocation: "Oh thou great and unscrupulous God!" If the orthodox religion be true, that prayer expressed with great accuracy the character of the Christian God.

Yours truly, R. G. Ingersoll

January 1st, 1883

Dear Mr. Holyoake,

We have missed you every day, and every day we talk about you and yours. You are the model man. You are so kind, candid, just, forgiving, and generous, and withal so uncompromising, so perfectly true to conviction, so ready to do and to suffer for the right, so severe with yourself and so easy with others, that we cannot help admiring and loving you. Besides, you have such a vein of genuine humour, such a keen sense of the ridiculous and absurd, that you are certainly the prince of companions. I am writing just what I feel, and it makes no difference whether you agree with me or not. I know what you are, and how infinitely true—how unspeakably honest and brave you have been, are, and always will be. There is no living man for whom I have greater respect and admiration.

Robert G. Ingersoll

Dear Mr. Ingersoll:

. . . My days have all been brighter since I received your letter. It is not necessary to take unto myself all the terms which your bountiful friendship employs—to feel proud of the generous partiality from which they proceed. As though I were still with you I watch all you do, and read all that Mr. Farrell in his kindness sends me that you say.

If you fight X [some controversial opponent], do it with a sword, when you can cleave him in twain with one blow, as from the arm of Gog or Magog. If pistols must be used, I crave to enter the lists for you. You are too palpable a mark, while I, attenuated and only semi-visible, could ill be seen by the mangy eyes of the adversary, and would be ill to hit if observed.

George Jacob Holyoake

99

Brooklyn, N. Y.,
78 Second Place
March 12th, 1883

Mr. Robert Ingersoll.

Dear Sir:

A strong impression came upon me last week to pray for your conversion to God. I obeyed the influence and have prayed for you, also have asked others to assist with their prayers. I believe it was God the Holy Spirit moved me to do this, and I expect to have answers to our prayers on your behalf. I believe you had some serious thoughts about your soul on last Sabbath evening about ten o'clock, as there were a company of faithful men on their knees praying for you. I want to see you " born again." " That which is born of the flesh is flesh, and that which is born of the Spirit is Spirit." " Except a man be born again he cannot see the Kingdom of God." And Christ has said " Him that cometh unto me I will in *no wise* cast out." I never had peace till I gave myself to Christ and obeyed my conscience. God does speak to us through our consciences and if we do not obey his Voice in our Souls we are unhappy and condemned.

I pray God to so change you that I will yet see you a preacher of the Gospel of Jesus Christ. All things are possible to God if he undertakes to do the work ; he can and will do it. He changed " Saul," and has power and love enough to change you. May God convert you and make you a blessing to the world.

Yours truly, John McGohie

Washington, D. C.
March 13, 1883

John McGohie, Esq.

Dear Sir:

No doubt about your honesty and your good intention. My own opinion is that prayer avails nothing. All the prayers in the world cannot add a blade of grass to the earth nor get one drop of rain from the sky. Certainly a God who failed to protect the martyrs—who allowed millions of men to be enslaved—who permitted babes to be sold from the breasts of mothers, cannot be relied on to take any particular pains to convert an infidel. Why should you depend upon a God who allows whole nations to be decimated by famine and pestilence to answer the prayers of a few gentlemen living in Brooklyn? Why should I desire the forgiveness of Christ? I never injured him. I want to be forgiven by those I have injured—not by those who lived nearly two thousand years before I was born.

I have examined the doctrines of the Christian system and am convinced that they are for the most part unsound.—Nothing can be more absurd than the idea that somebody else can be virtuous for me or bad for me.—I cannot be charged with the sins

of Adam nor credited with the goodness of Christ. The idea of eternal punishment is infamous and ought never to be taught. It has filled the world with horror and is as wretched [?] as foolish.—
The only thing for a man to do is to treat others justly, make as much happiness as he can—get superstition out of his mind—depend upon facts—get all he can out of this world and let the next wait until he gets there.—Labour is the right kind of prayer—and kindness is better than belief.—I am not depending on Christ to save me. I am depending wholly upon myself. If there be another world I shall do the best I can after I get there. In the meantime I have no fear.

Yours truly, R. G. Ingersoll

August 8th, 1883

To The Editor of *The Boston Investigator*.

Mr. Editor:

Two articles have appeared lately in *The Investigator* attacking the motives of George Jacob Holyoake. He is spoken of as a man governed by a desire to please the rich and powerful, as one afraid of public opinion, and who in the perilous hour, denies or conceals his convictions.

In these attacks, there is not one word of truth. They are based upon mistakes and misconceptions. There is not in this world a nobler, braver man. In England he has done as much for the great cause of intellectual liberty as any other man of this generation. He has done as much for the poor, for the children of toil, for the homeless and wretched, as any other living man. He has attacked all abuses, all tyranny, and all forms of hypocrisy. His weapons have been, reason, logic, facts, kindness, and above all, example. He has lived his creed. He has won the admiration and respect of his bitterest antagonists. He has had the simplicity of childhood, the enthusiasm of youth, and the wisdom of age. He is not abusive, but he is clear and conclusive. He is intense without violence—firm without anger. He has the strength of perfect kindness. He does not hate—he pities. He does not attack men and women, but dogmas and creeds. He does not attack them to get the better of people, but to enable people to get the better of them. He gives the light he has. He shares his intellectual wealth with the orthodox poor. He assists without insulting, guides without arrogance, and enlightens without outrage. Besides, he is eminent for the exercise of plain common sense. He knows that there are wrongs besides those born of superstition—that people are not necessarily happy because they have renounced the Thirty-nine Articles—and that the priest is not the only enemy of mankind.

He has for forty years been preaching and practising industry, economy, self-reliance, and kindness. He has done all within his power to give the working man a better home, better food, better wages, and better opportunities for the education of his children. He has demonstrated the success of co-operation—of intelligent combination for the common good. As a rule, his methods have been perfectly legal. In some instances he has knowingly violated the law, and did so with the intention to take the consequences. He would neither ask nor accept a pardon, because to receive a pardon carries with it the implied promise to keep the law, and an admission that you were in the wrong. He would not agree to desist from doing what he believed ought to be done, neither would he stain his past to brighten his future, nor imprison his soul to free his body. He has that happy mingling of gentleness and firmness found only in the highest type of moral heroes. He is an absolutely just man, and will never do an act that he would condemn in another. He admits that the most bigoted churchman has not only a perfect right to express his opinion, but that he must be met with argument couched in kind and candid terms. Mr. Holyoake is not only the enemy of the theological hierarchy, but he is also opposed to mental mobs. He will not use the bludgeon of epithets.

Perfect fairness is regarded by many as weakness. Some people have altogether more confidence in their beliefs than in their own arguments. They resort to assertion. If what they assert be denied, the " debate " becomes a question of veracity. On both sides of most questions there are plenty of persons who imagine that logic dwells only in adjectives, and that to speak kindly of an opponent is a virtual surrender.

Mr. Holyoake attacks the Church because it has been, is, and ever will be, the enemy of mental freedom, but he does not wish to deprive the Church even of its freedom to express its opinion against freedom. He is true to his own creed, knowing that when we have freedom we can take care of all its enemies.

In one of the articles to which I have referred, it is charged that Mr. Holyoake refused to sign a petition for the pardon of persons convicted of blasphemy. If this is true, he undoubtedly had a reason satisfactory to himself. You will find that his action, or his refusal to act rests upon a principle that he would not violate in his own behalf.

Why should we suspect the motives of this man who has given his life for the good of others? I know of no one who is his mental or moral superior. He is the most disinterested of men. His name is a synonym of candour. He is a natural logician—an intellectual marksman. Like an unerring arrow his thought flies to the heart and centre. He is governed by principle, and makes no exception in his own favour. He is intellectually honest. He shows you the cracks and flaws in his own wares. He calls attention to the open joints and to the weakest links. He does not want a victory for himself, but for truth. He wishes to expose and oppose, not men, but error. He is blessed with that cloudless mental vision that appearances cannot deceive, that interests cannot darken, and that even ingratitude cannot blur. Friends cannot induce, and enemies cannot drive this man to do an act that his heart and brain would not applaud. That such a character was formed without the aid of the Church, without the hope of harp or fear of flame, is a demonstration against the necessity of superstition.

Whoever is opposed to mental bondage, to the shackles wrought by cruelty and worn by fear, should be the friend of this heroic and unselfish man.

I know something of his life—something of what he has suffered—of what he has accomplished for his fellow-men. He has been maligned, imprisoned, and impoverished. " He bore the heat and burden of the unregarded day," and " remembered the misery of the many." For years his only recompense was ingratitude. At last he was understood. He was recognized as an earnest, honest, gifted, generous, sterling man, loving his country, sympathizing with the poor, honouring the useful, and holding in supreme abhorrence tyranny and falsehood in all their forms.

The idea that this man could for a moment be controlled by any selfish motive, by the hope of preferment, by fear of losing a supposed annuity, is simply absurd. The authors of these attacks are not acquainted with Mr. Holyoake. Whoever dislikes him does not know him.

Read his *Trial of Theism*—his history of *Co-operation in England* —if you wish to know his heart—to discover the motives of his life—the depth and tenderness of his sympathy—the nobleness of his nature—the subtlety of his thought—the beauty of his spirit— the force and volume of his brain—the extent of his information— his candour, his kindness, his genius, and the perfect integrity of his stainless soul. There is no man for whom I have greater respect, greater reverence, greater love, than George Jacob Holyoake.

Truly yours, Robert G. Ingersoll

Ingersoll believed that Emanuel Swedenborg suffered from insanity. But when it is recalled " that he was raised by a bishop and disappointed in love," you cease to be surprised at his mental condition, he said. " The trouble with Swedenborg " was that " he changed realities into dreams, and then out of the dreams made ' facts ' upon which he built . . . his system. . . . To him the material was the unreal, and things were definitions of the ideas of God."

Swedenborg, shocked by the literal interpretation of the Bible, sought to give new meanings to the old texts which would be " consistent with the decency and goodness of God." Ingersoll pointed out that if Swedenborg had " taken the ground that the Bible was not inspired, the ears of the world would have been stopped," because " his readers believed in the dogma of inspiration, and asked, not how to destroy the Scriptures, but for some way in which they might be preserved." Ingersoll believed that this philosopher and his followers rendered important service to the cause of intellectual progress and enlightenment by their efforts to demonstrate the necessity of giving new meanings to the cruel laws and commandments of Jehovah.

The Swedenborgians, he felt, " heightened in every way the absurdities, cruelties, and contradictions of the Scriptures for the purpose of showing that a new interpretation must be found, and that the way pointed out by Swedenborg was the only one by which the Bible could be saved." The method of Swedenborg permitted each person to construct his own " science of correspondence." " In this way and in no other," Ingersoll agreed, " can we explain the numberless mistakes and crimes ascribed to God "; and " thousands of most excellent people, afraid to throw away the idea of inspiration, hailed with joy a discovery that allowed them to write a Bible for themselves."

> Long Beach, Long Island,
> New York
> Aug. 8th, '83

My dear Mr. Ellis,
  I know that you are my sincere friend, and that you are prompted in all you say by the best and noblest motives.
  I have read a good deal of Swedenborg, and to me, and I say it in the kindest spirit—it is simply insanity. I can make nothing of it. It is ingenious, learned, subtle and sometimes interesting. But I am such an unbeliever in the supernatural that it makes not the slightest impression. I do not say that I am right—I do not know—I only think—suppose—guess—and my thoughts, suppositions, and guesses are all against Swedenborg.
  I am not at that point that I care nothing about the " future " world. It may be. It may not be. If it is—good! If it is not—good! I intend to make the best of this world—and if there be another I will make the best of that. The Bible to me is simply the barbarous record of a barbarous people. I do not care what it means. Whether inspired or not, I do not like it. And I do not believe it. If God is its author, then God is not good. If it was intended as a revelation it has been a failure, because none but the Swedenborgians have ever understood it. Consequently they are the only ones to whom God has revealed his will. In the time of Swedenborg it would not do to deny the Bible. The heart of Swedenborg revolted at the literal absurdity and cruelty of the " Sacred " Volume. So, he gave new meanings to old mistakes

and patched with mercy the torn and bloody garments of Jehovah. He made a new bible, far better than the old—but not as good as *none*.

Now do not misunderstand me. I think Swedenborg was mistaken. Probably we all are. In this world no man has a standard other than his own reason. My reason revolts at the supernatural, and yet, my reason may be wrong. This is the only planet I was ever on, and consequently my knowledge of the universe is limited, but judging by the little experience I have had, by the few things I am satisfied about, I have concluded that all religions are equally without any foundation in fact, and consequently reject them all.

There is enough to learn here—enough to occupy my mind without wandering into the unknown. The questions about origin and destiny have never been satisfactorily answered—and so I live happily within the territory bounded by the two questions of Whence and Whither.

I have a creed for this, the only world of which I know anything.

1. Happiness is the only good.
2. The way to be happy is to make others so.
3. The time to be happy is now.
4. Help for the living.—Hope for the dead.———

This belief satisfies me. I am free from the tyrants of the air, I have no fear. I wait, schooling myself to bear without complaint the miseries of life. The theories, the creeds, the " revelations "—these spider webs of the brain—have never bridged the gulf. We are on this side. If we ever cross, it will be time then to pay attention to the other side. Until that happens let us extract from this thistle, the world, all the sweetness we can.

Yours truly, R. G. Ingersoll

Washington, D. C.
Sept. 27, 1883

My dear Friend [George Jacob Holyoake],

Yours of the 10th recd today. To see your handwriting on the envelope sends a thrill through my blood. I feel the grasp of your hand & for an instant look into your eyes. You need not thank me for any words of mine. I was paid when I wrote them. It was a positive pleasure to say a sentence or two in favour of one of the best of men. I feel under personal obligation to you. You have shown me such a great & generous heart—such serenity—such candour—such trust, after all, in the blundering world & in even the *accidents* of this wondrous succession of stumbles towards the right.—

I see that Bradlaugh has taken the trouble to say a word in the *Investigator* about you.—It is of no consequence.—Let it go. I regret that so many Freethinkers find it necessary to attack each other.

Give my love to your daughter—we speak of her every day.

She was in all she said and did so gentle and loving that we all fell in love with her.

We are just home from the sea.—All in splendid health, and all send love to all.

Yrs always, R. G. Ingersoll

(Copy of letter in the possession of Mrs. E. Holyoake Marsh.)

Mistakes of Ingersoll, which was edited by James B. McClure, was a collection of sermons by prominent clergymen in answer to and criticism of the Colonel.

The general tone of the sermons varied from extreme, whole-sale criticism and condemnation, through more judicious, tempered judgment, to qualified praise and commendation.

Washington, D. C.
December 11, 1883

Mr. T. N. Mason,
Longstreet, La.

My dear Sir:

The book of which you speak, " Mistakes of Ingersoll," has, I think, many things that I never said, and never thought of saying. As a rule, it has seemed to be necessary to misquote in order to answer me.

I have no faith in the supernatural; neither do I think that miracles are done in accordance with natural laws, and for that reason they are in the domain of the natural, or they are nowhere. One thing is about as wonderful as another, and the only standard we have is the average of human experience. A thing may *seem* miraculous, yet if it happens often enough, it is not believed. There is no way of proving a miracle. It is a thorn in the flesh of reason. It produces perpetual irritation. A miracle is a denial of the certain. It undermines the foundation of things. It destroys the basis of consciousness. From that moment, in the intellectual world, the compass no longer points to the North; the sun no longer rises in the East. The shore of the certain crumbles and fades away; man is left a kind of wreck, expecting aid from the caprice of chance, or an infinite power—which is much the same.

In the olden times, an alchemist was seeking after a universal solvent—a something that would dissolve everything; and he was asked this question: " If you find it, what do you expect to keep it in? " One miracle changes to ashes all laws, causes, effects, facts.

I am not a materialist, because I do not know what matter is. I am not a spiritualist, because I do not know what spirit is. I am simply a naturalist—believe what I have to believe, what my senses certify is true, and my reason, after cross-examining the senses, approves.

Yours very truly, R. G. Ingersoll

Washington, D. C.
December 29th, 1884

Isaac T. Dyer, Esq.,
Quincy, Illinois.

My dear Sir:

I have just received your letter of the 26th inst., in which you say that you have published in the *Quincy Herald* a challenge to a debate with me, and that you hope I may accept, as you have " every reason to believe it will be a financial success, if nothing more."

As you did not sign your name " Rev. Isaac T. Dyer," nor " Isaac T. Dyer, D.D." I was at a loss to know why you should wish to have a discussion with me; but after reading the printed heading of your letter, which is as follows: " Office of I. T. Dyer, Patentee of the Eagle & National Refrigerator," I came to the conclusion that being in the Refrigerating business, you did not wish hell abolished, but hoped to carry on business in the next world!

Biased as you must be by your business; prejudiced by your own interest; I think it hardly worth while to discuss the question of eternal fire with you. What you say as to its being " a financial success " is hardly to my taste. I do not need your assistance to make a financial success, and certainly I am not under any obligation to give you mine.

Yours very truly, R. G. Ingersoll

Utica, New York
January 20th, 1885

J. A. Beardsley, Esq.
Dear Sir:

How can a space of time be holy? How can one day be better than another apart from the weather? A happy day is a good day. A day filled with loving deeds is a holy day. A day of innocent pleasure is a sacred day. A day given to superstition is a worthless day. A day filled with foolish prayer is a wasted day. A day spent in hearing an orthodox sermon is a lost day. It is far better to play cards than to play hypocrite. It is good to do anything at any time that adds to human happiness.

Yours truly, R. G. Ingersoll

To: August 17th, 1886
P. S. Banner and Committee,
De Leon, Comanche Co., Texas.

Gentlemen:

I hardly know why you saw fit to send " An Appeal " to me, to help rebuild the Baptist Church at De Leon. It seems, from your appeal, that you had a church—that it had been dedicated to " the Lord God of Israel," as you call him, but that afterwards this same

Lord God of Israel " tossed your church to the ground," leaving you without any place of worship.

I feel like acquiescing in what the Lord has done. He knows, better than I, whether he wants a Baptist Church; and, in my judgment he has given what might at least be called " an intimation," that a Baptist Church, in that particular locality, was not pleasing in his sight. Why should the "Lord God of Israel" destroy his own property? He is said to "hold the winds in his fists." Why did he open his hand at De Leon? Is it possible that the "Lord God of Israel" destroys that which he wished to see rebuilt? Maybe he is simply trying your faith. If so, you should not apply to others. You should furnish the evidence yourselves.

My position is this: If the "Lord God of Israel" wants a Baptist Church at De Leon, let him change the wind, and blow the old one back.

Yours truly, R. G. Ingersoll

New York City
November 23rd, 1886

Mrs. J. C. Euwer,
New Castle, Penn.

My dear Madam:

If there be an infinite God, who created and governs and controls all, then this infinite God is accountable for all that has happened, for all that is, and for all that will be. I have had some trouble in regarding evil as having been intended by infinite Goodness. When I remember all the slavery that has been in this world —all the people who have been devoured by other people,—when I remember that for thousands of ages my ancestors were cannibals— when one mother would steal and eat the babe of another—and when I remember that for thousands and thousands of years, they enslaved each other—and not only so, but sacrificed each other to this infinite God, so that hundreds and thousands of altars were red with the blood of men, women, and children—when I remember all of the famines that have covered the earth with skeletons—all of the wars that have reddened it with blood, and all of the death that has made it hollow with graves—I admit that my brain is not big enough to know all this, and yet say that it was all done and planned and executed by infinite Intelligence and Goodness.

A great many people say that they cannot believe the Bible, because in that book God is made to order wars of extermination —because he upheld slavery and polygamy. If you will think a moment, that is exactly what your God has been doing in the world, whether he ever wrote it down in the Bible, or not; and to my mind, the God of Nature is even worse than the God of the Bible.

Now, of course, I know nothing about how this is. I can only guess. You may have some way of knowing that I have not, but situated as I am, I may say:

First. There may be an infinite God, who made everything,

who does everything, and everything may be exactly right, and all the fault may be in my lack of wisdom.

Second. There may be a God, who has done the best he could, and is still doing the best he can, but who is not infinite; and if such a being exists, all good people ought to help him, and if I ever find that there is such a God, and he wants help, I shall go to work to help him. And,

Third. This is the thing I guess is right—nobody knows how it is. The human mind is not big enough to answer the questions of origin and destiny; and when we are all honest—when that day comes—popes and peasants, presidents of colleges and naked barbarians, will all admit, that one knows exactly as much as the other on this subject, and that all together know exactly nothing!

But of one thing I feel certain: that whether there be any God, or not, I ought to give to others the rights that I claim for myself; speech and thought should be free; and no matter whether we guess alike about Gods, or other worlds—here, we should be friends.

Very respectfully, R. G. Ingersoll

New York City
Dec. 11, 1886

S. W. Sparks, Esq.,
Camden, New Jersey.

Dear Sir:

You ask me whether the religion taught by Christ is practicable. The first thing to settle is, what was the religion taught by Christ? If I understand it at all, it is given in Matthew, Mark, and Luke, and is this: If you will forgive others, God will forgive you; and all of it, so far as I know, consists in the duties of man to man: Judge not, that ye be not judged. Give good measure. Do nothing from revenge. Live an honest and useful life.

Now, to this exceedingly simple religion, priests have made additions. If religion consisted only in this—treat others as you wish others to treat you, forgive others, and God will forgive you—there would be no need of a ministry of priests, cardinals, and popes. The machinery of superstition would be out of place, and all the ceremonials would become absurd, for this reason: Priests added the doctrine of the Trinity, the Atonement, the Incarnation, and a hundred other absurdities that require to be explained. To explain these things gave them business. That is to say, the priesthood became a profession. I do not think there is really a Christian church. I do not believe there is a church in the world that Christ, could he come again, would acknowledge. It would never occur to him, after hearing one of their sermons, that they were followers of his. But my doctrine is this: All true religion is embraced in the word Humanity.

Yours truly, R. G. Ingersoll

New York City, Dec. 11, 1886

Mrs. M. T. Burnette,
Olean, N. Y.

Dear Madam:

I am very much obliged to you for the interest you have taken in my case, and I have no doubt that you are perfectly sincere in asking the being whom you call your Heavenly Father to be pleased to spare me to my wife and children. Somehow, I cannot feel that there is any being in this universe who could have spared hundreds and thousands and millions of fathers for the sake of their families, and who did not; who allowed these millions of fathers to die and to leave wives and children in misery and want. It seems to me that if there were any being who could prevent the agony of this separation, he would. I cannot see how a God seeing a poor wife bending over the bed of a dying husband, can be hard enough and cold enough to deny her prayer. Neither can I understand why this God, infinite in wisdom, should in any manner be controlled by the prayers of men. The history of the world shows that millions and millions have been slaves; that millions and millions of innocent people have died in prisons; that the bravest and best have perished at the stake; that millions have died of famine; that pestilences have ravaged the world.

Now, under these circumstances, with these facts in mind, how can we ask this God to help an individual—he who was deaf to the cries of a whole race; he who allowed babes to be sold from the breasts of mothers; he who allowed his children to be pursued by bloodhounds over the Southern States [of the U.S.A.]? Why should we ask any favour of him? Why should we be egotistic enough to think that we can attract the notice of the Infinitely Negligent? Personally, I do not expect any help from on high. If it comes to me, it will come without asking. I rely upon what men have discovered. I rely upon the inherent forces of nature, and upon nothing else. And, if I recover, I shall thank no Heavenly Father, because I cannot believe that such a being exists.

At the same time, do not imagine that I, for one moment, even in my mind, deny to you absolute and perfect freedom of thought and speech. Neither do I imagine that I know. I only think. I think the best I can, and I can do no more.

Respectfully yours, R. G. Ingersoll

New York City
December 11th, 1886

D. M. Adams, Esq.,
Los Angeles, California.

My dear Sir:

I have read a good deal that has been written by Madam Blavatsky * among other things, two large volumes called *Isis*

* Helena Petrovna Blavatsky, co-founder of the Theosophical Society, wrote

Unveiled. I have read a great number of essays on the same subjects, and I am perfectly satisfied that what is called Theosophy is simply unadulterated nonsense; and, in that particular, it resembles what is called Esoteric Buddhism. In other words, I am perfectly satisfied that any doctrine founded upon what is called the supernatural is utterly and unqualifiedly false. All this slight-of-hand performance, all miracles and legerdemain, all tricks, all mystery, solemnity, ceremony, are simply the indications of dishonesty. The moral part of Buddhism no one can object to. The moral part of Theosophy is just as good as the moral part of anything else, and this moral part is always plain and above-board, easily comprehended, and can be told in words of one, two, and three syllables. There are no astronomical or astrological problems to be solved. But as to the rest, I have neither confidence in it nor patience with it. Undoubtedly we are surrounded by mysteries; and one thing is just as mysterious as another. Nobody knows what matter is, or what life is, or what thought is. Everything is a mystery, a mystery beyond our powers. We call a thing miraculous when it is contrary to our experience. If a man holding a stone in his hand should say that when he released this stone it would fall up, no human being could believe the statement; and if he afterwards said that when you were not looking it did fall up, certainly no one would credit the man. In my judgment, all things that ever happened had to happen, and everything has happened that has been possible, and everything will happen that is possible. Nothing more and nothing less. And there is no room in this Universe for interference, or for miracles; that is to say, for Theosophy, or Esoteric Buddhism.

Yours truly, R. G. Ingersoll

December 18th, 1886
New York, N. Y.

A. P. Agresta, Esq.,
New York City.

My dear Sir:

Of course a man who feels that the Pope stands in the place of God will not be true to his country as against the Pope. A man who believes that the Bible is the inspired word of God will be true to that book as against his country. And a man who believes that there is in the universe an infinite being who created all will be true to that being as against his fellow men. Those who live for another world are dangerous in this. Those who have any other standard than that given by observation, reason, and experience are unreliable. My hope in this country is that there always

---

widely on spiritualism and the occult philosophies. Her miraculous pretensions to communion with the other world have since been thoroughly discredited, although at her death she left approximately one hundred thousand disciples.

will be sensible men enough to keep the religious within bounds. The time may come when there will be a conflict, and I am doing what little I can, first, to prevent the conflict, and second, if it comes, to give victory to the hosts of freedom.

Yours very truly, R. G. Ingersoll

Robert Ingersoll looked upon Napoleon Bonaparte as " one of the most infamous of men." In his lecture, *The Liberty of Man, Woman, and Child*, is Ingersoll's celebrated *Apostrophe* to Napoleon:

A little while ago, I stood by the grave of the old Napoleon —a magnificent tomb of gilt and gold, fit almost for a dead deity —and gazed upon the sarcophagus of rare and nameless marble, where rest at last the ashes of that restless man. I leaned over the balustrade and thought about the career of the greatest soldier of the modern world.

I saw him walking upon the banks of the Seine, contemplating suicide. I saw him at Toulon—I saw him putting down the mob in the streets of Paris—I saw him at the head of the army of Italy —I saw him crossing the bridge of Lodi with the tricolour in his hand—I saw him in Egypt in the shadows of the pyramids—I saw him conquer the Alps and mingle the eagles of France with the eagles of the crags. I saw him at Marengo—at Ulm and Austerlitz. I saw him in Russia, where the infantry of the snow and the cavalry of the wild blast scattered his legions like winter's withered leaves. I saw him at Leipsic in defeat and disaster—driven by a million bayonets back upon Paris—clutched like a wild beast—banished to Elba. I saw him escape and retake an empire by the force of his genius. I saw him upon the frightful field of Waterloo, where Chance and Fate combined to wreck the fortunes of their former king. And I saw him at St. Helena, with his hands crossed behind him, gazing out upon the sad and solemn sea.

I thought of the orphans and widows he had made—of the tears that had been shed for his glory, and of the only woman who ever loved him, pushed from his heart by the cold hand of ambition. And I said I would rather have been a French peasant and worn wooden shoes. I would rather have lived in a hut with a vine growing over the door, and the grapes growing purple in the kisses of the autumn sun. I would rather have been that poor peasant with my loving wife by my side, knitting as the day died out of the sky—with my children upon my knees and their arms about me—I would rather have been that man and gone down to the tongueless silence of the dreamless dust, than to have been that imperial impersonation of force and murder, known as "Napoleon the Great."

New York City
Jan'y 17th, 1887

Dr. J. B. Reed,
Washington, D. C.

My dear Sir,
Of course, I have always known that nearly all the Christian churches of the world believe in the divinity of Jesus Christ. That, however, has not the slightest effect upon my mind. I do not believe that Jesus Christ was divine, any more than I believe that you are divine, or that any other human being is divine. Neither do I believe it necessary to believe in the Lord Jesus Christ, to be happy in this world, or in any other.

It is far better to do justly, than to believe in the divinity of Jesus Christ.

I do not believe that any book is inspired. Many things, in many books, are true. Many things in most books are false—and the Bible is no exception to this general rule.

You send me a pamphlet, the object of which is to show that Napoleon the Great was a Christian, and that he believed in the divinity of Christ. Admitting that Napoleon did believe in the divinity of Christ, I think you can see that such belief did not prevent Napoleon from living the life of a cruel monster. This belief did not prevent his sacrificing all that was best and greatest in France, on the altar of personal ambition. I am perfectly willing to admit that Napoleon was a Christian, and that he acted like one.

My creed is this:
1. Happiness is the only good.
2. The time to be happy is *now*.
3. The way to be happy, is to make others so.
4. The supernatural does not, and cannot exist.

Yours very truly, R. G. Ingersoll

New York City
February 21, 1887

J. B. Cooper, Esq.,
Coleo, Moultrie Co., Illinois.

My dear Sir:
The statements of Mr. Talmage in reference to Thomas Paine are of course untrue. It is impossible for any minister to tell the truth about the author of *Common Sense*. The Church has been busy manufacturing and telling lies about Thomas Paine for nearly a hundred years, and will no doubt go right on just the same as long as the Church exists. Whenever the Church stops lying, nothing will be left. To stop is to commit suicide.

Thomas Paine had the misfortune to be an honest man, the misfortune to tell what he really thought, and the misfortune to overthrow and defeat the priests of his day. For this the Church never forgave him. Ministers like Talmage will keep on repeating falsehoods just as long as there is malice and ignorance and prejudice and credulity in the pews. If Mr. Talmage says that Thomas Paine was a drunkard, and so filthy and loathsome in his habits that he was too bad to be picked from the gutter, and that his last words were, " O Lord! Have mercy on my soul," nothing could be more natural than for such a man as Mr. Talmage describes to use the language he puts in his mouth in his last moments. If he had been a drunkard, if he had been a filthy sot and beast, in all probability he would have cried out, " O Lord! Have mercy on my soul." But not being a drunkard, and not being a filthy beast, but a sensible, honest, patriotic, truth-loving man, he died as he lived—without fear and without asking alms, even of God.

Yours truly, R. G. Ingersoll

New York City
February 21st, 1887

F. Van Dresar, Esq.,
Westernville, Oneida Co., N. Y.

My dear Sir:
I have received yours of February 16th, in which you say that you want to meet me in Heaven. You certainly will if you are there.

Yours truly, R. G. Ingersoll

New York, N. Y.
March 18th, 1887

Joseph Lewes, Esq.,
Milwaukee, Wis.

My dear Sir:
I have no doubt that you were prompted by kindness, and by kindness alone, to write me.

It gives me pleasure to state that my health is excellent, and that there is no immediate prospect of my leaving this world.

There is not as much responsibility in dying as in living. When a man is dying, he can do little else—he can do little to help, or harm, his fellow men. Consequently, but little responsibility attaches to this, the last act; whereas, in life, he has the power to do every moment, and for the use of this power he is every moment responsible—responsible to himself and to those he injures, or to those he refuses to help.

I think it was quite unfortunate that you should have alluded to the parable of Lazarus and the Rich man. According to this parable, the people in hell are much better than those in heaven. When this rich man asked Abraham to send Lazarus with a little water, you will notice that Abraham did not express the least regret that he could not comply with the request—not one word of sympathy—and yet the rich man in the flames of torment remembered his brethren on the earth. From this it would seem that there is more sympathy in hell than in heaven, and for my part I have altogether more respect for the rich man than for the polygamous patriarch or the transfigured pauper.

But, my dear Sir, my anxieties are all about this world—the next will take care of itself.

Very truly yours, R. G. Ingersoll

New York
March 18, 1887

Theo. F. Wolf, M.D.,
New York City.

My dear Doctor:
Somebody had the kindness to publish a statement that I had purchased a large number of gods—all kinds.

The fact is, I have never had but a few genuine gods, and I think all of them have been given away, with one exception. A few days ago I was presented with a Hindoo god—a little fellow —but I was assured, small as he is, he had answered prayers as well as any God that ever lived.

If you will call sometime, at the house, I will lend you this god, for a few moments, and I have no doubt but he will help you to the extent of his power, and what more could you expect from any God?

There is one good thing about this little fellow: he does not frighten anybody. I have never heard him mention hell, and he does not seem to care whether we stand up, or kneel; and I must say, that I have never had a better behaved god in the house.

Very truly yours, R. G. Ingersoll

April 28th, 1887

B. W. Lewis, Esq.,
Dayton, Ohio.

My dear Sir:
It is very gratifying to me to know that my books are being read in India—glad to know that they are in the way of the hypocritical and idiotic missionaries who are endeavouring to get these people to exchange one superstition for another.

You may rest assured, that while I live, I shall do what little I can to destroy what is known as " orthodox religion." In my judgment, it has covered the face of the world with tears, and the greatest possible good would be its utter destruction.

You say in your letter that you hope some time I will " do something for God." I never shall—but I do intend to do something for humanity. If God is infinite, he does not need my help. I believe in living in this world for this world, and doing what little we can for ourselves and our fellow men. If there is another world, when we get there we can do the same.

Very truly yours, R. G. Ingersoll

[No date of month given] 1887

Miss Gertrude Spinney,
Ashland, Schuylkill Co., Pa.

Dear Miss,

You ask me how it is that Christianity has succeeded—how it is that it grew in spite of persecution? I suppose, of course, that the answer in your mind is, that it must have received assistance from on high, and must have been under the peculiar care of a Supreme Being.

Before answering you I will take the liberty of asking a few questions. How is it that Mohammedanism grew and flourished in spite of the opposition of the world? How is it that Mohammed exercised a greater influence upon mankind for a thousand years, than any other human being? How is it that his armies, and the armies battling for his faith, wrested from Christianity two-thirds of its territory? If you answer that all these victories were gained by force, then must you not admit that this force was under the special care of a Supreme Being?—just as God was on the side of the Jews when they conquered the Canaanites?

Another question. Here in our own day, and land, is a religion —a horrible religion—that started in the United States, and is founded on the grossest and most ignorant superstition, and imposition. It has been persecuted in New York, in Illinois, in Missouri, and on the plains of the far west. Its founder was murdered. Hundreds of its disciples have been assassinated, and yet it continues steadily to grow. Mormonism is a thousand times stronger today—forty years after the death of its founder, than Christianity was two centuries after [the death of] Christ. This religion has been persecuted, and is now being persecuted by the United States—that is, the Mormons call it persecution—and yet it continually gains ground; converts by the thousand even today flocking from this land, and from other Christian lands to these shores, to join the followers of Joseph Smith.

Now success does not necessarily mean the result of supernatural aid. Tyrannies of all kinds have succeeded in this world; and for hundreds and thousands of years hundreds of millions of people have suffered the burdens and agonies put upon them by injustice and power—and yet they have been rescued by no God. Your argument proves entirely too much. It would prove that every religion that has succeeded was divinely defended and sustained.

Thousands of causes produced what we call Christianity. Influences almost infinite have produced everything that exists. Those opposed to the Roman Empire at first gathered about the Christian standard. It was a political movement gaining strength from the tyranny of Rome. Born mostly of hatred, when it became strong it appealed to the sword. It flourished through cunning, cruelty, and force. It became the greatest scourge of the human race. For a thousand years it kept Europe in intellectual night.

If you will read Mr. Draper's *History of the Intellectual Development of Europe* you will find that there are no words strong enough to express the depth of the crime called Christianity. There was some good in it, as there is in all systems, but not good enough to save it. Christianity is slowly being civilized by Science, and by the countless influences born of discovery, of investigation, of reason, of experience. I advise you to read also, Buckle's *History of Civilization in England*, and you will find how baseless the claims of Christianity are.

One word more. If success is to be the measure of inspiration, then why should not all Protestant denominations immediately become Catholic? Would not your argument, had it been used by Paganism, have closed the mouth of Christianity? Paganism was at one time a success, and if success means inspiration, Paganism was inspired. Hoping that I have said nothing to hurt your feelings, and something towards creating a desire in your mind to ascertain the real truth, apart from the sentimentalities of superstition, I am respectfully yours,

R. G. Ingersoll

New York, May 24, 1887

I. H. Priffle, Esq.,
Ladonia, Mo.

My dear Sir:

I just received your letter of the 21st inst., in which you say that a Methodist clergyman had informed you that I had expressed regret for my assaults on Christianity, and that I had also said that if God would forgive me for what I had done, I would never again say a word against religion.

There is not one word of truth in what the Methodist minister said. If I have any regret at all, it is that I have not said more against the superstition called Christianity. I believe that religion, so-called, is the greatest curse and blight that ever fell upon the hearts of men. It has shed more blood, caused more grief, than all other things combined. It has not only made a hell of this world, but predicted another in the next.

With every drop of my blood I despise this superstition.

Tell your Methodist friend that he should wait until I am dead, because, as long as I have breath to speak, these lies will be denied.

Yours very truly, R. G. Ingersoll

New York, June 3rd, '87

Lucien I. Chapman, Esq.,
New York City.

My dear Sir:

1. In answer to your first question: "Do you believe that Jesus of Nazareth and Mohammed were messengers from the Creator of the world—from the First Great Cause to the created—or mere fanatics?"

117

I am not sure that Jesus of Nazareth ever lived. I am perfectly certain that the Jesus described in the New Testament, never could, by any possibility, have existed. There may have been a Jewish peasant by that name, who was a very great and good man, who became indignant at the absurdities and cruelties, at the formality and heartlessness, of the Hebrew religion, and who endeavoured to do what little he could for its destruction—and it may be that afterwards, hundreds of things were ascribed to him that he never said—hundreds of things related of him that he never did.

As to Mohammed, his intentions may have been honest. He may have deceived himself. He may have been on the edge of insanity—and probably was. He exerted a wonderful influence upon mankind. No man in the history of the world made a deeper impression on his fellow men—when we take into consideration the circumstances and the shortness of time in which he accomplished such marvels.

Of course I have not the slightest idea that either of them was a " messenger from the Creator of the world, or from the First Great Cause."

2. In answer to your second question: " Does death to you mean total annihilation? " I can only say this:

I have no evidence that man lives again—any more than I have that he lived for an eternity before his birth. Neither have I any evidence that he will not live again. It may be that it is just as reasonable that he will live again, as that he does live. Perhaps, after all, the greatest of all wonders is that we do live.

Upon this question, I simply say that I do not know. To those who hope for another life, I have no word of doubt, no word of fault—but to those who preach that a majority of mankind are to be eternally miserable, I have had something, and I still have something, to say. In my judgment, no human being knows whether there is another life or not—and whether there is or not should make no particular difference with us. If there is no other life, we should make the best of this—if there is another life, we should still make the best of this.

3. In answer to your third question: " Is the Hebrew Bible to you a message from the Creator, or only a history of the Jews? "

I think the Bible would be a history of the Jews, if it were true. It is like most other ancient books—a mingling of falsehood and truth, of philosophy and folly—all written by men, and most of the men only partially civilized. Some of its laws are good—some infinitely barbarous. None of the miracles related were performed —all of the wonders are simply falsehoods. It could be made much better by leaving a good deal of it out. Take out the absurdities, the miracles, all that pertains to the supernatural— all the cruel and barbaric laws—and to the remainder I have no objection. Neither would I have for it any great admiration.

Yours very truly, R. G. Ingersoll

New York, July 1, 1887

Mary R. Thomas, Nashville, Tenn.

My dear Madam:

I am greatly obliged to you for your favour of the 22nd inst. You felt it your duty to write such a letter, and did it undoubtedly for my good.

You are right in saying that I have often said that if one can gain eternal joy by forgiving his enemies, I am perfectly willing to forgive mine—every one; and I have often called attention to the fact that in the New Testament God promises to forgive those who will forgive others, and I have always insisted that that was a very good kind of religion, so far as it applies to man.

Every man should forgive his enemies—that is to say, he cannot afford to make his heart a den of vipers. He should not forgive others simply because God promises to forgive him; he should forgive others because forgiveness is right, because it is the better and nobler way.

You will see also that the offer of God involves an inconsistency on his part, in this: He says to man: " I will forgive you, if you will forgive others." But suppose the man does not forgive others; is God then to be unforgiving because the man is unforgiving? A good man forgives his enemies, although his enemies have injured him. No one can injure God. How much easier, then, for God to forgive his enemies than for man!

So far as I am concerned, I do not want the forgiveness of God, because I have never injured him. I want the forgiveness of those people whom I have wronged, if any such there be.

I have a very short creed, and it is this:

Happiness is the only good. The time to be happy is now. The way to be happy is to make others so.

If I only live in accordance with this creed, I shall have no fears.

Yours respectfully, R. G. Ingersoll

New York, July 6th, 1887

To Mrs. H. H. Jenkins,
Hardin Co., Ohio.

My dear Madam:

No doubt your letter was written to me in perfect kindness and with the best possible motive.

My idea is, that it is much better to make people happy, than to trouble yourself about any particular form or kind of religion, or about the truth or falsity of any creed whatever. If there be a God, certainly he is as good as we are, and if he is, he will punish none of his creatures for having treated others of his children with kindness. There is nothing we can do for the Infinite, and it is necessarily a matter of very little concern to God—if there be one—what we believe. This is evident from the fact that he has taken so little pains to inform us on a great variety of subjects. If he is really anxious that we should all believe in his existence, he could convince us all. A statement to that effect could grow on every leaf, on every spear of grass. It could be reflected from every star, and be read even on the shifting, changing clouds. So too, if the Bible be true, and if a belief in that book be important, that fact could be communicated to the whole human race in a thousand ways, any one of which would be an absolute demonstration.

So you see, my dear madam, I am convinced that God takes but very little interest in this matter, and I presume his lack of interest proceeds from the lack of importance of the subject.

Thanking you for your expressions of kindness, and hoping that some day you may see the error of your creed, and that before you die you may feel the joy that springs from a feeling of liberty—from a feeling that there is no world of pain, and that not a single human being is to suffer forever—

Very respectfully yours, R. G. Ingersoll

New York
July 6, 1887

K. A. Brock, Esq.,
Jefferson Co., Alabama.

My dear Sir:

Two hundred and eighty-seven years ago—that is to say, in February, 1600, Giordano Bruno, an Atheist, was burned by the Catholic Church. He was offered his freedom if he would recant his opinions. According to his doctrine, there was no God to be pleased or enraged. He could not be rewarded with heaven, neither could he be punished with hell. The only reason he had for standing firm and suffering death was to preserve the whiteness of his soul. He was one of the greatest men who ever lived.

Yours always, R. G. Ingersoll

New York
July 13th, 1887

F. M. Terry, Esq.,
Liverpool, N. Y.

My dear Sir:

It is hard to read the history of the world without coming to the conclusion that it was a mistake to make man. One of the greatest arguments against the existence of an infinitely wise and benevolent God, is the existence of man.

But we are here, and let us be as happy as we can. The highest philosophy is to enjoy today, without any regret for yesterday, or any fear for tomorrow.

Very truly yours, R. G. Ingersoll

November 9, 1887

S. C. Windsor,
Pittsburgh.

My dear Sir:
In reply to your letter of September 30th, in which you say that you have heard that my father's unkind treatment of me caused me, when a boy, to lose confidence in the Christian religion, and ask me if there is any truth in the story, I have to say:
That there is not the shadow of truth in the statement. My father was one of the most affectionate of men, and in his treatment of his children was kindness itself. There never were two better friends than my father and myself. We were together for years. I loved him with all my heart, and to me his memory is sacred.

But my father was willing that his children should think and investigate for themselves. He taught me to be intellectually honest.

To me, it is a matter of amazement that Christians should be willing to calumniate a fellow believer who sleeps in death, for the purpose of answering the arguments of his son.

Yours truly, R. G. Ingersoll

December 2nd, 1887

E. H. Sandford, Esq.,
Morris, Illinois.

My dear Sir:
Of course, I do not think people are bad because they are Presbyterians, or Methodists, or Catholics. There are good and bad people of all religions, and all forms of irreligion. I do not believe that an intelligent man ought to judge another by the church he belongs to, or by what he professes; and if there be a God, I do not believe he will judge that way.

You know that an incorporation will act meaner than any one of its stockholders. I think a church, as a church, will do meaner things than any of its individual members. A church seems to be a personality apart from its members, and possessed by a strange devil of its own. There are no trials in which it is as hard to ascertain the truth, as in church trials. Quarrels between members of churches, or other corporations, are the bitterest and most malicious.

I hope however, the time will come when churches will turn their attention to the affairs of this world, and to the great work of civilizing their members.

Yours very truly, R. G. Ingersoll

New York, May 7th, 1888

W. H. Rhinehart, Esq.,
Wheeling, West Virginia.

My dear Sir:

I am glad to know that you appreciate the tribute that I paid to the memory of Abraham Lincoln.

I do not know how you came to think that I had said anything derogatory to the character of Jesus Christ. I deny the supernatural origin of Christ—deny that an Infinite God was his Father, or that he was in fact a God.

If such a man existed, he was a human being—a Jewish peasant—and judging him by my standard—that is to say, accounting for many things in the New Testament as interpolations and mistakes—he was a great and tender soul, and I believe that I have said the best things of him that I am able. I do not agree with his philosophy as expressed in the New Testament; but behind all the mistakes and interpolations, I see a great character, and to that character I have paid, on many occasions, the tribute of my respect and admiration.

Yours truly, R. G. Ingersoll

New York
May 17th, 1888

R. B. Berkeley, Esq.,
Farmville, Va.

My dear Sir:

The words of which you speak I think were uttered in the same spirit that like words were uttered thousands and thousands of years ago, by Zoroaster, by Zeno, by Buddha, by Epicurus, by Socrates, by Epictetus, by Confucius, by Christ and many others.

The spirit that prompts these expressions is that of humanity, kindness, human affection. It does not come from the clouds. It is born of the earth—it is a blossom of the human heart.

There were millions of generous and just men—charitable and loving women—thousands and thousands of ages before Christ was born. You must admit that man loved women thousands of years before the birth of Christ. You must admit that mothers loved their babes. In other words, you are compelled to admit that love has always dwelt among the sons of men.

Now this thing called love expresses itself in an infinite number of ways, and it is called, of course, by various names—but all charity, justice, fairness, goodness—all these are born of that.

I do not wish to take anything from Christ, except that which has been falsely ascribed to him. He could not have been more than man, and he said nothing and did nothing that man had not said, and had not done, long before he lived. I do not wish to give the honour and glory that belongs to so many millions, to one.

In order that you may know that the spirit of which you speak did not commence with Christ, let me call your attention to a few words:

Buddha said, " If a man strike thee, and in striking drops his staff, pick it up and hand it to him again "; " Return kindness for injury." So Laotze, of China, said, " Return benefits for injuries." Confucius, however, in my judgment said a far wiser thing: " If you return benefits for injuries, what do you propose to return for benefits? "

My doctrine is this: For benefits return benefits, and for injuries return justice.

Epictetus said the same, precisely, as Christ afterwards said. So did Zoroaster, so did Thales, and hundreds of others.

Yours very truly, R. G. Ingersoll

New York
May 23rd, 1888

Mrs. Ellen B. Dietrick, President,
Women's Ed'l. & Industrial Union,
Covington, Ky.

My dear Madam:

I return your MS. I do not know whether it could be published or not. I really have no time to attend to it.

I think it makes but very little difference what the Methodist Conference does. As long as the women are foolish enough to believe in the creed of that Church, and to fry chickens for wandering preachers, and then humble enough to take their pay in kicks, it is hardly worth while to say anything on the subject.

If it were not for the women the Methodist Church could not live a day. They collect the money—they induce their husbands to pay—they take care of the preachers—they get up the Fairs, and are the only attraction at the Camp Meetings—as no one would think of going on a picnic without the girls.

Yours respectfully, R. G. Ingersoll

Rev. Henry M. Field and Colonel Ingersoll were good friends; and Rev. Mr. Field was one of the very few ministers who treated Ingersoll with justice and fairness.

New York
September 27, 1888

My dear Mr. Field:

With great pleasure I have read *You Are My Brother*. Of course, I recognize heroism, love, and self-denial in the labour of all honest missionaries. I know that the Jesuits endured countless hardships in all parts of the world, and suffered everything that one can suffer for the spread of their religion; and while I respect and admire all this, I hold the religion they taught in abhorrence. Heads may be wrong, and hearts right. . . . So when I said (speaking of the good bishop), there never was such a priest, I did not intend to say that there never was, or could have been, such a man. I do not see how a man, looking at sin as something so horrible that the sinner deserves to suffer eternal pain, can feelingly say to the criminal " you are my brother." The man believing this fearful dogma is not only wrong in his head, but in his heart. I feel that you have outgrown this creed, that your heart has protested against the infamies of a former age. I don't mean by this that you have failed to give your thought. You have given it, and no one can read what you say on the question without feeling and knowing that you have hope for all the world.— If all the ministers were like you—if they had hearts and sympathies, a sense of justice, and a feeling of comradeship—how much better and grander they would be, and how the bitterness would fall out of discussion.

I have great hope for the future of the world—great hope in social reforms—and this hope has been made stronger by my knowledge of you—by what you have said and written.

To become acquainted with a good, honest, generous man, lays a foundation for the hope that the race may become good, honest, and generous. If one clergyman can treat an unbeliever with fairness, with kindness, can one not say that the rest may follow his example? All this being within the possible, let us hope for the civilization of the race.

I thank you sincerely for the kind words you have written. You have not always understood me, but you have always been candid and generous, and you have won the friendship and admiration of

Yours always, R. G. Ingersoll

September 29, 1888

H. L. Suydam, Esq.,
Geneva, N. Y.

My dear friend:

I have read your lecture on Restitution, and of course agree with you about the falsity of the infamous dogma of eternal punishment; but I do not agree with you as to the inspiration or truth of the Bible. Neither have I the slightest interest in the second coming of the Lord. To tell you the honest truth, I hope he won't come.

You know, according to the doctrine, he came about 1800 years ago, and, in consequence, at least one hundred and fifty millions of human beings have been sacrificed to establish what is called the Christian religion.

I am opposed to the whole business. I want to get rid of the old religions, and I want no new ones in their place.

Yours very truly, R. G. Ingersoll

New York, Oct. 12th, 1888

Rev. Henry B. Walbridge,
Brooklyn, L.I.

My dear Sir:

I have just received your question, and will answer it.

Question. "Do you believe there is a God—Creator of all things?"

Answer. I do not. It does not seem possible that the universe was created. If it was, then there was a time when it was not, and back of that there must have been an eternity. We can hardly conceive of a being of infinite power and wisdom living, as Shelley puts it, "in an eternity of idleness." I do not put back of the universe another power. I do not regard the universe as an effect. The universe comprises all causes and all effects. The idea of a personal Deity who created, or caused, the universe, is to me infinitely absurd. So far as I am personally concerned, I am unable to conceive of such a being. An infinite personality, an unconditioned Creator, is to my mind a contradiction in terms.

I do not say that such a Being does not exist, or cannot exist, for the reason that I do not know that what *seems* to me impossible, or absurd, *is* impossible or absurd. All I can say is, that my mind is so, that I am driven to the conclusion I have stated.

Yours truly, R. G. Ingersoll

New York, October 15th, 1888

Mrs. Nancy E. Kennedy,
Riverdale, Tenn.

Dear Madam:

You have been misinformed. I am not " on the side of the Lord." I am still on the side of the human race. I am still doing what little I can to destroy a belief in the eternity of pain.

Nothing could be more terrible than for us to know that the Christian religion is true. If it is true, we know that there are hundreds and thousands, and thousands of millions, who are to suffer for ever. It would have been a thousand times better for God to have remained " in eternal idleness " if a majority of the human beings that he called into existence are to be eternally lost.

You do not understand me. I attack only the bad, the cruel, the infamous. I defend the good. I believe in justice, mercy, kindness, and above all, in liberty.

I judge people, not by what they believe, but by what they do— not by their creed, but by their conduct. I do not wish to be saved by any God who will damn anybody else.

Yours respectfully, R. G. Ingersoll

New York, November 5th, 1888

Dr. T. S. Hodgson,
Middleboro, Mass.

My dear Sir:
While I do not believe that all religion has had an astronomical origin, I do believe that all [religions] have had the same origin.

Every religion has been an attempt to account for the phenomena of nature—that is to say, at first it was an honest attempt in that direction. Afterwards, it was made an instrument for the oppression of man—a means by which the few could live on the labour of the many.

I think all religions have had the same origin, and that all will perish in the same way.

Yours very truly, R. G. Ingersoll

December 12th, 1888

Miss Alice Eskel,
Portland, Oregon.

My dear Miss:
I received your letter this morning and have read the article enclosed. I hardly think it possible to come to a definite conclusion upon the subject touched, without far greater experience than we now have and without the ascertainment of a vast number of facts.

It may be true that every atom has intelligence; but as we have never seen an atom, it is hardly possible to say. It may be true that there is a certain intelligence in all vegetation, and that the form of the leaf and fruit is determined by desire.

It may be that all chemistry depends on the loves and hatreds of atoms. I do not know. It is impossible for me to say why three atoms of one kind will harmonize with five atoms of another kind, and refuse to have anything to do with the sixth.

It may be that the planets—that is to say, all the stars—are the atoms that compose one being.

I believe that it has been said by some scientist that, taking into consideration the size of the planets, they are as near together as the atoms are in a ball of glass taking into consideration their size; but it gives me pleasure to admit that I know nothing on this subject.

It seems to me that sun worship is a very natural religion, and my own idea is that the nomenclature, ceremonies, ideas, and worship connected with that religion were afterwards transferred to others.

Years ago I took the ground that shutting the eyes in prayer is a souvenir of sun worship. People who addressed the sun had to close their eyes and afterwards, when they worshipped images adorned with jewels, they pretended that their faces were so bright that they could not look upon them. So it was a kind of flattery to close the eyes, and this habit was persisted in, although no one now pretends to see the God, or object worshipped.

I also agree with you that the images of men and women have represented gods and goddesses—that is to say, gods and goddesses have been represented as men and women. But back of that, gods and goddesses were represented as animals, because there was a time when man regarded the animals as his superiors. The eagle could fly, the lion and tiger and many other animals excelled him in strength. The serpent excited his admiration; it travelled without feet, it climbed without claws, and it could live an indefinite time without food. Besides all this, it was the simplest form of life.

As man advanced, he became superior to some animals. He then made his gods by a combination—that is to say, he gave to his god the body of a lion. On this body he placed the wings of an eagle for the purpose of representing the two things, swiftness and strength; and sometimes he gave to this strange mixture the head of a serpent, representing wisdom.

Man advanced. He became superior to all animals. He then represented his gods and goddesses as men and women, for the reason that intellectual strength became the highest, and the human form was associated with mind. Consequently, it became impossible for him to represent his god except in that form which to him represented the highest phase of thought.

No one now could represent God with four legs, or with a mane and tail, or as any animal whatever, because no animal form is associated with the highest intelligence.

I cannot say as to whether there is any planetary god or not. You have no idea how little I know on that subject.

To me, the most wonderful thing in the world is thought, the impalpable, the invisible, the noiseless—the something that can neither be seen, nor touched, nor heard—and yet it is the great force so far as we know.

All these questions are beyond my mind, so I am willing to wait. I feel like a passenger on a ship, unacquainted with the captain or any of the officers—without knowing the port the ship left, and without having the slightest idea as to the harbour to which it is going. If it goes down, I shall not be surprised. If it lands on fairer shores, beneath blue skies, I shall be rejoiced. But whatever it does, I intend to do my level best to have a pleasant voyage, and get along as well as I can with the other passengers.

I am, Yours very truly, R. G. Ingersoll

The Hon. Andrew D. White was one of America's most illustrious educators, scholars, and diplomats. After a period as Professor of English Literature at the University of Michigan and Senator from New York, he became President of Cornell University, which he had founded. Both during and after his presidency he served the country in the diplomatic service in Germany, Russia, and Venezuela.

Mr. White was the author of numerous books, the most important of which was the *History of the Warfare of Science with Theology in Christendom*, which Ingersoll considered one of the comparatively few indispensable works of critical religious scholarship with which he was acquainted.

December 27th, 1888

Hon. Andrew D. White,
Ithaca, Tompkins Co., N. Y.

My dear Sir:

I have read with great pleasure the *New Chapters of the Warfare of Science*.

How any one could help seeing that the Church in all modern ages, to say the least, has been the enemy of progress, is a mystery to me.

The Church pretended to have the word of God—pretended to have all truth worth knowing—and as a consequence it was obliged to say: " Obey! Believe! " It could not say: " Investigate—Think! "

For my part, I do not see how man can be free, or worthy of freedom, until he ceases to imagine that a Master exists. The only " power in the universe strong enough to make truth-seeking safe," is man. No other power has interfered. Millions of men found to their cost that truth-seeking was not safe. No power above nature—above man—interfered. The fires were not quenched —the prisons were not opened—the victims were not rescued. If God makes truth-seeking safe now, why did he allow it for thousands of years to be dangerous? Was not truth as valuable then as now?

All orthodox churches have taught, and still teach, that investigation is dangerous. The Christian virtues are the slave virtues: meekness, obedience, credulity, and mental non-resistance.

The power that makes for righteousness is exceedingly weak where bigots are in the majority.

And yet, what you have written will do good. The tendency will be to increase intellectual hospitality—to do away with the provincialism of creed, and the egotism of ignorance.

We know now, if we know anything, that our religion was produced like others, and that the supernatural is the superstitious —that the superstitious is untrue. We know now, if we know anything, that a religion is worth the truth that is in it, and that the truth will be much more effective—much better—without the alloy.

Yours very truly, Robert G. Ingersoll

On June 9, 1889, through the joint efforts of the Rationalists and Freethinkers of Europe and America, a life-sized statue of the noble and heroic philosopher and martyr Giordano Bruno was unveiled in the Campo dei Fiori, at Rome, on the spot where he was burned at the stake by order of the papal Inquisition.

Colonel Ingersoll was invited by the International Monument Committee to deliver the oration at the ceremonies of dedication of the Bruno statue. However, he was unable to accept the invitation owing to his legal and lecture commitments at home. Professor Giovanni Bovio, a brilliant Italian jurist, statesman, and Rationalist, delivered an eloquent and moving dedicatory address in Ingersoll's stead.

40 Wall Street, New York
Feb. 8, 1889

T. B. Wakeman, Esq.,
Treasurer of the Bruno Monument Committee.

My dear Sir:

It gives me great pleasure to inclose my check for one hundred dollars ($100). I shall never be quite satisfied until there is a monument to Bruno higher than the dome of St. Peter's.

Yours very truly, R. G. Ingersoll

New York, Mch 4th, 1889

Dr. A. A. Bell,
Madison, Ga.

My dear Sir:

There was a time when the physician and theologian were on an equality. In fact, there was a time when they were both united in the same rascals. In the ancient days, the " medicine man " was also the priest. Gradually, the business was divided— the priests fighting with all their might those who had become physicians.

There is an account in the Bible of a certain king who abandoned the priests and called in the physicians, and the priests who wrote an account of it, closed with the information that he was " gathered to his fathers." But as man has been slowly civilized, the physician has entirely given up the supernatural—he at last is a disciple of Science.

The priest, however, is still on the old leg, and wants it understood that he belongs to a firm of which God is the Senior Member. (A gentleman in the office suggests that they regard God, not as the Senior, but as the Junior member of the firm.) I am inclined to think he is right.

Yours very truly, R. G. Ingersoll

Thomas Henry Huxley was one of the greatest scientists and biologists, and probably the greatest exponent and popularizer of science and the scientific method, that England has produced.

After the publication of Darwin's immortal work, *The Origin of Species*, Huxley sprang into spectacular fame as the most fearless and powerful champion of Darwinism. It might justly be said of Huxley that he forced the theories and facts of Darwinism upon England and the rest of the civilized world at the point of his pen. He repudiated both Materialism and Theism, and he coined the term " Agnostic."

Frederic Harrison was the author of many distinguished and scholarly works; and his views on religion are best revealed in his *The Creed of a Layman*, and *The Positive Evolution of Religion*. He was the leading Positivist of his time.

In Ingersoll's article in the *North American Review* for April, 1889, entitled *Professor Huxley and Agnosticism*, Colonel Ingersoll wrote: " Professor Huxley has stated with great clearness the attitude of the Agnostic. It seems that he is somewhat severe on the Positive philosophy. While it is hard to see the propriety of worshipping Humanity as a being, it is easy to understand the splendid dream of Auguste Comte. Is the human race worthy to be worshipped by itself—that is to say, should the individual worship himself? Certainly the religion of humanity is better than the religion of the inhuman. The Positive Philosophy is better far than Catholicism. It does not fill the heavens with monsters, nor the future with pain.

" . . The mission of Positivism is, in the language of its founder, 'to generalize science and to systematize sociality'. . . .

" Although I am not a believer in the philosophy of Auguste Comte, I cannot shut my eyes to the value of his thought," said Ingersoll. " Neither is it possible for me not to applaud his candour, his intelligence, and the courage it required even to attempt to lay the foundation of the Positive Philosophy."

Ingersoll paid enthusiastic tribute to Huxley and Harrison as " splendid soldiers in the army of Progress "; for their having " attacked with signal success the sacred and solemn stupidities of superstition "; because they appealed " to that which is highest and noblest in man "; because they were " the destroyers of prejudice . shedding light," and winning " great victories on the fields of intellectual conflict." Ingersoll also felt that they could not " afford to waste time in attacking each other," because " the Agnostic and the Positivist have the same end in view—both believe in living for this world.   "

In the characteristically witty letter given below, Professor Huxley congratulated Colonel Ingersoll on his controversial triumph over Mr. Gladstone and Cardinal Manning in what might be described as the most important and widely publicized controversy of the nineteenth century.   This controversy was started through the efforts of Allen Thorndike Rice, the editor of the *North American Review*, and began with *An Open Letter to Robert G. Ingersoll* by Rev. Henry M. Field in the August, 1887, number of the *Review*; Gladstone and Manning contributed an article each, Field two articles, and Ingersoll five—the last being his *Reply to Cardinal Manning* in the November, 1888, issue.

4 Marlborough Place, Abbey Road, London
May (?) 1889

Dear Colonel Ingersoll:
Some unknown benefactor has sent me a series of numbers of the *North American Review* containing your battles with various " Bulls of Bashan," in 1888—and the very kindly and appreciative article of last April about my picador work over here.

I write mainly to thank you for it and to say that I feel the force of your admonition to [Frederic] Harrison and myself—to leave off quarrelling with one another and to join forces against the common enemy.   The excuse of, " Please sir, it was the other boy began," is somewhat ignoble; but really if you will look at Harrison's article again, I think you will see there was no help for it.

However, he is far too good a man to quarrel with for long, and I have hope we shall arrive at a treaty of peace and even cooperation before long.   In the meanwhile, I am glad to say that we are, personally, excellent friends.

You are to be congratulated on your opponents.   The Rabbi is the only one with any stuff in him—though, by the way, I have not read Manning, and do not mean to.   I have had many opportunities of taking his measure—and he is a parlous windbag—and nothing else, absolutely.   Gladstone's attack on you is one of the best things he has written.   I do not think there is more than 50 per cent more verbiage than necessary, nor any sentence with *more* than two meanings.   If he goes on improving at this rate, he will be an English classic by the time he is ninety. . . .

Do not answer this letter, I beg, unless the spirit should move you.   My life has been made a burden to me by letter writing, and now I do as little as possible.

Yours very faithfully, T. H. Huxley

New York,
July 25, '89

My dear Mr. Huxley,

For many years I have read your books, lectures, and essays with the keenest pleasure. You are one of my mental creditors and will always remain so. It is hardly necessary to say that your letter was gladly received. In the first place I apologize for what I said about you and Mr. Frederic Harrison. I know nothing of the controversy—having never read Harrison's article. Since receiving your letter I have read what Mr. Harrison had to say and I agree with you that " the other boy began it " and that the other boy's tone was somewhat overbearing. Most of the followers of Comte claim too much and while the objects they seek to attain are good the means seem inadequate. They think that they hold the " eel of science by the tail "—so much for that.

Mr. Rice asked me to write a few words about your splendid article in reply to Dr. Wace. You answered the absurd theologian to the last echo. And I wrote simply to call attention to what you had done. Your reply was in every respect admirable and overwhelming.

Your estimate of Mr. Gladstone is generous. It does not seem to me that he can live long enough to become a classic.

Your description of the Cardinal is perfect. I was greatly disappointed in both of these men. It is hard to have any respect for an intellect that in this age accepts the orthodox creed.—I feel that the brand of intellectual inferiority is over the theological brain.

You need care nothing for what you saw in the Washington paper. The intelligent people of America know that you are the friend of liberty and progress, and they regard you as one who bravely tells what he knows and modestly says what he thinks.

A friend of mine published a volume of collections from my speeches and essays which I take the liberty to send you. It may be well enough to say that the flattering title was given by the publisher. Do not trouble yourself to even acknowledge its receipt. I know that the little scraps and shreds of time you save from labour are of great value to you.

Thanking you again and again for your kind letter and hoping that you may live for many years to shed light.

Your friend and admirer, R. G. Ingersoll

New York, Sept. 9, 1889

Mrs. M. P. Ferris,
Garden City, L. I.

Dear Madam:

A Gnostic is one who professes to know—that is to say, one who is acquainted with the supernatural—who knows about God, about the origin and destiny of things.

An Agnostic is one who says that he does not know—that he knows nothing about the supernatural—nothing as to origin— nothing as to destiny—and consequently does not pretend to know and willingly waits.

Yours respectfully, R. G. Ingersoll

New York, Dec. 13, '89

F. M. Atwood, Esq.,
Chicago, Ill.

My dear Sir:

I did not attack Christianity until I was perfectly convinced that it was not only a false system, but that it had done and was doing an immense harm to the human race.

The great trouble with that system is that it sells crime on a credit. It says to any man: "No matter what you do, you can be forgiven, and in this way you can escape the consequences of your actions." This I believe to be exceedingly harmful. Every human being should be taught that he must suffer the consequences of his actions—in this world, as long as he lives, and in another world, if there be one.

An action is bad because the consequences are bad, and an action is good because the consequences are good—and there is no power on earth or in heaven that can step between an action and its consequences. That is one objection.

There is still another. According to the Christian religion, a large majority of mankind are destined to suffer eternal pain. This dogma, to me, is the most infamous that has ever found expression in human language. If it be true, the God of this universe—if there be one—is not good. No God would have the right to create a human being knowing that that human being's life was to be the source of everlasting grief. It would have been far better to have left all such persons unconscious dust. If you had the power to create a human being out of a stone, and you knew that that human being would commit murder—that finally he would be executed on the scaffold, and that he would be eternally damned, do you not see and clearly see, that you had altogether better leave the stone, stone?

These are at least two of my objections to Christianity. There is still another. Christianity rests upon miracles, and miracles cannot be established by human testimony—they can only be established by other miracles—and as the age of miracles has passed, it is impossible to substantiate the truth of Christianity. There is still another objection. Christianity rests upon the idea that the Bible is an inspired work. It is impossible to prove the fact—if it be a fact—of inspiration. Even the inspired could not certainly know that he had been inspired by an infinite being, and as to all others, this testimony must be merely hearsay.

Let us hope for better things. Let us hope that the Christian religion is false—because, if it is true, it would have been far better that no universe existed.

I wish to be in such a frame of mind that I can stand by the grave of the lost, and hope that the poor inhabitant below is not destined to suffer eternal grief. I wish to be in such a state of mind that I can prophesy good of all the children of men. Instead of softening towards the Christian religion, as the years roll by my hostility to the entire system increases—and, instead of having simply a dislike to some of its dogmas, I think of them with passionate hatred. All that is good in Christianity I like; all the morality of it, and all the forgiveness of it, is good; but the damnation of it is entirely bad.

Yours sincerely, R. G. Ingersoll

New York, Dec. 23, 1889

C. Palmer, Esq.,
Escanaba, Mich.

My dear Sir:

I see no objection to saying that there has been " intelligence " from eternity—any more than that there has been what we call " substance " from eternity. I do not know whether there is any difference between substance and force, or not. I am satisfied that substance cannot exist apart from what we call force, and that force cannot exist apart from what we call substance—but I am not prepared to say that force and substance are not the same. I suppose that what we call intelligence is a form of force, or to say the least of it, that it does not exist except in connection with what we call substance. I am not prepared to say that what we call the order of nature is intelligent, or that it is controlled by what we call intelligence. Neither do I know that what you are pleased to call " chaos " could not evolve order. It may be that order is simply the necessary action of substance on substance, and the necessary effects resulting therefrom.

You will see from this that I cannot admit that what you call " order " must be inseparable from what you call " intelligence."

So, it may be that we can conceive of infinite space, and that such a conception is a necessity of the mind, for the reason that we cannot conceive of any substance so great but when there will be space beyond it. So, it may be true that the conception of infinite space is a necessity.

After all, I think that you, with the rest, will be compelled to say: " I do not know."

Yours truly, R. G. Ingersoll

Rev. Hugh O. Pentecost (1847–1907), brother of a widely known evangelist, George F. Pentecost, pronounced himself an Agnostic in 1888. He published a Freethought paper called

The Twentieth Century, and at the time of his death was the leader of a Freethought congregation in Lyric (later Bryant) Hall, in New York City.

Rev. Minot J. Savage (1841–1918), was one of the most liberal of all Unitarian ministers of his day. When the following letter was written he was minister of the Church of the Unity, in Boston. From 1896 until 1906 he presided over the Church of the Messiah in New York. Dr. Savage was probably the first minister in the United States to champion the theory of evolution. He delivered a highly eulogistic sermon on Ingersoll at the time of the Colonel's death.

Jan. 25, '90

Mr. Hugh O. Pentecost,
New York.

My dear Friend:
First. I will never antagonize anybody who is going my way.
Second. I will never antagonize anybody who, on the main question, is going my way, although on minor matters he takes to the woods.
Third. I cannot bear to find fault with, or to criticize a liberal Christian: he is headed in the right direction, and is doing more good than harm. I do not want to drive him back, neither do I want to put it in the mouths of those he has left to say that he has found no friends.
Mr. Savage is a liberal. He fights the Christian's God and the Christian's Bible—and in addition to that, the Christian's Hell. Taking into consideration his conditions, and the effect of heredity, climate, and habitation, I think he is doing exceedingly well. Under these circumstances, I prefer not to antagonize him.
Of course it is impossible for him to conceive of any argument in favour of a personal God—in favour of any God who wants anything, or who ever did want anything—or of one who knows right from wrong.
But I do not care to answer him, for the reason that there are plenty of enemies in the field wearing the orthodox uniform, that I might prefer to shoot.

Very truly your friend, R. G. Ingersoll

Feb. 6, '90

Joseph Stidham, Esq.,
Hopkins Co., Texas.

My dear Sir:
You ought by this time to know that not the least dependence can be placed on any orthodox assertion. The Church having been founded on falsehood and mistake, it must be supported in the

K

same way. Take from every orthodox creed the falsehoods and mistakes, and nothing of importance will be left.

There is no truth in the reports you have heard, to the effect that I have changed my belief. The fact is that if I have changed at all, it is only to be more thoroughly convinced of the utter absurdity of all religions.

It is not true that Thomas Paine professed religion, or changed his views before his death. He died as he had lived.

Yours very truly, R. G. Ingersoll

Charles Watts, a leading English Rationalist lecturer, editor, and writer, was born on February 27, 1836. " The son of a Wesleyan minister, he was at an early age converted to Freethought by Southwell and G. J. Holyoake. . . . He came under the influence of R. Cooper, Bradlaugh, and other prominent men in the Secularist movement. In 1864 . . . he became sub-editor of the *National Reformer.* . . In 1877 he acquired the *Secular Review* from G. J. Holyoake. He edited the paper for some years, at first without assistance, then with G. W. Foote, and finally with W. Stewart Ross (' Saladin '). . . . In 1886 Mr. Watts accepted a Rationalist pastorate in Toronto, where he founded *Secular Thought,* and conducted a vigorous Freethought propaganda for several years. In 1891 he returned to England . . . and became a regular contributor to the *Freethinker.* In his closing years he was a lecturer for the Rationalist Press Association. . . . He excelled as a debater, and his opponents included nearly every leading Christian representative who was willing to defend his religion on the public platform. Mr. Watts was responsible for one volume of *The Freethinker's Textbook,* and was also the author of *The Meaning of Rationalism,* and numerous brochures expository of the teachings of Secularism. He died on February 16, 1906." (*A Biographical Dictionary of Modern Rationalists,* compiled by Joseph McCabe, London, 1920.)

New York, February 9, 1890

My dear Mr. Watts:

I have just received the debate between yourself and the editor of the *Halifax Evening Mail,* N. S. Your statement as to what Secularism is could not be improved and your definitions of certain terms are accurate and lucid. I have never read better. The Editor of the *Mail* does not understand you. He has not enough intelligence to grasp your meaning. When you ask for a better guide than *Reason,* he does not see that he cannot *even deny* that reason is the best of all guides without admitting *that it is.* Suppose he had said that the Bible is a better guide than reason, he would have been compelled to give his *reasons* for the assertion, and in doing this would have admitted that reason had been his guide. I can hardly call this a debate that you had with the Editor of the *Mail.* In a debate there ought to be arguments on *both* sides. All the argument is on your side. Your antagonist refused to come into the ring. He kept outside the ropes, and even in that place, threw up the sponge.

You are doing a great and splendid work in Canada. Every Freethinker ought to stand by you, and no one can afford to do without *Secular Thought.* Best regards to Mrs. Watts from us all, and to you.

Yours always, R. G. Ingersoll

June 2, '90

Rev. Henry H. Lipes,
Penn Yan, N. Y.

My dear Sir:

Of course you know that I do not believe in what is known as the Christian religion, and that I do not believe in the preaching of the Gospels—do not believe that it tends to civilize mankind.

On the other hand, you know that it is my opinion, that such preaching tends to harden the human heart. I am not a believer in the inspiration, or truth, of the scriptures. Neither do I believe in the dogma of the atonement—and least of all in an eternity of pain. I wish to do what little I can to increase the happiness of man. The tendency of orthodox religion, in my judgment, is to increase sorrow and insanity. I have spent the most of my life in endeavouring to destroy what I believe to be superstition, and you can readily see that I cannot now do anything to support that which I believe is wrong, and that which I have been endeavouring to kill.

You must not think that I am saying this to hurt your feelings. I am saying it simply because I must say it to justify my own conduct.

Yours respectfully, R. G. Ingersoll

Mr. Edgar Lee Masters, at the time this letter was written, was an unknown, struggling young attorney. Many years later he became famous overnight, with the publication of his brilliant *Spoon River Anthology.* He was the author of several works of historical and literary criticism, and biographies, and many volumes of poetry, notably, *Domesday Book,* and *The Great Valley* (1916), the latter containing a memorable poem to "Robert G. Ingersoll."

45 Wall Street
November 8, 1890

Edgar Lee Masters, Esq.,
Lewistown, Illinois.

My dear Friend:
Whoever attacks the Church, must expect to be attacked. Ministers, unable to answer arguments, will resort to personalities. They invent falsehoods about his (the unbeliever's) life, misconstrue and misinterpret his expressions, and in every way endeavour to destroy his influence.

All I can say is, that if I have changed at all in the last 25 years, it is in the direction of free thought.

I am more firmly convinced, if possible, from year to year, of the utter falsity of all religions—and never in my life did I more perfectly see than I do today, the absurdity of what is called Christianity. I have for many years done what little I could to destroy what I believe to be superstition, and I expect to continue in the same work as long as I live. I regard the Bible as the work of man, and for the most part, of barbarian man, and feel that the only hope for the human race lies in the destruction of superstition.

Your friend, R. G. Ingersoll

Nov. 20, 1890

Mark M. Aiken, Esq.,
Peoria, Ill.

My dear Friend:
I received your letter today in reference to the Baptist church. You say it is nearly completed, with the exception of the roof. I do not see why there should be any roof on a Baptist church. They believe in salvation by water, and why they should fight the " means of grace " with a roof is beyond my comprehension.

R. G. Ingersoll

P. S.   Motto for the Baptist church:
" The wetter, the better."

Decem. 26, 1890

To the Editor of *The Toledo Blade*,
Toledo, Ohio.

My dear Sir:
My attention was called to an article in your paper in reference to a conversation claimed to have taken place between the late Washington McLean and myself.

Nothing of the kind ever occurred. The same story was told, with Henry Ward Beecher in the place of Mr. McLean. Mr. Beecher denied it, and I did the same.

As a matter of fact, nothing could be more idiotic than the idea that men who are destroying superstition are taking crutches from Christian cripples. Will the Christians admit that they are cripples, and will they admit that their creeds are crutches? Will they also admit that the free thinker takes away their crutches and leaves them helpless cripples? It would be cruel to take crutches from a cripple; on the other hand, it would be exceedingly philanthropic and humane to cure the cripple, so that he would throw away the crutches himself.

My effort has been to make man superior to superstition—to educate him to that degree that he shall need no crutches, and to convince him that a good cause never has, and never will, need the assistance of falsehood.

There is not one word of truth in the story. No such conversation ever occurred.

Yours very truly, R. G. Ingersoll

May 7, 1891

Jno. B. Fidlar, Esq.,
Davenport, Iowa.

My dear Sir:

Much obliged to you for your letter of the 3rd. I never could persuade myself that any human being could be infamous enough to inflict eternal torment on any animal or man capable of suffering. How any human being ever imagined it, or believed it, or preached it, is beyond my comprehension.

The infamous dogma is dying out, and the Church must either give up hell, or, figuratively speaking, catch it.

Yours very truly, R. G. Ingersoll

From a symposium in *The New York World*, on the subject of "How to Spend Sunday," June 14, 1891 : Colonel Ingersoll's contribution runs:

To the Editor of *The World*.

Sir: The question of Sunday-keeping is one to be determined by its effect upon man in this world and no other.

In my judgment, every one should spend Sunday as he spends Monday—to the best advantage. But as there is a custom by which most people cease from labour on Sunday, I think it should be set apart as a day of enjoyment—a day for the working-man, not only to rest, but to take his wife and children to the park, or to the woods, or to the seashore.

So I think Sunday is a good day to cultivate the amenities of life, a good day to get acquainted with your family, a good day to see your best girl, to read old letters, old poems, to write letters, to have dreams—a good day to enjoy yourself in every way in which you may feel inclined, provided you do not in any way interfere with the happiness of others.

Nothing could be more cowardly than the effort to compel

the observance of the Sabbath by law. We of America have out-grown the childishness of the last century; we laugh at the super-stitions of our fathers. We have made up our minds to be as happy as we can be, knowing that the way to be happy is to make others so, that the time to be happy is now, whether that now is Sunday or any other day in the week.

R. G. Ingersoll

Dec. 31, 1891

Mrs. M. B. Freeley,
Chicago, Ill.

My dear Madam:

I have read with great pleasure your sketches: *How Eve Seduced the Serpent*, also *The Abraham–Hagar Scandal, Lot's Wife, Reckless Rebekah*, and *Sorry We Didn't Take the Preacher's Say-so*, and I think you have made out a case.

You have shown clearly that the women of the Bible had their way—that they were disobedient then as now, and that the writers in the New Testament knew very little about the women of the old.

Your style is exceedingly graceful, and many of your descriptions beautiful.

Yours very truly, R. G. Ingersoll

Feb. 2, 1892

R. B. Berkeley, Esq.,
Pulaski, Va.

My dear Sir:

It is exceedingly wonderful that we live. Whether we live beyond this world, or not, nobody, so far as I know, knows.

Most people dread annihilation, consequently, they would like to live forever; but as others are constantly dying, they are satis-fied that they, too, must die. The wish to live here is then changed to a wish to live in another world.

It may be that the tears of sorrow are prismatic—making the future beautiful. I would not take any hope from the human heart. I have been warring against the doctrine or the dogma of eternal pain—of endless agony. I do not regard immortality as a Christian's hope. Immortality was believed in, and hoped for, thousands of ages before Christianity existed; and this hope of immortality was not born of any religion, but of human affection, of the human desire to live, not only, but to meet the loved gone. This hope rests on no book, but is the child of the heart.

Yours very truly, R. G. Ingersoll

N. Y., Feb'y 2, 1892

William C. DeWitt, Esq.,
Brooklyn, N. Y.

My dear Friend:
    I read with great pleasure what you have to say of Burns. It is exceedingly beautiful, poetic, and pathetic.
    I have always wondered how a rose like Burns could have grown among the thistles of Calvinism. He was probably a protest and re-action.
    I dislike Knox exceedingly, and have not the slightest sympathy with any form of religion that ever flourished in Scotland.
    I am a little in doubt about one thing you mention: I hardly think that Scotland ever adopted the family of Burns, or provided for their future. I have always loved Burns, and there is one thing about him that I like especially, and that is, that in his day and generation he preferred the tavern to the church.

Your friend, R. G. Ingersoll

Colonel Ingersoll had an article published in the *New York Evening Telegram* on the general subject of Christianity, to which he and the newspaper received many replies.

One of the most vitriolic attacks upon Ingersoll's position came from Dr. DeCosta, who argued that " Christianity has taught the value of freedom . . . established the fact of human brotherhood, encouraged the advancement of science, art, philosophy, letters, and learning," and has been responsible for " all events for many centuries, especially the good ones."

The following letter by Ingersoll closed the discussion.

New York, N. Y.
Feb. 5, 1892

The Editor of *The Evening Telegram*.

    Time and space are lacking to answer all who have replied to me. Several of the replies contain substantially the same lack of argument, and need not be noticed separately. A few are exceedingly absurd, and while reading them I thought of a saying of Thomas Paine: " To argue with a man who has renounced his reason, is like giving medicine to the dead." This applies with great force to the author of one of the last and longest of these replies.

    The Rev. Dr. DeCosta, drawing a distinction between Christianity and Churchianity—claiming, of course, to be governed himself by Christianity—calls me, in an exceedingly argumentative way, " A tiger," and then, to clinch the argument, suggests that, after all, I may be " an ass under a tiger's skin." Fearing that a loophole might still be left, he asserts that " some go so far as to assert that he (meaning myself), holds a brief for Satan, and is doing the best he can for his client."

He makes the familiar assertion that " by its fruits we may know Christianity." Now, if by Christianity he means kindness, candour, the spirit of investigation, observation, reason—in other words, if he aggregates what are called the virtues and calls them Christianity—then there need be no dispute.

But is this true? Every religion teaches a code of morals, plus something else, and it is this " something else " that determines what each religion is.

Buddhism is a code of morals, plus a belief in the transmigration of souls; in the illumination of Buddha; in certain prayers, ceremonies, genuflections, and superstitions.

So, Christianity is a code of morals, plus the belief that the God of the Old Testament is the Creator of the universe; that the Christ of the New Testament is the same God, and that his death and atonement were made for all who should believe in him in a certain way, plus certain ceremonies and superstitions.

R. G. Ingersoll

March 18, 1892

Mrs. Sarah H. Greenleaf,
Flushing, N. Y.

My dear Madam:

This morning I received your curious letter, in which occurs the following: " Tell me your object in attacking what you call Christianity! There is an immeasurable gulf between the Christianity you attack and the Christianity we, who love its founder, believe in."

From this, it seems that I have not attacked real Christianity. Then it follows, as a matter of course, that I have attacked a false Christianity. Why do those who believe in the true Christianity find fault with me for attacking a false Christianity? It seems to me that I should receive your thanks for endeavouring to destroy that which you admit to be false.

In the light of your question and of your statement, you will easily see that the rest of your letter is a *non sequitur*, and that you have fallen into the error of finding fault with me for attacking what you admit is false.

Yours respectfully, R. G. Ingersoll

March 26, 1892

Rev. William C. Hall,
Diana Mills, Va.

My dear Sir:

I have not the least doubt as to your kindness of heart, and sincerity. I do not think that you understand just what I am endeavouring to do.

I have never attacked anything in Christianity that is good. I have said what I could against the miraculous, the cruel, and the absurd—nothing against charity or justice, and nothing to dim the hope of the world.

I object to orthodox Christianity because it is infinitely cruel, and because it teaches the doctrine that this little life, filled with darkness, is a probationary state, and that the life here settles an eternal life to come. This doctrine has added greatly to the sorrows of this world. It has furrowed the cheeks of the really good and tender, with tears. It has cast a shadow upon every cradle and upon every grave.

I am doing and have done what I could do to destroy what I believe to be a very absurd and cruel falsehood.

Yours very truly, R. G. Ingersoll

April 19, 1892

Bronson Murray, Esq.,
New York City, N. Y.

My dear Sir:

I am much obliged to you for the work of Prof. Turner. A copy was sent me several weeks ago by a Chicago friend.

I think that Prof. Turner has very much over-stated the case. In the first place, we live in a very small world, and I suppose there are many billions of worlds many millions of times larger than ours. Under these circumstances, it is quite difficult to say what is the only good, in all the worlds.

Of course I believe there can be nothing better in any world than justice, charity, love, provided we have intelligence enough to know and they have intelligence enough to know what justice really is, and what charity really is, and what love really is.

Neither do I think that all the goodness of humanity was concentrated in one man. I believe that just as good men and women are alive today as ever walked on earth.

Professor Turner is an excellent man—perfectly honest in his opinions—but it does not seem to me that Christ, in his teachings, covered the entire intellectual field. In fact, I think he covered but little—very little.

Yours very truly, R. G. Ingersoll

April 29, 1892

F. McCarthy, Esq.,
Chicago, Illinois.

My dear Friend:

You have not quoted me exactly right. I did not say that the Gospels contained only one reference to salvation by faith. I did say that Matthew, Mark, and Luke said nothing on the subject —insisting that I thought that Mark 16 was an interpolation.

Of course I admitted that much was found in John on the subject of salvation by faith.

My own opinion is, that that faith business, and the atonement idea, and the regeneration dogma, were all produced long after Christ was dead. As a matter of fact, I do not believe that such a man ever existed.

Yours very truly, R. G. Ingersoll

Eugene Victor Debs was the great leader of the Socialist Party in America for many years, and a candidate for the presidency of that ticket in several campaigns. He was one of the Colonel's warmest admirers, an admiration that was fully reciprocated by Ingersoll.

New York, N. Y.
June 17, 1892

Eugene V. Debs, Esq.,
Terre Haute, Indiana.

My dear Friend:

I have read your answer to the parson on the Sunday opening, and you have answered him conclusively on every point. All the working-men in this country should resent the impudence and arrogance of the gentlemen who live on the labour of others. The people can hardly afford to hire masters. They are able to take care of themselves, and they know what to do with their time.

It is absurd that people in the nineteenth century should still be the victims of a Roman Emperor who has been dead for nearly sixteen hundred years, and who established Sunday, not as a Christian Sabbath, but as the " venerable day of the sun." I hope that you will keep drawing attention to this matter in your magazine [*Debs Magazine*].

What the people want is light. It gives me great pleasure to know that the priest is losing his power. In this country, the majority rules, and we all know that there are more pews than pulpits.

Your sincere friend, R. G. Ingersoll

July 15, 1892

Frank C. Richardson, Esq.,
Boston, Mass.

My dear Sir:

You are right in what you say. The *Age of Reason* was not written until three years after Franklin's death.

Paine left the United States in 1784, and did not return until 1802. Franklin never saw the MS. of the *Age of Reason*, as he had been dead some three years before it was written.

Moncure D. Conway has just published a life of Thomas Paine, and this matter, among others, is fully explained. As a matter of fact, Franklin and Paine agreed about religious matters. Franklin did not believe in the inspiration of the Scriptures, or the divinity of Christ, but he did believe in the existence of God, and hoped for immortality.

Yours very truly, R. G. Ingersoll

July 15, 1892

To J. O. Clifton, Greenville, S. C.

My dear Sir:

I do not say that there is no God—that is, no infinite personality—because I do not know. But I do say, that I do not believe there is; I have no evidence upon that subject.

To my mind, an infinite personality is an infinite absurdity. Neither can I conceive of a conditionless being. Still, I do not say that no such being exists—I simply say that I do not believe such a being exists.

So with regard to immortality. I have no evidence showing that man is immortal—neither have I any evidence showing that he is not immortal. If eternal life is a good, I hope that it will be enjoyed by all men, but whether it is a fact in Nature or not, I do not know.

Yours very truly, R. G. Ingersoll

July 15, 1892

A. E. Ganning, Esq.,
Lansing, Michigan.

My dear Sir:

You ask for my views on the subject of opening the World's Fair on Sunday.

1st. There are two reasons given in the Bible for " keeping the Sabbath." The fact is, that God, having made the world in six days, and having rested on the seventh, therefore, man shall rest on the seventh.

We know that this is not true. We know, if we know anything, that God did not make the world in six days, and rest on the seventh. It will not do to say that he made the world in six " periods," and rested on the seventh. This would be no argument in favour of keeping the Sabbath.

2nd. The second reason given in the Bible for keeping the Sabbath is, that God had brought out the Jews from Egypt. If this is the real reason, it applies to no people except the Jews. It certainly could not have been expected that the Egyptians would think a day sacred for that reason. The reason given applied only to the Jewish people, and if that be the real reason, then the Sabbath is for the Jews and for no others.

3rd. There is another point. The day that was made sacred, according to the Bible, was Saturday, and not the day we keep.

There is nothing in the Old or New Testaments to show that God ever changed the day, and there is no warrant to be found in the " Sacred Scriptures " for keeping the day we call Sunday. The day we keep was kept by Pagans long before the Jewish people were released from Egypt. It was a day sacred to the Sun—not sacred in the sense that people were not to enjoy themselves, but sacred in the sense that they were on that day to enjoy themselves. That day was a festival, not a penitentiary.

This worship of Sunday is of modern growth. It seems to have reached its height in Scotland, then in England, and from England it was brought by the Pilgrims and Puritans to the New World. It is a relic of asceticism—of the idea that man can please God by making himself miserable. The Jews at one time kept the Sabbath so strictly that if anyone, by accident, fell down, he would not rise until after sunset. On Sunday they built no fires in their houses—they shivered and thanked God. They ate cold victuals with pious gratitude, and longed with all their hearts for the next day.

At one time, in Scotland, it was discussed whether it was right to rescue drowning men on Sunday. The most pious took the ground that they should not be rescued, that the drowning was God's punishment for the violation of the day, and that man should not endeavour to rescue his fellow man from the judgment of God.

The question now is whether here, in this country, in this Nineteenth Century, the World's Fair should be closed on Sunday.

Admit for the sake of the argument, that the day is absolutely sacred—ought the Fair to be closed? What will be the effect of looking upon great pictures or statues, of seeing the wonderful machines that man has invented? Will the tendency be to degrade, or elevate?—to demoralize, or to enlighten?

If looking at these pictures, at these statues, at these machines, enlarges the mind, educates the brain, cultivates the tastes—certainly there can be no objection to opening the Fair on Sunday, no matter how sacred the day is. Can anyone conceive of a better way to keep Sunday—admitting the day to be sacred—than to develop the brain and civilize the heart?

From this it follows that whether the day is sacred or not, the Fair should be open.

There will be many thousands of people in Chicago. They must do something on Sunday. They will not remain in their rooms and read Baxter's *Call to the Unconverted,* neither will they attend church. They must do something, and it is impossible to conceive of a better thing for them to do than to examine and study the triumphs of genius. Even the most devout will hardly object to looking at the world about us, on Sunday—at the undulating fields, the green and spreading trees, the rivers and clouds. Neither will they think it wrong on Sunday night to gaze on heaven's dome inlaid with stars. And yet, all things are from the same source. Nature works through man, and the great painting and the great statue are and have been as naturally produced as rivers and trees and stars.

Of course, the idea that one day is better than another is infinitely absurd—that a space of time can be " holy," or that man is under any more obligation one day than another, to do good, to love mercy, and to increase the happiness of his fellowman.

All things that man ought to do on any day of the week, certainly can be done on Sunday, without sin. The whole matter may be summed up thus: It is never right to do wrong, and it is never wrong to do right.

Most people imagine that Sunday should be kept sacred by not doing anything on that day for the good of man, but by devoting your entire time in [to?] the worship of God—that is to say, in doing something for God. There is nothing a man can do for God, as God needs nothing; but there are many things we can do for our fellowmen, because many of them are in constant need.

All days should be for the good of man, and that day in which the most people are really happy, is the best day.

Yours very truly, R. G. Ingersoll

Robert Ingersoll and Dr. Moncure D. Conway (see page 81) were pioneer champions of Thomas Paine. Ingersoll enjoyed Conway's society and companionship enormously, and rejoiced that at long last his good friend gave the public a fine and fair biography of the much-maligned Thomas Paine. " The real history of Thomas Paine, of what he attempted and accomplished, of what he taught and suffered, has been intelligently, truthfully, and candidly given to the world," Ingersoll declared. " Henceforth the slanderer will be without excuse."

July 18, 1892

Isaac H. Julian, Esq.,
San Marcos, Texas.

My dear Sir:

I have read Mr. Conway's *Life of Thomas Paine* and consider it a good book—well and candidly written, and whoever will read it will, I think, become a friend of Paine.

The people of this country are hardly civilized enough, as yet, to appreciate the services of that great man. We are in the stage to appreciate force, to worship the physical conqueror—but we have hardly arrived at the stage to hold in high esteem " the still and mental parts ". . . .

Yours very truly, R. G. Ingersoll

New York, N. Y., Dec. 11, (?) '92

To the Editor of *The Liberal Christian.*

Dear Sir:

I have for a long time wondered why somebody didn't start a church on a sensible basis. My idea is this: There are, of course, in every community, lawyers, doctors, merchants, and people of all trades and professions, who have not the time during the week to pay any particular attention to history, poetry, art, or song. Now, it seems to me that it would be a good thing to have a church, and for these men to employ a man of ability, of talent, to preach to them Sundays, and let this man say to this congregation: " Now, I am going to preach to you for the first few Sundays—eight or ten or twenty, we will say—on the art, poetry, and intellectual achivements of the Greeks." Let this man study all the week and tell this congregation Sundays what he has ascertained. Let him give to his people the history of such men as Plato, as Socrates, what they did; of Aristotle, of his philosophy; of the great Greeks, their statesmen, their dramatists, their poets, actors, and sculptors, and let him show the debt that modern civilization owes to these people. Let him, too, give their religions, their mythology—a mythology that has sown the seeds of beauty in every land. Then let him take up Rome. Let him show what a wonderful and practical people they were; let him give an idea of their statesmen, orators, poets, lawyers—because probably the Romans were the greatest lawyers. And so let him go through with nation after nation, biography after biography, and at the same time let there be a Sunday-school connected with this church where the children shall be taught something of importance. For instance, teach them botany, and when a Sunday is fair, clear, and beautiful, let them go to the fields and woods with their teachers, and in a little while they will become acquainted with all kinds of trees and shrubs, and flowering plants. They could also be taught entomology, so that every bug would be interesting, for they would see the facts in science—something of use to them.

I believe that such a church and such a Sunday-school would at the end of a few years be the most intelligent collection of people in the United States.

To teach the children all of these things and to teach their parents too, the outlines of every science so that every listener would know something of geology, something of astronomy, so that every member could tell the manner in which they find the distance of a star—how much better that would be than the old talk about Abraham, Isaac, and Jacob, and quotations from Haggai and Zephaniah, and all this eternal talk about the fall of man and the garden of Eden, and the flood, and the atonement, and the wonders of Revelation!

R. G. Ingersoll

New York, June 3, 1894

R. M. McKinney,
Burlington, Iowa.

My dear Sir:
The real question is this: If God commands men to love their enemies, will he not forgive his? My enemies can hurt me; and yet I am told that I ought to forgive them. God's enemies cannot hurt him; why should he not forgive them?

If Christ is in fact God, is he not as good-natured now, as when he lived in Jerusalem? He then forgave his murderers. Will he not now forgive honest men for expressing their honest thoughts? Did it change his nature to go back to heaven?

If Christ was God why did he ask his Father to forgive his murderers; why would he ask a favour of himself? Why did he say "My God why hast thou forsaken me?" Did he forsake himself? Was he in doubt as to the reason why he did forsake himself? What reason did he expect he would give to himself for having forsaken himself?

Again, why should God make any man knowing that he was to be eternally unhappy? How can God be justified for having made failures? You claim that He is infinitely wise and powerful; why then are there any failures of His making? Do not try to saddle these failures on man, or on the devil, because then you will be asked why God made man weak and liable to err, and why did he make the devil to tempt man and fill the earth with evil? You see, my friend, you have not thought upon these subjects; and I beseech you to examine some of these questions—all of them—for yourself. If you do, you will find that all the theologians and "divines" simply know nothing, and that all religions are based upon falsehood and assumption of a superior knowledge which man has not.

Yours truly, R. G. Ingersoll

April 3rd, '95

Mrs. J. E. Oliver,
Waterloo, Iowa.

My dear Madam:
Theosophy seems to me without the slightest foundation in fact. I am a believer in the natural. The supernatural does not, and cannot exist. So, you will see I reject all religions based on the miraculous—the supernatural—including Theosophy and Christianity.

Very truly yours, Robt. G. Ingersoll

220 Madison Avenue, Feb. 2, 1897

My dear Mr. Hoskett:
I received and read the sermon and thank you for your kindness. The truth is that I have no desire to be a Christian—no

desire to be "saved." I have no fear as to the future and care nothing about gods.

I am satisfied that we can find nothing about origin or destiny and consequently we should turn our attention to this life. We should be ambitious to be useful—to be happy ourselves and to make others so. There may be another life, and if there is, and it is good, so much the better.

All this talk about Christ being God—about the fall of man, the atonement and the redemption of true believers, is to me nothing but superstition. I know that good men believe these things, and good men reject them.

After all, the best way is for each man to live to his ideal and be of real use to himself and others.

I feel that you are actuated by kindness and therefore I thank you.

Yours truly, R. G. Ingersoll

Charles Henry Tucky Collis was a lawyer, a General in the Civil War, and the author of two books which created considerable interest, namely, *The Religion of Abraham Lincoln* and *I Died*, a spiritualistic fantasy.

Feb. 15th, 1893

Gen. Charles H. T. Collis.

My dear Sir:

I have just received your letter in which you criticize a statement made by me to the effect that Lincoln's religion was the religion of Voltaire and Thomas Paine, and you add, " I know not where you got your authority for this, but if the statement be true, Lincoln himself was untrue, for no man ever evoked the gracious favour of Almighty God in every effort of his life with more apparent fervour than did he."

You seem to be labouring under the impression that Voltaire was not a believer in God, and that he could not have " invoked the gracious favour of Almighty God." The truth is that Voltaire was not only a believer in God, but even in Special Providence. I know that the clergy have always denounced Voltaire as an atheist, but this can be accounted for in two ways: 1st by the ignorance of the clergy, and 2ndly, by their contempt of truth. Thomas Paine was also a believer in God, and wrote his creed as follows: " I believe in one God and no more, and hope for immortality." The ministers have also denounced Paine as an atheist.

You will therefore see that your first statement is without the slightest foundation in fact. Lincoln could be perfectly true to himself if he agreed with the religious sentiments of Voltaire and Paine, and yet invoke the gracious favour of Almighty God.

You also say: " This God (meaning the God whose favour Lincoln invoked) was not the Deists' God."

The Deists believe in an infinite being who created and preserves the universe. The Christians believe no more. Deists and Christians believe in the same God, but they differ as to what this God has done, and as to what this God will do.

You further say that " Lincoln worshipped his God under the forms of the Christian Church, of which he was a member."

Again you are mistaken. Lincoln was never a member of any church. Mrs. Lincoln stated a few years ago that Mr. Lincoln was not a Christian. Hundreds of his acquaintances have said the same thing. Not only so, but many of them have testified that he was a Freethinker; that he denied the inspiration of the Scriptures, and that he always insisted that Christ was not the Son of God, and that the dogma of the atonement was, and is, an absurdity.

I will very gladly pay you a thousand dollars for your trouble to show that one statement in your letter is correct—even one. And now, to quote you, " Do you not think it were better for the truth of history that you should state the facts about Lincoln, and that you should commend him for what he was, rather than for what he was not? "

Yours truly, R. G. Ingersoll

General Collis answered as follows :

1055 Fifth Ave.
Feb. 21, 1893

Dear Col. Ingersoll :

I trust that you and I can assert our respective views of Abraham Lincoln's religion without requiring the stimulus of a $1,000 prize.

You have publicly made the broad statement that his (Lincoln's) religion was that of Voltaire and Thomas Paine. This you do not deny. Upon that, and that alone, I take issue with you, and I want to discuss without wandering outside the record. I do not care whether you select Voltaire's Voltaire, or Ingersoll's Voltaire, or Carlyle's, or Voltaire as mankind has accepted him. Lincoln's religion bore no resemblance to either [any ?]. Voltaire called himself a " master Deist." Your Voltaire led a crusade against superstition and religious persecution. Carlyle's fought the Christian Church. The world generally regards him as a mocker and a scoffer.

I am not " labouring under the impression that Voltaire was not a believer in God." You will agree with me, I presume, that he was a Deist. I say that Mr. Lincoln was not a Deist. That is the issue, as I understand it.

Had you said that if Mr. Lincoln [had] lived in the time of Louis Fifteenth he would have been a disciple of Voltaire, I would have respected your opinion though I could not subscribe to it; but what Mr. Lincoln really was is a substantial fact, easily established, and not dependent upon mere conjecture and speculation.

You proselyte him because you say " Mrs. Lincoln stated he was not a Christian "; because " hundreds of his acquaintances have said the same thing "; because " many of them have testified he was a freethinker and denied the inspiration of the Scriptures," etc. As a lawyer you accepted such secondary evidence as this, when Mr. Lincoln's own testimony to the contrary was in existence and abundant.

If I find that Mr. Lincoln professed Christianity, worshipped at a Christian Church, admitted his belief in the Divinity of Christ, and boldly asserted the doctrine of the inspiration of the Scriptures, I am compelled to deny that " his religion was the religion of Voltaire and Tom Paine," or to confess that he was an impostor. There is no middle course.

That Mr. Lincoln regularly attended a Christian Church in Washington, is a historical fact. Though not a " member," as we technically understand it, he was a constant attendant of Dr. Gurley's Presbyterian Church, near the corner of 14th Street and New York Avenue. Dr. Gurley was his pastor, and was present at his death-bed. He also frequently attended Dr. Sutherland's Church.

That he was a Christian at heart as well as in form, and believed in the efficacy of the prayers and support of Christian denominations let extracts from his addresses verify.

Leaving his home at Springfield with a full—a sorrowful— appreciation of the awful responsibility devolving upon him . . . he thus addressed his friends and neighbours: " I now leave, not knowing when or whether ever I may return; with a task before me greater than that which rested upon Washington. Without the assistance of that Divine Being who ever attended him, I cannot succeed. With that assistance I cannot fail. Trusting in Him, who can go with me and remain with you, and be everywhere for good, let us confidently hope that all will yet be well. To His care commending you, as I hope in your prayers you will commend me, I bid you an affectionate farewell."

To the Presbyterians he said: " It has been my happiness to receive testimonies of a similar nature from, I believe, all denominations of Christians. This to me is most gratifying, because from the beginning I saw that the issues of the great struggle depended on the Divine interposition and favour. Relying as I do upon the Almighty power, and encouraged as I am by these resolutions which you have just read, with support which I receive from Christian men, I shall not hesitate to use all means to secure the termination of the rebellion, and will hope for success."

To the Methodists he said: " Nobly sustained as the Government has been by all the churches, I would utter nothing which might in the least appear invidious against any, yet, without this, it may fairly be said that the Methodist Episcopal Church, not less devoted than the best, is, by its greatest numbers, the most important of all   . God bless the Methodist Church, bless all the churches, and blessed be God, who in this our great trial giveth us the churches."

If on September 4, 1864, you had served him (Lincoln) with notice that thirty years later you would claim him as a Voltairian because he disbelieved in the inspiration of the Bible and the divinity of Christ, he could not more emphatically have repudiated the honour than he did when he then said to the coloured men of Baltimore who presented him with a Bible: " In regard to the Great Book, I have only to say that it is the best gift which God has given to man. All the good from the Saviour of the world is communicated in this book. . . ." You must not proclaim Lincoln's honesty in one sentence and ask us in another to believe that his real faith soared no higher than that of the man who wrote: " Nobody thinks of giving an immortal soul to a flea; why should you give one to an elephant or a monkey, or my champagne valet, or a village steward, who has a trifle more instinct than my valet? " Nor must you expect us to couple the man who, in guileless love, exclaims: " God bless the churches," with him whose shibboleth of malignant hate was *Écrasez l'infâme*.

Let me say to you, in all kindness, that if your cause is imperilled for lack of recruits, you neither strengthen your own nor weaken that of Christianity by resorting to conscriptions of this character, for you can no more easily make Lincoln a Deist than I can make Voltaire a Christian. Mankind will estimate the life of Abraham Lincoln for what it was, and not for what you or I would have it.

Sincerely yours, Charles H. T. Collis

400 Fifth Ave., Feb. 23, 1893

My dear Collis:

You are getting away from the issue.

You wrote me that Lincoln belonged to a church. Do you still insist that he did? Do you admit that you were wrong?

You insisted that Lincoln was a Christian. Have you any evidence to show that he was a believer in any orthodox creed?

Did he believe in the divinity of Christ, in the Atonement, in the inspiration of the Bible? You must stick to your original charges.

All that you say about Voltaire is as far from the facts as what you said about Lincoln—" but no matter."

I again call for the evidence of your two statements.

First, that Lincoln was a Christian, and, second, that he was a member of a church. Stick to your charges. Do not wander.

Yours truly, R. G. Ingersoll

George W. Foote, the prominent English lecturer and founder and editor of *The Freethinker*, and Ingersoll were warm friends and colleagues in the Freethought cause, and the former was entertained on a number of occasions by the Colonel and his family.

Robert Ingersoll was a great admirer and friend of Mr. Charles Watts (see letter of February 9, 1890, to Mr. Watts, quoted on page 136); they had a good deal of correspondence throughout the years, and met on a number of occasions; and this is the high opinion Ingersoll held of him: " Mr. Watts is an extremely logical man, with a direct and straightforward manner and mind. He has paid great attention to what is called 'Secularism.' He . . is undoubtedly one of the strongest debaters in the field. . . He has demolished more divines than any man of my acquaintance. . . . In discussion he is quick, pertinent, logical, and above all, goodnatured. There is not in all he says a touch of malice. He can afford to be generous to his antagonists because he is always the victor."

(No month given) 1897

To George Jacob Holyoake:
Thanks for your good letter. Messrs. Foote and Watts spoke to me in the highest terms about you. They knew that I was your friend. And I say to you that nothing that any human being could say would *decrease* or *increase* my respect, admiration, and love for you. I know you. I know how sincere, candid, and courageous you are. I know that your head is full of wisdom and your heart of kindness. You are the ideal reformer. You see all sides and pierce the centre. There is no better intellectual marksman. Your arrows, like those of Ulysses, fly through all the rings, and cleave the question's heart.

New York, May 27, '97

My dear Mr. Wertheimer,
Many people have had your experience. They have sought and suffered.—They have tried to guess the riddle—tried to know the absolute—to find origin—to know destiny. They have all failed. These things are beyond our intellectual horizon—beyond the " reaches of our souls." Our life is a little journey from mystery to mystery. We emerge from darkness—we are lost in night, we must give our attention to the journey. We cannot get behind the beginning or see beyond the end. We know many things about force and substance, but we know not what they are. We know something of relations, qualities, forms, but the absolute eludes all our senses and our thoughts. I have ceased looking for the unfindable.—I let " determined things to destiny hold unbewailed their way." I know that the walls cannot be scaled, and so I adorn my cell, cultivate patience, cheerfulness, and above all courage. I

know that virtue is the mother of happiness and that vice breeds grief, failure, and despair. This knowledge is enough for this life. If there is another it is enough for that.

Yours always, R. G. Ingersoll

Horace Traubel was Walt Whitman's constant companion and secretary, and one of the executors of his estate. He was also the editor of *The Conservator*, a liberal magazine, and a distinguished poet and man-of-letters.

New York
Dec. 25, '97

My dear Traubel,

Your are too flattering in the *Conservator* but I thank you with all my heart.

" What of Christ " is exceedingly noble. " You have faced (or defaced) the Christ of your lips with the mammon of your deeds." This is the whole case.

For hundreds of years Christians have loved with their mouths and hated with their hearts. But they are slowly becoming civilized in spite of their creeds. You have done much to hasten the coming of the better day and I congratulate you. You have succeeded in rising above all prejudice and the clouds are below you. After all we know that all that is has been naturally and necessarily produced. So, we need not blame or hate. If we wish to change people we must change conditions. A man is the stone and environment is the sculptor.

Yours always, R. G. Ingersoll

New York
June 18th, 1898

Dr. R. H. Bell.

My dear Bell:

A thousand thanks for your generous defence. It is too flattering—too partial. You are a little hard on the minister. As a matter of fact, I care very little for what comes from the pulpit. Of course I hate to be thought badly of by good people, but as a rule I let the preachers alone. Mr. Jones [Rev. Sam Jones of Georgia] seems to talk without thinking. The other day, a man speaking about an address made by a lawyer, said:—He began speaking at two and kept on until six, but his brain stopped working at two-ten.

Do not, I pray you, take any trouble to defend me. Do not make enemies. Your article is splendid—covers the case and leaves nothing of Mr. Jones.

R. G. Ingersoll

New York, N. Y.
Aug. 28, '98

Rev. J. E. Roberts.

My dear Mr. Roberts,

I feel that you are doing great good—setting an example for all the preachers in the world. You have established a church on a foundation of fact, instead of faith, and you are preparing people for this world—showing them how to be happy before they are dead.

I will have the extracts from Confucius sent you. I know that you will agree with the wretched heathen who found out so much without being told by Jehovah.

Well, you must take the best care of yourself. Real preachers —those who are teachers—are very scarce. Cling to the willows and keep talking.

Yours always, R. G. Ingersoll

In 1898 George J. Holyoake wrote a pamphlet about Bradlaugh entitled *The Warpath*, to which Ingersoll refers in the letter quoted below.

(No month given) 1898

My dear, dear Friend:

I read your book about Bradlaugh and a few others, and I think I appreciate what they intended, and realize what your feelings must be. Organization always brings envy and all sorts of *littleness* to the front. It is easy to work for a cause, but it is generally hard to work with others. They become jealous and hostile. I want just as little as possible to do with folks. I do not care to lead, but I hate to follow the egotistic and idiotic. You have always been for the right—for the cause without regard to yourself. It was enough for you to be useful—useful in the highest sense. There are many Freethinkers who have but little humour, but little real *heart*. . . . But no matter. You have done well. You have earned the right to be serene and satisfied.

R. G. Ingersoll

Mr. Edward R. Johnes was a prominent attorney, and author of *Circumstantial Evidence of Personal Immortality, and a Reasonable View of Future Existence*, which he presented to Colonel Ingersoll.

June 25th, 1899

E. R. Johnes, Esq.

My dear Sir:

Accept my thanks for your Essay on Immortality. It is very beautifully written, and you have brought forward, in support of your doctrines, all the argument there is, and you have stated your case with much force and clearness. In addition to this, you have abandoned many positions that cannot, in this age of the world, be maintained.

You admit that the hope of immortality cannot, with safety, rest upon the inspiration of the Old and New Testaments, or upon any form of superstition. .If we admit the existence of a God of infinite wisdom and compassion, we may say that there must be a world better than this; but how do we account for one worse than that—that is to say, for this? If injustice triumphs here, why not there? If honesty goes without bread, in this world, why not in another? Certainly God will be no better then than now.

Still it may be possible that a God of infinite wisdom and compassion will so reward those who suffer—through suffering itself—that all that happens will be consistent with wisdom and compassion.

I do not see any evidence in this world that it was created by either wisdom or compassion. Neither do I see what right we have to say that man has a spiritual body, any more than trees have. The tree springs from a seed; so does man. The trees produce others, and then perish from the earth; the same is true of the human race. You have had the courage to accept the logic of your position, and give to all life the immortality that Christians give to man.

I hardly know the meaning of the words " spiritualist " and " materialist." I do not see that it makes the slightest difference with the argument to admit that everything is " spiritual," or to assert that everything is " material." He who asserts that all is " spiritual," admits the existence of everything that another calls " material "; and he who insists that all is " material," admits the existence of everything that is by the other called " spiritual." Call it what you will, it remains beyond the grasp of our mind.

The weakest parts of your Essay are the quotations from others. What Greenleaf says upon the subject seems to me a *non sequitur*.

If man had believed only in his own experience, why could the world be " neither governed nor improved "? The first man obtained something by experience, which he could convey to another, to which the other might add by his own exertions, his own experience—and so on from generation to generation, until there would be a vast and splendid capital of human experience.

So, what Mr. Drummond has to say may be more ingenious, but is equally without foundation. Of all the men who have written upon this subject, I know of no one so shallow and insincere as Dr. Young. I congratulate you on what you have said concerning the " wax figures " of Milton. If any one is open to the charge of barren materialism, it is Milton. His " heaven " was simply another England—with a government somewhat worse.

You have endeavoured to establish your doctrine by reason— by something universal—and you have wisely left out the provincialisms, the prejudices, and the puerilities of Christianity.

Love and hope are universal. As long as men love, and as long as they hope, there will probably be in heart and brain the splendid dream of immortality.

It may be that we live no more—that we go back to the unconscious dust, and yet, the heart will always say, " perhaps there is another life."

But whether there is or not, let us all paint on the canvas of the future the pictures that delight and satisfy the soul.

We know that in this world, after joy comes grief, as after day comes night; and it may be there is some world where after grief comes joy, as after night comes day.

Thanking you again for your beautiful and poetic Essay,

Sincerely yours, R. G. Ingersoll

New York
July 13, 1899

Clinton J. Robins, Esq.,
Dayton, Ohio.

Dear Sir:

First accept a thousand thanks for your good letter. The only trouble is that it is too flattering. You are right in thinking that I have not changed. I still believe that all religions are based on falsehoods and mistakes. I still deny the existence of the supernatural, and I still say that real religion is usefulness. Thanking you again,

Yours always, R. G. Ingersoll

PART FOUR

Ingersoll—Lay Critic and Lover of the Arts

T HE FACT THAT Robert Ingersoll was a natural poet in thought, feeling, and expression contributed vitally to his power as a critic and lover of poetry, literature, and the other arts. All the rhythms of his heart and soul were informed with poetry and artless art. It was instinctive and inevitable for him to express himself in terms of verbal beauty and music. His æsthetic sense was delicately attuned to the right cadence of line and phrase; and countless passages in his works scan like pure blank verse. While Ingersoll wrote no more than a dozen poems in his life, his lectures and orations are poetic in the highest meaning of the word; and in simple justice it must be said that he was the author of poetic prose that will live as long as beauty of language is cherished by mankind.

Refreshingly free from all trammels of pedantry and traditionalism in his artistic attitudes and judgments, Ingersoll approached beauty in all forms of art—literature, music, painting, sculpture, architecture—with pristine intellectual honesty and directness, and warm-hearted emotion.

His imagination penetrated to the roots and secrets of human psychology and situation, to the hidden springs of motive and action. He identified himself with the lives and personalities of his fellowmen—their problems, hopes, fears, frustrations, defeats, sorrows, agonies, joys, and fulfilments became his own. He thought in terms of individuals, never in terms of masses of people; he was concerned with individual working-men, not with Labour—with individual bankers, barbers, politicians, and mechanics, not with Capital, Investment, Management, or any other abstract category. He knew that art, to fulfil its true mission, must bring understanding, sympathy, empathy, and illumination to the Human Dilemma by means of the myriad little individual human dilemmas, as well as by means of symbol, idealization, and abstraction.

Ingersoll worshipped beauty and art, which is the outward form as well as the inner spirit of beauty. He said that " at the foundation of the beautiful will be found the fact of happiness, the gratification of the senses, the delight of intellectual discovery, and the surprise and thrill of appreciation." Beauty is " the flower of the association of ideas, of memories, of experiences . . . and the perception that the prophecies of the ideal have been and will be fulfilled."

Ingersoll gave this significant and somewhat metaphysical description of art: " There is something called soul; something that thinks, and hopes, and loves. It is never seen. It occupies a world that we call the brain, and is for ever, so far as we know, invisible. Each soul lives in a world of its own, and endeavours to communicate with another soul living in a world of its own, each invisible to the other, and it does this in a variety of ways. That is the noblest art which expresses the noblest thought, that gives to another the noblest emotions that this unseen soul has. In order to do this, we have to seize upon the seen, the visible. In other words, nature is a vast dictionary that we use simply to convey from one invisible world to another what happens in our invisible world. The man that lives in the greatest world and succeeds in letting other worlds know what happens in his world, is the greatest artist."

One can hardly fail to note the delightful paradox of the Agnostic's apparent preoccupation with the soul! He uses the word over and over again, not only in connection with man's strivings and achievements in the arts, but in his contemplation and consideration of all aspects of the human drama. However, the concept of soul did not mean precisely the same thing to Ingersoll that it did, and still does, to orthodox minds. No one can really define soul, but to this heretical philosopher it signified something equivalent to the sacred, inviolate essence of moral beauty—the pure, passionate, and holy principle of mental and spiritual life.

Ingersoll maintained that art should portray life in its wholeness and truth. " Art," he believed, " to be great, must deal with the human. The great artist holds the mirror up to nature, and the mirror reflects with absolute accuracy. The lesser artists distort nature, and deal either with the impossible or the exceptional. The men of genius touch the universal.

Their words and works throb in unison with the great ebb and flow of things. They write and work for all races and for all time." However, our critic emphasized that while art must be faithful to life, to reality, it must never be merely a slavish copy of reality; it must always enhance and "transfigure the common." He held that "the real sustains the same relation to the ideal that a stone does to a statue, or that paint does to a painting. Realism degrades and impoverishes. . . . According to the realist's philosophy, the wax that receives and retains an image is an artist." The artist in Ingersoll was aware that "back of forms, are the desire, the longing, the brooding, creative instinct, the maternity of mind, and the passion that gives pose and swell, outline and colour." Ingersoll felt that perhaps the most satisfying statement which he had discovered concerning the technique of great art is the following: "As nature unconsciously produces that which appears to be the result of consciousness, so the greatest artist consciously produces that which appears the unconscious result."

This connoisseur was keenly alive to the elevating influence and power of true art; knew that it is both cause and effect of man's cultural and spiritual growth. For art and beauty, like truth and morality, are not absolute, but relative to human experience and understanding. "Art cultivates and kindles the imagination and quickens the conscience." He felt it to be the most potent of all bonds which unite men to one another; a universal language that eliminates prejudices and barriers of nation, race, and class; the supreme instrument of understanding and empathy, because "it is by imagination that we put ourselves in the place of another."

However, "art has nothing to do directly with morality or immorality. It is its own excuse for being," Ingersoll affirmed. "There is the same difference between moral art and the product of true genius that there is between prudery and virtue." He said that "prudery is the nastiest of all things. Most people having obtained their ideas from the Church, regard the passion of love as degrading." Ingersoll believed that to propagandize directly through art is to betray both truth and beauty. "Art," he felt, "teaches by indirection." However, in the ultimate sense, art, or beauty, and morality are one, for "morality is the harmony between act and circumstance; it is the melody of conduct "; and " a wonderful statue is the melody of proportion; a great picture is the melody of form and colour."

Thus proportion—" the married harmony of form and function "—would appear to have been Ingersoll's basic standard of æsthetic appreciation and judgment; and aside from this single criterion of value, he seems not to have had any formal, hard-and-fast rules which determined his attitude as a non-professional critic and lover of the arts.

Ingersoll's critical and poetic intuitions and insights came to his mind as clear, fresh, and radiant as morning comes to the sky. There was a seminal quality about them, a simplicity and spontaneity, and often a naïveté, which reveal that he was guided primarily, if not always consciously, by the unwritten code of his heart. Therefore, his opinion of a work of art depended to an incalculable degree upon how deeply his emotions were " touched and kindled " in its presence. But it should not be forgotten that Ingersoll's heart was an educated heart, and that his emotions were as mature as they were ardent.

" To express desires, longings, ecstasies, prophecies, and passions in form and colour; to put love, hope, heroism, and triumph in marble; to paint dreams and memories with words; to portray the purity of dawn, the intensity and glory of noon, the tenderness of twilight, the splendour and mystery of night, with sounds; to give the invisible to sight and touch, and to enrich the common things of earth with gems and jewels of the mind—this is Art," said Ingersoll.

SHAKESPEARE

Shakespeare, Ingersoll regarded as " the greatest genius of our world." It was in the works of this supreme dramatist that he found everything he sought in art—freedom, imagination, understanding, truth, sympathy, love, and beauty. " There was nothing within the range of human thought, within the horizon of intellectual effort, that he [Shakespeare] did not touch. He knew the brain and heart of man—the theories, customs, superstitions, hopes, fears, hatreds, vices, and virtues of the human race. He knew the thrills and ecstasies of love, the savage joys of hatred and revenge. . . . There was no hope that did not put its star above his head—no fear he had not felt

—no joy that had not shed its sunshine on his face. He experienced the emotions of mankind. He was the intellectual spendthrift of the world . . ." said Ingersoll. Shakespeare's fecundity of invention and imagination was unbounded. " Read one play, and you are impressed with the idea that the wealth of the brain of a god has been exhausted—that there are no more comparisons, no more passions to be expressed, no more definitions, no more philosophy, beauty, or sublimity to be put in words—and yet, the next play opens as fresh as the dewy gates of another day."

Ingersoll has given us a glowing picture of the occasion of his first discovery of the poet-dramatist who was to become the supreme intellectual and æsthetic inspiration in his life: " One night I stopped at a little hotel in Illinois many years ago when we were not quite civilized, when the footsteps of the Red man were still in the prairies. While I was waiting for supper, an old man was reading from a book, and among others who were listening, was myself. I was filled with wonder. I had never heard anything like it. I was ashamed to ask him what he was reading; I supposed that an intelligent boy ought to know. So I waited, and when the little bell rang for supper, I hung back and they went out. I picked up the book; it was Sam Johnson's edition of Shakespeare. The next day I bought a copy for four dollars. My God! More than the National Debt. You talk about the present straits of the Treasury. For days, for nights, for months, for years, I read those books, two volumes, and I commenced with the introduction. I haven't read that introduction for nearly fifty years, certainly forty-five, but I remember it still.

" Other writers are like a garden, diligently planted and watered, but Shakespeare is a forest where the oaks and elms toss their branches to the storm, where the pine towers, where the vine bursts into blossom at its foot. That book opened to me a new world, another nature." And Ingersoll went on to say that: " Whenever I read Shakespeare, if it ever happens that I fail to find some new beauty, some new presentation of some wonderful truth, or another word that bursts into blossom, I shall make up my mind that my mental faculties are failing, that it is not the fault of the book." Hardly a day passed that the Colonel did not read at least a few passages from the plays or the sonnets; they became a vital part of his spiritual being. He grew to think and feel and to express himself as Shakespeare thought and felt and wrote. Of course he did not write plays or sonnets as his master did, but he was Shakespearean all the same. He lived and moved and had his being in the Shakespearean atmosphere; Shakespearean heights and depths and amplitudes were his own heights and depths and amplitudes as well; and some of the quintessential elements of Shakespeare's genius were transmuted into the soul of Ingersoll.

> Love is not love
> Which alters when it alteration finds

Ingersoll considered the loftiest and noblest lines in all literature. His heart vibrated to that tender strain, as it did to the other multitudinous harmonies of the poet, and, since his heart was the touchstone of his critical judgment, he placed Shakespeare above all the other creative artists of the world. "Shakespeare alone has delineated love in every possible phase—has ascended to the very top, and actually reached heights that no other has imagined," declared Ingersoll.

"I once had a dream, and in this dream I was discussing a subject with another man," the Colonel tells us. "It occurred to me that I was dreaming, and I then said to myself: ' If this is a dream, I am doing the talking for both sides—consequently I ought to know in advance what the other man is going to say.' In my dream I tried the experiment. I then asked the other man a question, and before he answered made up my mind what the answer was to be. To my surprise, the man did not say what I expected he would, and so great was my astonishment that I awoke.

"It then occurred to me that I had discovered the secret of Shakespeare," concludes Ingersoll. "He did, when awake, what I did when asleep—that is, he threw off a character so perfect that it acted independently of him."

Ingersoll felt that Shakespeare's ability to transform old materials by putting his own creative imagination to work first in one character and then in another absolved him from all blame as a robber of plots. He had no need of the artifice of plot which is needed by lesser artists to conceal their shallowness and poverty of invention and thought. In Ingersoll's estimation Shakespeare was great in the three dimensions of thought, feeling, and action; and that is why he has occupied a unique position in the creative world of art and beauty through the centuries. He created characters so true that they appear unconscious of their creator and he " compresses lives into hours, tells us the secrets of the heart, shows us the springs of action— how desire bribes the judgment and corrupts the will—how weak the reason is when passion pleads, and how grand it is to stand for the right against the world." In the spirit of the true artist, Shakespeare " pursued the highway of the right and did not seek to put his characters in a position where it was right to do wrong. He was sound and healthy to the centre—he was an idealist. He did not, like most writers of our time, take refuge in the real, hiding a lack of genius behind a pretended love of truth."

Ingersoll felt that Shakespeare, by means of the miraculous power of his imagination, had the genius " to give the generalization, the result, without the process of thought. . . . He seems to be always at the conclusion—standing where all truths meet."

Shakespeare was a man of imagination . . . of genius, and having seen a leaf and a drop of water, he could construct the forests, the rivers and the seas. . . . Looking at a coat of mail, he instantly imagined the society, the conditions that produced it, and what it, in turn, produced. He lived the life of all. He was a citizen of Athens in the days of Pericles. . . . He saw Socrates thrust the spear of question through the shield and heart of falsehood. He was present when the great man drank hemlock, and met the night of death, tranquil as a star meets morning. . . . He knew the very thought that wrought the form and features of the Sphinx. . . . He walked the ways of mighty Rome, and saw great Cæsar with his legions in the field. . . . He heard the shout that shook the Coliseum's roofless walls, when from the reeling gladiator's hand the short sword fell, while from his bosom gushed the stream of wasted life. . . . He knew all crimes and all regrets, all virtues and their rich rewards. He was victim and victor, pursuer and pursued, outcast and king. He heard the applause and curses of the world, and on his heart had fallen all the nights and noons of failure and success.

Completeness and wholeness of vision, and the touch of the universal, which Ingersoll recognized as essential elements of the highest art, were the very stuff of Shakespeare's genius.

Shakespeare was an intellectual ocean, whose waves touched all the shores of thought; within which were all the tides and waves of destiny and will; over which swept all the storms of fate, ambition, and revenge; upon which fell the darkness of despair and death, and all the sunlight of content and love, and within which was the inverted sky lit with the eternal stars—an intellectual ocean—towards which all rivers ran, and from which now the isles and continents of thought receive their dew and rain.

It was ordained of the fates that Ingersoll should visit Stratford, the birthplace of his idol, and Westminster, the shrine of his memory. On his visit to Westminster Abbey, standing there beside the statue of the poet, it appeared that—

Shakespeare was not alone; that his brain-begotten children were about him, and, while looking upon him, the Abbey faded away, and in its place came Prospero with his magic wand; Ariel, running on the sharp North wind; Caliban, the foot-licker, son of the blue-eyed hag; Ferdinand, saying that " most poor matters point to rich ends "; Miranda, extending her " hand with her heart in it! " . . . Portia and Shylock . . . Lorenzo and Jessica, sitting on the moonlit bank; the melancholy Jacques, with his seven ages of man; and Adam, who once was Shakespeare's self; Orlando, carving the trees with love's carving; Rosalind, natural as light; Beatrice, all fire and joy and dawn; Benedict, the married man; Dogberry and Verges, and the whole " dissembly " . . . There came Isabella, pure as a star; Hamlet, with " thought beyond the reaches of (his) soul "; Ophelia, from whose " pure and unpolluted flesh " the violets sprang . . . Lear, in the storm and tempest; and poor, mad Tom, riding trotting-horses over the four-inch bridge; the eyeless Kent, and the stony-bosomed Goneril and Regan; Cordelia, too, her eyes jewelled with pity's holy tears; . . . Theseus and his fair bride; love-sick Titania; fairy Puck; Starveling and Snout, and Bully Bottom, " roaring like a sucking dove " . . . Romeo and Juliet, and the garrulous old nurse; and the poor apothecary, with his " beggarly account of empty boxes."

William Henry Burr (1819–1908), official reporter of the United States Senate, wrote in advocacy of the theory that Thomas Paine was the author of the famous *Letters of Junius* as well as of the Declaration of Independence, and that Francis Bacon was the author of the works of Shakespeare. Ingersoll is said to have called Mr. Burr " the greatest literary detective."

166

October 1st, 1887

William Henry Burr,
Washington, D. C.

My dear Sir:

I am perfectly satisfied that no man with whom the world is acquainted could have been the author of Shakespeare's plays. They must have been written by somebody whose acquaintance the world has never made. The fact that Shakespeare is unknown renders it possible for the imagination to say that he may have been the author. The world knows Bacon, and I think is satisfied that he could not have been the author of *Lear*. For my part, I do not see the slightest evidence in any of his writings that he had sufficient intellect to produce even a good play, or that he had any real dramatic talent.

Of course I could not accept Voltaire's judgment as to the literary men of England. Voltaire regarded Shakespeare as a kind of barbarian. He was raised in the classic school. He believed that nothing should be introduced that did not tend to the catastrophe, and he had the idea that all nature sympathized with the drama. He believed in Racine, and consequently looked upon Shakespeare as a literary outlaw. I do not wonder that that was his opinion, if he had read only *Titus Andronicus*, as I do not believe Shakespeare wrote a line of that play.

Now as to the Sonnets. Of course I do not know what reason Mr. O'Connor has for thinking they were written by Sir Walter Raleigh, and I do not wish to know the reason your sixteenth cousin has for saying that they are " poor trash." Some of the finest lines of literature are in the Sonnets. Take, for instance, this one line that has in it all the philosophy of the human heart:

Love is not love which alters when it alteration finds.

But as you say, " enough "—because, if Mr. Donnelly * has a cipher that demonstrates it, there is no need of wasting arguments, but let me tell you that in my judgment Mr. Donnelly has no cipher, and all that he has written so far, that I have read, is to my mind exactly what your cousin thinks the Sonnets are.

I stand by Shakespeare—the man unspoiled by Oxford—the greatest, the sublimest, of the human race.

I will gladly accept one of the two copies of the brochure of which you speak, and will give you my thanks in advance. It is only fair to say that I am so prejudiced on this Bacon–Shakespeare controversy that nothing except an absolute demonstration could by any possibility change my opinion. " Though one rose from the dead," I should not be convinced that Bacon is the author of *Midsummer Night's Dream*.

Yours very truly, R. G. Ingersoll

Ignatius Donnelly, American author and politician. Author of *The Great Cryptogram; Francis Bacon's Cipher in the So-called Shakespeare Plays*, etc.

May 18th, 1888, New York

Charles F. Steele, Esq.,
Philadelphia, Pa.

My dear Sir:

I am much obliged to you for the book *Is There Any Resemblance Between Shakespeare and Bacon?* I have read it. I think it is a demonstration that Bacon was entirely unable to write Shakespeare. He had no capacity of that kind. He was not a poet—not a dramatist, and he had no more imagination than an average English judge—which is saying as little upon that subject as could be well expressed in words. Long ago, I called attention to his poetry—that which he dedicated to George Herbert—for the purpose of showing that he had not the slightest capacity in that direction.

Yours very truly, R. G. Ingersoll

December 31st, 1890

William S. Loomis, Esq.,
Holyoake, Mass.

My dear Sir:

It has been claimed that Shakespeare was a Catholic—that he was an infidel—and some people have gone so far as to claim that he was a Presbyterian.

The fact is, that Shakespeare could have had no religion. He knew that all religions were subject to change, and consequently he introduced no religious questions into his dramas, knowing that they were simple phases of human thought, or the lack of thought and of emotion. He dealt more with the elemental things—knowing that as long as the race lived, the passions would survive.

If you wish to find what Shakespeare's opinion really was, I suppose there is no better test than the words he puts into the mouths of his greatest characters, especially when dying. This is not a demonstration—but it throws some light on the subject.

Yours very truly, R. G. Ingersoll

Elbert Hubbard was a distinguished and brilliant popular author, editor, publisher, and lecturer of the late nineteenth century. He founded the Roycroft Shop, in East Aurora, New York, for the revival of handicrafts; edited a monthly magazine, entitled *The Philistine*, for many years; wrote *Little Journeys to the Homes of Great Americans*, and to the homes of great men and women, living and dead, throughout the world, that had enormous popular appeal. One of the *Little Journeys* was dedicated to the life and works of Colonel Ingersoll. Elbert Hubbard was a great admirer and friend of Ingersoll, and shared his views on orthodox religion, as well as on many other subjects.

New York
April 8, 1892

Elbert Hubbard, Esq.,
East Aurora, Erie Co., N. Y.

My dear Friend:
I have just read the pages you sent me from your book called *The Man*. I was much struck with what you say about Shakespeare's education, and about his language " taking every hue of thought or feeling, of good and base alike, as the sky takes shade or shadow, or as the forest takes storm or calm, to remain for ever the emblem of the multitudinous life," etc.

And on the next page you have expressed the thought that I have had, and that I have expressed, when you say: " It is impossible to suppress a sense of satisfaction at the thought that the greatest author of all mankind was not learned." I have said on the same subject: " How fortunate that Shakespeare was not educated at Oxford; that the winged God within him never bowed to the professor; that he was not caught and tethered by the literary lilliputians of his time."

Of course I was greatly interested in all that you have said with regard to the woman in the case. I suppose you have drawn on your fancy. I think every man of genius has a feminine mind, and every woman of genius has a masculine mind.

Yours truly, R. G. Ingersoll

ROBERT BURNS

In the opinion of Ingersoll, poetry, in common with all the other arts, " must rest on the experience of men . . . it must sit by the fireside of the heart. . . . Poetry cannot be written by rule; it is not a trade or profession. Let the critics lay down the laws, and the true poet will violate them all. . . .

" A poem is something like a mountain stream that flashes in light, then lost in shadow, leaps with a kind of wild joy into the abyss, emerges victorious and winding runs amid meadows, lingers in quiet places, holding within its breast the hills and vales and clouds—then running by the cottage door, babbling of joy, and murmuring delight, then sweeping on to join its old mother the sea. . . . Poetry must have to do with this world . . . with the men and women we know; with their loves, their hopes, their fears, and their joys."

169

It was because the poetry of Robert Burns fulfilled Ingersoll's ideas of what poetry should be—and because the Scottish bard was the most human and compassionate and tender of men —that the Critic placed him second only to Shakespeare as a poet, but second to none as a man. Ingersoll loved Burns for his sympathy and pity that embraced all sentient creatures— because he hated the sight of suffering and cruelty, and lamented the death of even a humble field-mouse. Ingersoll's admiration went out to him, also, for his intellectual integrity, courage, and independence; and on account of his having given expression to the basic human virtues and verities in his sweet and moving songs.

Burns "kept close to the grass," knowing that "above the clouds it is too cold. In his heart there was the perpetual climate of spring—a poetic April and May, and all the poetic seeds burst into sudden life. In a moment the seed is a plant, and the plant is in blossom, and the fruit is given to the world." Ingersoll was impressed by the fact that "Burns seems to have done everything without effort. His poems wrote themselves. . . . He was a real poet of nature; he put fields and woods in his lines. There were principles like oaks, and there were thoughts, hints, and suggestions as shy as violets beneath the withered leaves. There were the warmth of home, the social virtues born of equal state, that touch the heart, and soften grief . . . that make the rich and poor clasp hands and feel like comrades warm and true." Was there ever a sweeter song than *Bonnie Doon*, or than *My Love is Like a Red, Red Rose?* he asks. Ingersoll considered *To Mary in Heaven* the most perfect of all love-poems; and *The Cotter's Saturday Night* one of the noblest poems in the literature of the world. He felt that domestic love was never set to such entrancing music as in these lines:

> To make a happy fireside clime
> To weans and wife ;
> That's the true pathos and sublime,
> Of human life.

" ' A Man's a Man For a' That ' is as grand a declaration of independence as has ever been uttered," Ingersoll declared. "It is the apotheosis of honesty, independence, sense, and worth —a prophecy of that better day when men will be brothers the world over."

It was through Robert Burns that Robert Ingersoll first saw the light of intellectual emancipation and artistic beauty. The great event shook his inner world to its foundations, and yet, like many momentous things, it occurred quite casually. Robert had taken some old shoes to be repaired. The cobbler, an elderly Glasgow Scot, was reading a book with much apparent relish as Robert entered his shop. When the cobbler took the shoes he turned the book over to Robert, who was thus introduced to Burns for the first time. Immediately there was flung wide before his enchanted vision a new earth and a new heaven! It seemed to him as if he had been waiting for this moment, this book, this revelation, ever since he had come to mental consciousness; as if he had been looking for Burns all his life and had found him at last.

Upon his shoes being mended Robert inquired excitedly of the old cobbler where he might obtain a copy, and as to the price, of this truly priceless volume, and upon being given the desired information betook himself homeward post-haste to apprise his brother Clark of the new-found treasure. And a week later, thanks to a joint accumulation of small savings, the two brothers became the proud and happy possessors of a reprinted copy of the Kilmarnock edition; and in an incredibly short time after that, they had committed to memory a great majority of the poems. If Shakespeare was a few years later to become, and ever to remain, Robert Ingersoll's Bible, Burns was his hymn-book from the time of that unforgettable first meeting with him at the old Scottish shoemaker's until the end of his days.

In 1878 the Colonel realized one of his fondest dreams and desires when he visited the birthplace of Robert Burns, in the little village of [Alloway, near] Ayr, in Scotland; and so deep were his emotions that in a genuine flash of inspiration he wrote, as he stood in that humble cottage, the following poem:

THE BIRTHPLACE OF BURNS

Though Scotland boasts a thousand names
　　Of patriot, king and peer,
The noblest, grandest of them all
　　Was loved and cradled here.
Here lived the gentle peasant-prince,
　　The loving cotter-king,
Compared with whom the greatest lord
　　Is but a titled thing.

A hovel made of clay;
  One door shuts out the snow and storm,
    One window greets the day;
And yet I stand within this room
    And hold all thrones in scorn;
For here beneath this lowly thatch,
    Love's sweetest bard was born.
Within this hallowed hut I feel
    Like one who clasps a shrine,
When the glad lips at last have touched
    The something deemed divine.
And here the world through all the years,
    As long as day returns,
The tribute of its love and tears,
    Will pay to Robert Burns.

Some years later these verses were placed in the birthplace cottage, but with the author's name omitted. This injustice was rectified through the intercession of Mr. John E. Milholland, of New York, an old and dear friend of Ingersoll, and Ian Maclaren (Rev. John Watson), distinguished Scottish clergyman and poet, who saw to it that a photographic copy of the original poem with Ingersoll's name on it was substituted for the version in ordinary print without a signature.

Mount Vernon [Ill.], Sept. 29th, '52

My very Dear Bro. [John] & Sister,

 I recd your letter yesterday & I was glad enough I tell you, because I have waited for it about five weeks. I am well & weigh one hundred & fifty three lbs, so you see I'm quite fat. . . . You ask me what I think of Burns. You may be supprised [sic] when I tell you that I know more than three fourths of all Burns ever wrote by heart. I like him the best of all because he wrote the most natural of all. His *Cotters Saturday Night* is his best, and the . . . next best is *Tam o'Shanter*. . . . Or you may like the last verse of the little piece on Sensibility, written to Mrs. Dunlop. . . .

 Well so much for Burns. I like Byron too & Shelly [sic] and Shakespeare. I have now before me Coleridges, Keats, Shelly's [sic] & Shakespeares entire works, so you see I have Books if I did not read them but I do. I read in old Billy Shakespeare almost every night I like to read. *Richard 3rd*, also *Taming of the Shrew*, I have read them so often that I have learned them by heart. I think a good deal of the song you sent me. I like it first rate. Thems my sentiments them is.

Robert G. I.

172

Ayr Arms Hotel, Ayr
Aug. 19th, 1878

Dear All of You,

Today we have visited the little cottage where Burns was born. It is made of clay and straw—the walls, are thatched with straw. It is about twelve feet by sixteen. It had one window about a foot square, one fireplace, and one bed.—Upon this bed Burns was born. This fact makes this mud hut a palace. It is about two miles from Ayr and in a lovely country.

All went to Auld Kirk, Alloway, where Tam O'Shanter saw the devil and the witch with the short chemise (sark) on. There is buried Wm. Burns, father of the poet, and "Souter" Johnny, the fellow who drank with O'Shanter. We then went to Burns' Monument on the banks of the bonnie Doon, and over the bridge that "Tam" rode, and down by the mill where Burns went to school, and then to the cottage where now live Agnes and Isabella Begg, nieces of Robert Burns. They are the children of his youngest sister Isabella. They were delighted to see us and we were to see them. Right across the street from the hotel is the saloon where the Souter Johnny & Tam O'Shanter drank on that memorable night.

Kisses & hugs—Robert

London
Aug. 24th, 1878

Dear All,

Here we are again at the Royal Hotel, Blackfriars.

We visited Stratford-upon-Avon yesterday. We were at the house where Shakespeare was born & in the old church where his dust sleeps.—

. . . We got back here yesterday. We went to every place connected with Burns. Ayr, where he was born, Mt. Oliphant where he lived from seven to seventeen. Lochlea where his father died—Mossgiel where he ploughed up the daisy and the field mouse's nest and where he saw the wounded hare. We were at Tarbolton where Burns joined the Masons, also at Willie's Mill, and the hill where Burns met Death and had the talk about Dr. Hornbook. We were by the Castle of Montgomery and stood beneath the old thorn tree where Burns last met Highland Mary. We were at Mauchline, stood in the room where he was married to Jean Armour, were in the *one* room where they commenced keeping house. We were at Dumfries in the room where he died and we went and stood beside his grave.

Good-bye, Robert

New York, Nov. 3, 1889

W. C. Angus, Esq.

My dear Sir:

I love Robert Burns with all my heart. As a poet he stands next to Shakespeare; but as a real, true, loving, natural man he is second to none.

Yours always, R. G. Ingersoll

Andrew Carnegie and Colonel Ingersoll were warm friends. They had many interests in common—notably, religious freedom and intellectual liberalism. But the one mutual bond which transcended all the rest was their love for Robert Burns.

Each knew an amazing number of the poems, and was able to quote from memory stanza after stanza. Ingersoll declared that if all the works of Burns were destroyed he could reproduce more than half of them, word for word, and, not to be outdone, Mr. Carnegie made a similar claim.

400 Fifth Avenue, May 6, '91

My dear Mr. Carnegie,

I have not touched it. Both bottles are as they were. You must be present when they are opened. We four must have an evening—I mean Burns, Carnegie, the whisky and myself.—

I feel that I have two bottles of real poetry—of good fellowship—of royal ceremonies of the King of Song—I am not selfish enough to open these treasures alone. We did pass one evening long ago at the St. Nicholas talking about Burns—we must have one more, and then the bottled bliss will be released.

Thanking you again and again for each bottle—and swearing to keep dry until you come.

Yours Always, R. G. Ingersoll

45 Wall Street, New York
Feb'y 2, 1892

William C. DeWitt, Esq.,
Brooklyn, New York.

My dear Friend:

I read with great pleasure what you had to say of Burns. It is exceedingly beautiful, poetic, and pathetic.

I have always wondered how a rose like Burns could have grown among the thistles of Calvinism. He was probably a protest and a re-action.

I dislike Knox exceedingly, and have not the slightest sympathy with any form of religion that ever flourished in Scotland.

I am a little in doubt about one thing you mention: I hardly think that Scotland accepted the family of Burns, or provided for their future.

I have always loved Burns and there is one thing about him that I like especially, and that is, that in his day and generation he preferred the tavern to the church. . . .

Your friend, R. G. Ingersoll

SHELLEY

Ingersoll loved the free, unfettered, ethereal spirit of Shelley. He thought that "in a few poems he reached almost the perfect; but many are weak, feeble, fragmentary, almost meaningless." He considered the *Skylark* infinitely beautiful and poetic, and said that Shelley's soul "was winged like his own skylark." Our Critic was enchanted by "the subtle delicacy, the aerial footstep, the flamelike motion" of his poetry. *Queen Mab* held a special appeal for him, with its ardent idealism and atheism, and its fearless liberation of outlook—"a poem filled with beauty, courage, thought, sympathy, tears, and scorn, in which a brave soul tears down the prison walls and floods the cells with light."

In these lyric lines Ingersoll has endeavoured to convey what this poet at his exquisite best meant to him:

"Shelley:—The light of morn beyond the purple hills—a palm that lifts its coronet of leaves above the desert's sands—an isle of green in some far sea—a spring that waits for lips of thirst—a strain of music heard within some palace wrought of dreams—a cloud of gold above a setting sun—a fragrance wafted from some unseen shore."

As for Burns's poem, *A Mountain Daisy*, referred to in the letter to G. Henry (see next page), Ingersoll thought that one stanza of that poem is "the daintiest and nearest perfect in our language." This is the stanza:

Alas! it's no thy neebor sweet,
The bonnie lark, companion meet,
Bending thee 'mang the dewy weet,
Wi' speckl'd breast
When upward-springing, blythe, to greet
The purpling east.

[Fragment]

Mount Vernon [Ill.], January 14th, '53

My very Dear Bro. [John],
I received your very good letter a few days ago or yesterday rather & so you see that I answer your letters about as soon as I

175

receive them. Mary is teaching school & has about 20 scholars at 3 dollars per quarter for each scholar. I have towards thirty scholars at 2·50 per quarter & each quarter consists of twelve weeks and I teach five days in each week. I am not making money very fast but can manage to get enough to eat & thats all Well I believe I have told you most the news & now we can talk about something else. You spoke about Goldsmith's poem the *Deserted Village*. I have not read it for more than a year but it struck me at the time as being very fine poetry. There are four lines which I can never forget. They are brought in to describe the minister (who was Goldsmith's own father) and are as follows

> As some proud cliff that lifts its awful form
> Swells from the vale & midway leaves the storm,
> Though round its base the rolling clouds are spread
> Eternal sunshine settles on its head

I have read most of Goldsmith's works, his plays, such as *The Good Natured Man, The Mistake of a Night* or *She Stoops to Conquer*. And his novel the *Vicar of Wakefield*. I like his works first rate. Have you ever read Shelley's *Queen Mab* ? I think it is one of the finest compositions in the world. . . . I'll tell you what John ! Edgar Poe's *Raven* takes my eye. He begins it so,

> Once upon a midnight dreary
> As I pondered weak & weary
> Oer many a quaint & curious volume
> Of forgotten lore
> Suddenly I heard a tapping as of some one gently rapping
> Tapping at my chamber door
> Only that and nothing more.

New York, June 8th, 1892

Jno. G. Henry, Esq.,
Jersey City Heights, N. J.
My dear Sir :
The poems were the *Skylark* and the *Daisy*. The *Skylark* was written by Shelley, and you will find it in any edition of his works. The *Daisy* was written by Robert Burns.
I did not say that these contain all the poetry I cared for, but I did say that between the *Skylark* and the *Daisy* you will find all the poetry—the meaning being that we need not go above the skylark for the sublime, nor beneath the daisy for the profound.
Yours truly, R. G. Ingersoll

LORD BYRON

That Ingersoll, the worshipper of the purest and tenderest sentiment and loftiest idealism in poetry, should be an ardent admirer of the sensual and cynical Lord Byron, would seem a strange paradox! However, Ingersoll's warm and generous emotions were seduced by what he described as " the amplitude, sweep, and passion, the strength and beauty, the courage and royal recklessness of Byron." Indeed, he went so far as to assert that Byron was " one of the greatest poets this world has produced." But the fact that *The Prisoner of Chillon* was his favourite selection from this poet's works shows that he regarded Byron as a gallant and fearless champion of liberty; and Ingersoll honoured him for fighting for the liberation of oppressed peoples. *The Prisoner of Chillon* filled his heart with tenderness, pity, and eternal hatred of tyranny.

ROBERT BROWNING AND MRS. BROWNING

Ingersoll entertained no particular enthusiasm for the poetry of Robert Browning, although he ardently admired that of Mrs. Browning. He thought the former greatly overrated; but Elizabeth Barrett Browning in his estimation was " a marvellous poet—and the lyric beauty of her *Mother and Poet* is greater than anything her husband ever wrote." He considered that her love poems dedicated to Robert Browning, entitled *Sonnets From the Portuguese*, were among the few immortal and supremely beautiful sonnets ever written; and that they were worthy even of Shakespeare himself.

But Robert Browning never satisfied Ingersoll's æsthetic tastes or standards. He felt that this poet " lacked form "; and that " that is as great a lack in poetry as in sculpture." And yet Ingersoll had extravagant admiration for Walt Whitman, whose poetry has always been conceded to the most " formless " in all great creative literature up to his time. What is more, Browning's poems were wrought according to a peculiarly elaborate and intricate pattern. It seems even more surprising that Ingersoll, who placed such emphasis upon the primacy of content over form, and upon the paramount importance of thought and feeling in poetry and all literature, should have so signally failed to appreciate these very qualities in Browning.

The Colonel does give him the credit of being " the author of some great lines, some great thoughts," and he insisted rightly that " he was obscure, uneven, and was always mixing the poetic with the commonplace . . . " and that " he cannot be compared with Shelley or Keats or Walt Whitman."

> 400 Fifth Avenue,
> New York, Mch 6, '90

Dear Frank,*
   Much obliged for the outline of what you said about Browning. I have hardly made up my mind as to whether Browning was a great poet or a strange one. Some authors hide defects of thought in curious verbal embroideries. Straight lines are the hardest to make. A full, round, soft note in singing is more difficult than trills. Browning has a certain affectation. His mental garments and jewels are quaint—sometimes *loud*—a wonderful collection of scarf pins and antique rings. His clothes attract rather by the *cut* than the quality.—He has more intellectual curiosity than sympathy. His emotions are well behaved and feel the chill of propriety. He is an engraver—rather than a sculptor. Besides, he preaches too much.—To me Mrs. Browning was far greater. Her husband wrote nothing as great as *Mother and Poet*. Her prose is more poetic than his poetry. You have said the best that can be said on your side with your conception—but

> I remain yours Always, Robert

Walt Whitman

It is probable that Robert Ingersoll first became acquainted with Walt Whitman's *Leaves of Grass* in the 1860s, although he did not meet the poet until many years later. This magnificent and unique work of creative genius brought him new and rousing revelations of Beauty and Truth. He felt once again, as he had felt upon first encountering Burns and Shakespeare—transfigured with spiritual illumination and ecstasy! Whitman entranced Ingersoll's opulent senses and warm, tender heart. *Leaves of Grass* did not wholly satisfy him—there were many passages which he thought should never have been written because of what he considered to be their coarseness and vulgarity. The Colonel was an uncompromising believer in sexual purity—in severe standards of sex-ethics, consequently some of the poems of Whitman horrified his sense of delicacy and good taste. Nevertheless, his poetic soul was ravished by

* Frank Gilbert was political editor of the Chicago *Inter-Ocean* for many years; and a beloved cousin of Colonel Ingersoll. At the outset of his career he was a Congregationalist minister, but after hearing and associating with the Colonel he became completely emancipated religiously.

the elemental, cosmic genius of the *Good Gray Bard*; and the quality for which Ingersoll loved him most of all was his boundless compassion and tenderness for all human-kind—a compassion and tenderness which flowed in literary perfection in these lines: " Not till the sun excludes you, will I exclude you! " " When Lilac Last in the Dooryard Bloomed," and " Out of the Cradle Endlessly Rocking," were the Colonel's favourite selections; he said that the former poem " will live as long as our language . . . one who reads this will never forget the odour of the lilacs, ' the lustrous Western star ' and the ' grey-brown bird singing in the pines and cedars.' " Never can one forget " the solemn journey of the coffin through the day and night, with the great cloud darkening the land, nor the pomp of inlooped flags, the processions long and winding, the flambeaus of night, the torches' flames, the silent sea of faces, the unbared heads, the thousand voices rising strong and solemn, the dirges, the shuddering organs, the tolling bells—and the sprig of lilac. And then for a moment they will hear the grey-brown bird singing in the cedars, bashful and tender, while the lustrous star lingers in the West

" But most of all, the song of the bird translated and becoming the chant for death . . .

" This poem, in memory of ' the sweetest, wisest soul of all our days and lands,' and for whose sake lilac and star and bird entwined, will last as long as the memory of Lincoln," declared Ingersoll.

It is not known just when and where Ingersoll and Whitman first met one another in person; however, the warm and profound friendship between the two kindred spirits was of many years' duration. They met very infrequently, but were often in each other's minds and hearts. Ingersoll was always chanting pæons of praise of the poet because " Whitman's charity was as wide as the sky, and wherever there was human suffering, the sympathy of Whitman bent above it as the firmament bends above the earth. . . . He was the poet of that divine democracy which gives equal rights to all the sons and daughters of men. He uttered the great American voice; uttered a song worthy of the great Republican."

In the opinion of this Critic, no profounder poem exists in the English language than *Elemental Drifts*. Whitman preached and lived the highest philosophy, Ingersoll felt: the cheerful even joyous acceptance of whatever fate may have in store for us, greeting the inevitable with a smile, a serene, undaunted nonchalance. He knew that to be satisfied—content—is to have achieved a success *beyond* success—the ultimate triumph, through and in, rather than over, life and destiny.

The Colonel's affection and admiration for Whitman was reciprocated in full heaped and rounded measure by the poet. He declared (to quote from Horace Traubel's *With Walt Whitman in Camden*) that " Ingersoll is a man whose importance to the time could not be over-figured; not literal importance, not argumentative importance, not anti-theological Republican party importance: but spiritual importance—importance as a force, as a consuming energy—a fiery blast for the new virtues, which are only the old virtues done over for honest use again. . . ." To quote Traubel again, Whitman exclaims: "What a substantial, rounded fellow the Colonel certainly proves to be! He is in a way a chosen man. There always was something in the idea that the prophets are called. Ingersoll is a prophet—he, too, is called. He is far, far deeper than he is supposed to be, even by radicals; we get lots of deep sea fruit out of him. . . .

" Whitman got hold of a San Francisco portrait of Ingersoll, . . . and regarded it long and intently. ' That is a grand brow, and the face—look at the face (see the mouth): it is the head, the face, the poise, of a noble human being. America don't know today how proud she ought to be of Ingersoll.' " Whitman rhapsodized about his beloved Colonel to his intimate circle of friends on any and every occasion: " Damn if I don't think the Colonel is always magnificent . there is always something ample, sufficient, about Bob's ways and means: he always seems big enough to go as high and as deep and as far around as anybody. He is the same man today (1888), only a little more so if anything: inevitably, tremendously, yet almost lethargically forceful, like a law of nature. . . ." Or: " Ingersoll stands for perfect poise, nonchalance, equability; he is non-conventional: runs on like a stream: is sweet, fluid—as they say in the Bible, like precious ointment."

Ingersoll was not able to attend the celebration of Whitman's seventieth birthday. However, he was present at the poet's seventy-first birthday dinner, at Reisser's Restaurant in Philadelphia. On this occasion, says Traubel, Ingersoll "impromptued across the table to Whitman for fifty-five minutes, in a speech which Whitman thought the most consummate piece of oratory he had ever enjoyed. Sitting opposite Whitman, he (Ingersoll) held a long discussion with him on immortality, the orator finding no evidence for it, and the poet asserting it with a tenacious instinct. Reporters scribbled shorthand notes while the two celebrities debated."

Five months later, Ingersoll delivered a lecture in Philadelphia from which nearly nine hundred dollars was raised for the Whitman benefit fund. This address is the famous *Testimonial to Walt Whitman*, or *Liberty in Literature*, which is one of the Colonel's most poetically beautiful and imaginative efforts. After the lecture, Ingersoll and the great poet sat together for a brief hour, and this proved to be their last meeting.

"As you read the marvellous book, or the person, called *Leaves of Grass*, you feel the freedom of the antique world," Ingersoll cried. "You hear the voices of the morning, of the first great singers—voices elemental as those of sea and storm. The horizon enlarges, the heavens grow ample, limitations are forgotten—the realization of the will, the accomplishment of the ideal, seem to be within your power. Obstructions become petty and disappear. The chains and bars are broken, and the distinctions of caste are lost. The soul is in the open air, under the blue and stars—the flag of Nature. Creeds, theories, and philosophies ask to be examined, contradicted, reconstructed. Prejudices disappear, superstitions vanish and custom abdicates. The sacred places become highways, duties and desires clasp hands and become comrades and friends. Authority drops the sceptre, the priest the mitre, and the purple falls from kings. The inanimate becomes articulate, the meanest and humblest things utter speech, and the dumb and voiceless burst into song. A feeling of independence takes possession of the soul, the body expands, the blood flows full and free, superiors vanish, flattery is a lost art, and life becomes rich, royal, and superb. The world becomes a personal possession, and the oceans, the continents, and constellations belong to you. You are in the centre, everything radiates from you, and in your veins beats and throbs the pulse of all life. You become a rover, careless and free. You wander by the shores of all seas and hear the eternal psalm. You feel the silence of the wide forest, and stand beneath the intertwined and over-arching boughs, entranced with symphonies of winds and woods. You are borne on the tides of eager and swift rivers, hear the rush and roar of cataracts as they fall beneath the seven-hued arch, and watch the eagles as they circling soar. You traverse gorges dark and dim, and climb the scarred and threatening cliffs. You stand in orchards where the blossoms fall like snow, where the birds nest and sing, and painted moths make aimless journeys through the happy air. You live the lives of those who till the earth, and walk amid the perfumed fields, hear the reapers' song, and feel the breadth and scope of earth and sky. You are in the great cities, in the midst of multitudes, of the endless processions. You are on the wide plains—the prairies—with hunter and trapper, with savage and pioneer, and you feel the soft grass yielding under your feet. You sail in many ships, and breathe the free air of the sea. You travel many roads, and countless paths. You visit palaces and prisons, hospitals and courts; you pity kings and convicts, and your sympathy goes out to all the suffering and insane, the oppressed and enslaved, and even to the infamous. You hear the din of labour, all sounds of factory, field, and forest, of all tools, instruments, and machines. You become familiar with men and women of all employments, trades, and professions—with birth and burial, with wedding feast and funeral chant. You see the cloud and flame of war, and you enjoy the ineffable, perfect days of peace.

"In this one book, in these wondrous *Leaves of Grass*, you find hints and suggestions, touches and fragments, of all there is of life that lies between the babe, whose rounded cheeks dimple beneath his mother's laughing, loving eyes, and the old man, snow-crowned, who, with a smile, extends his hand to death."

On March 30, 1892, Ingersoll was bidden to Camden, to place a last offering of love on the dead poet's tomb. Whitman, he said, was the poet of Life and Love, and supremely, " The poet of Death." But " he was above all things, a man; and above genius, above all the snow-capped peaks of intelligence, above all art, rises the true man. . . . He wrote a liturgy for mankind . . . and gave to us the gospel of humanity—the greatest gospel that can be preached."

My dear Whitman :—[no date given]
     A thousand thanks for your good letter and for the beautiful Second Annex of *Leaves of Grass*, filled with the splendour of sunset, the far west of a superb life. There is something more than beauty in the last rays and in the last thoughts. As I read, I saw the picture of an old man sitting in the afterglow—rich in memory, the dross all out of his heart, filled with hope, not so much for himself as for the race, and with content, not so much with the race as with himself, clinging to life, but with no fear of departure. Longing to get the last sheaf of harvest, even that which had been dropped in the gleaning; he who sits in the deepening twilight as the sun disappears and countless stars emerge, has at least the

memory of the morning. In him, there is the divine mingling of dawn and dusk, the loving nymphs of day have gone, but the veiled and silent sisters of the night have noiselessly approached. On the frontier from the wave-tossed shore, his last words, his last messages, all contain a hope, and these come to us like strains of music. He who is old has lived the poem of the four seasons. The snows are upon him but in his heart, spring, summer, and autumn have left their buds, their blossoms, and their bounties, and so he sits by the fireside on the last days near the glowing embers of winter and drinks the wine of life. In youth the heart is but a scorner of the brain, and in manhood's prime, the brain usurps control, but in old age the brain and heart become comrades, and so remain to the journey's end.

Yours always, R. G. Ingersoll

December 29th, 1891

My dear Whitman:

I am glad that you have lived long enough to know that *Leaves of Grass* will live forever—long enough to know that your life has been a success—that you have sown with brave and generous hands the seeds of liberty and love. This is enough—and this is a radiance that even the darkness of death cannot extinguish.

May be the end of the journey is the best of all, and may be the end of this is the beginning of another, and maybe the beginning of that is better than the ending of this.

But however and whatever the fact may be, you have lightened the journey *here*, for millions of your fellow-men. In the great desert you have dug wells and have planted palms. As long as water and shade are welcome to the faint and weary, your memory will live.

Wishing you many, many days of health and happiness, and with a heart full of love.

Yours always, R. G. Ingersoll

This was Colonel Ingersoll's last letter to Walt Whitman:

New York, N. Y., March 24th, 1892

My dear Friend:

I was pained to hear that you are suffering more and more, but was glad to know that your brave spirit has never been bowed —and that in all your agony your heart keeps sweet and strong.

I think of you a thousand times a day,—and of the great good you have done the world. You have uttered such brave, free, and winged words—words that have thrilled and ennobled the hearts and lives of millions—that my admiration has deepened to obligation.

Again I thank you for your courage, and again I lovingly say farewell—and yet I hope to see you soon.

Yours always, R. G. Ingersoll

In certain poetic moods, Ingersoll felt an indefinable sympathy with Pantheism. At other times he regarded it as a sort of sublime intellectual nonsense, an incoherent, meaningless mysticism.

He felt that the Pantheists, the Accepters of the Universe, fell inevitably into moral confusion, for they failed to discriminate among values, to choose the true and reject the false. Instead they accepted all things—the good and the bad—with a certain sentimental, unreasoning smugness. All was *not* for the best in the best of all possible worlds, Ingersoll insisted, and accordingly took issue with Whitman and Traubel on what he considered their intellectual apostasy concerning the " God belief."

June 29, '96

My dear Traubel,
Your poem, *The Wild Rose*, is good and I guess, true,—in a few thousand years. There is one line that ought to be changed: " Where priests chant the old truths to the new lie." It ought to be: " Where priests chant the old lies to the truth."

The only answer to your poem is that Nature produces failures—that millions and millions of people are failures—and these failures produce misery and crime. This is the disheartening fact. Still, I have my dream that the failures are to grow fewer and fewer.

In the *Wild Rose* are some beautiful thoughts and the dream is good, but after all, science is the only Saviour. Let us develop the brain.

The weakest part of Whitman was his God belief—that in some way all is good.

Yours always, R. G. Ingersoll

John Burroughs

John Burroughs, the great and beloved naturalist, was one of Robert Ingersoll's warmest and most affectionate admirers. The two had many precious intellectual and spiritual bonds uniting them, evident in their correspondence.

220 Madison Avenue
Dec. 3, '96

My Dear Mr. Burroughs,
Accept my best thanks for your beautiful book on Whitman. You understand Whitman and his work perfectly. You appreciate his elemental quality—his sun-burnt philosophy—his appalling

candour—his nude naturalness—his kinship with Nature in all her forms,—his perfect courage and above all, his sympathy!

You have written a great book and have built a lasting monument to the memory of your friend. I read every page with delight—all are filled with thought, poetry, and philosophy. You have exhausted the subject and have said the final word about Whitman and his work.

Yours always, R. G. Ingersoll

LITERARY MISCELLANY

Tennyson was " undoubtedly a great writer," in the view of Ingersoll, despite the fact that " he had no flame or storm, no tidal wave, nothing volcanic. He never overflowed the banks. He wrote nothing as intense, as noble and pathetic as *The Prisoner of Chillon*; nothing as purely poetic as *The Skylark*; nothing as perfect as *The Grecian Urn*; and yet he was one of the greatest of poets." Indeed, Ingersoll felt that, " viewed from all sides, he was far greater than Shelley, far nobler than Keats. Tennyson's imagination lived in a palace, ample, wondrous fair, with dome and spire and galleries, where eyes of proud old pedigree grew dim with gazing at the portraits of the worthless dead; and there were parks and labyrinths of walks and ways and artificial lakes where sailed the ' double swans.' . . . Tennyson was ingenious—Burns, ingenuous. One was exclusive, and in his exclusiveness was a little disdain. The other pressed the world against his heart   . . Tennyson was a piece of rare China. Burns was made of honest human clay, moulded by sympathy and love.   Tennyson had the art born of intellectual taste, of the sense of mental proportion, knowing the colour of adjectives and the gradations of emphasis. . . . Burns's brain was the servant of his heart. His melody was a rhythm taught by love. He was touched by the misery, the injustice, the agony of his time. While Tennyson wrote of the past—of kings long dead, of ladies who had been dust for many centuries, Burns melted with his love the walls of caste—the cruel walls that divide the rich and poor. Tennyson was the poet of the . . . twilight, of the sunset, of decorous regret, of the vanished glories of barbarous times, of the age of chivalry. . . . Burns was the poet of the dawn, glad that the night was fading from the East. . . ."

Ingersoll warmly admired the poet Thomas Hood, responding to his compassionate, humorous, gentle spirit, his warm and generous human emotions.

He also loved some of the poetry of Leigh Hunt, notably *Abou Ben Adhem*, which he considered as nearly perfect as a poem could well be, in respect to length, sustained, heightened emotion, and idealistic, exalted sentiment.

In three poems "Keats reached a great height. . . . *St. Agnes' Eve* is a story told with such artless art that this poor common world is changed to fairy-land; *The Grecian Urn* fills the soul with ever eager love, with all the rapture of imagined song. *The Nightingale* is a melody in which there is the memory of morn—a melody that dies away in dusk and tears, paining the senses with its perfectness."

However, Ingersoll felt that most of Keats's poetry "is insipid, without thought, beauty, or sincerity." This is a startlingly heretical and unjust judgment to pronounce upon such a poet as Keats, whose æsthetic stature is now recognized to be higher than that of most of the other great creative writers of the world; and who was even more outstanding in nobility of character than in poetic genius!

Ingersoll enthusiastically admired the genius of George Eliot, both as poet and novelist, but particularly as a poet. He felt that "there is no poem in our language more beautiful than *The Lovers*, and none loftier or purer than *The Choir Invisible*."

He considered George Sand a great writer; however, he did not place her in the same category with Ouida, whom he said was "probably the greatest living novelist, man or woman." "In *Ariadne*," he continued, "you find the aroma of all art. It is a classic dream. And there, too, you will find the hot blood of full and ample life . Some of her [Ouida's] books I do not like. If you wish to know what Ouida really is, read *Wanda*, *The Dog of Flanders*, and *The Leaf in a Storm*. In these you will hear the beating of her heart.

"Most of the novelists of our time write good stories," Ingersoll thought. "They are ingenious, the characters are well drawn, but they lack life, energy. They do not appear to act for themselves, impelled by inner force. They seem to be pushed and pulled," and he felt that "the same may be said of the poets."

It appears that Ralph Waldo Emerson was one of Ingersoll's

intellectual blind spots. In his attitude towards this great poet and philosopher there was an odd mixture of tempered, if not tepid, admiration, and a certain condescension not in the least characteristic of his generous spirit. For some unaccountable reason Ingersoll did not put Emerson in the first category of greatness. He liked him better as a poet than as a philosopher, and thought that " his doctrine of compensation would be delightful if it had the facts to support it." The Colonel cheerfully conceded that " Emerson was the author of many poetic and philosophic lines "; that " he uttered some great and splendid truths, and sowed countless seeds of suggestion." At the same time, he seemed to reproach Emerson for being " always perfectly self-possessed," and for " keeping his passions under control." He could say this of one who declared that: " He who would be a man, must be a non-conformist! " Ingersoll's usually keen critical judgment certainly was not functioning when he alluded to Emerson as being quite a remarkable man indeed, considering that he was descended from a long line of New England preachers!

Thoreau was recognized by the Colonel as not only a fine naturalist, but an original genius of the first order as well as a supreme literary stylist.

Our Critic loved Hawthorne for his magnificent psychological and emotional insight, richness, and depth.

The Colonel's intellectual independence was as unique in the literary as in all other fields. He had had instilled into his mind from his earliest years that Milton was the greatest and sublimest of poets, yet, in spite of his indoctrination, he demurred most strenuously from the orthodox judgment concerning the formidable author of *Paradise Lost*. With characteristically incorrigible wit he declared: " I have read Milton once. Few have read him twice. With splendid words, with magnificent mythological imagery, he musters the heavenly militia—puts epaulets on the shoulders of God, and describes the Devil as an artillery officer of the highest rank. Then he describes the battles in which immortals undertake the impossible task of killing each other." The Colonel asserted that " Milton gave to the Protestant Church the most outrageously materialistic ideas of the Deity. He turned all the angels into soldiers—made heaven a battlefield, put Christ in uniform, and described God as a militia general. His works were considered by the Protestants nearly as sacred as the Bible itself, and the imagination of the people was thoroughly polluted by the horrible imagery, the sublime absurdity of the blind Milton."

Ingersoll's antipathy for Milton, the theological poet, is perhaps understandable, but how may one account for his lack of appreciation of Milton, the courageous apostle of freedom—free speech, press, and assembly, and the separation of church and state? How could Ingersoll have failed to honour the author of the epoch-making *Areopagitica*?

Another daring Ingersollian literary heresy was his lack of enthusiasm for the resplendent Dante. It seems that about the only thing that appealed to him in connection with the Italian poet was that " he (Dante) had the courage, and what might be called the religious democracy, to put a pope in hell! "

Dec. 30, 1885

Dear Palmer,

I send you the greatest novel in the world [Victor Hugo's *Les Misérables*]—a novel filled with philosophy, beauty, pathos—with all that is tender, heroic, and dramatic. You will find all the lights and shadows that fall upon the heart—all the buds and blossoms, and all the withered leaves that belong to hope and memory. This novel goes over the whole field of human experience—war, religion, politics, love, government, crime, punishment, education, history, and prophecy. It is filled with the divine, that is to say, with pity—with love.

The good bishop—the nobler convict—the pure " Sister " Simplice—the purer Fantine. All these contradictions are higher forms of truth.

No man can read this book without becoming much better or much worse. This great light will either illumine the soul or deepen the shadow. You will read it with wonder and tears. You will finish it with a sigh.

Yours, R. G. Ingersoll

September 1, 1887

William H. Leff, Esq.,
Burlington, Montana.

My dear Sir:

It is exceedingly difficult to give a list of books—minds and temperaments are so different.

Among the poets: Shakespeare, Burns, Byron, Shelley, and Hood.

Among the historians: Gibbon, Lecky, and Buckle.

Among the novelists: Dickens, Hugo, George Sand, and George Eliot.

Among the scientists: Humboldt, Darwin, Haeckel, and Büchner. Of Haeckel's works—*The History of Creation*; of Darwin's works, *The Descent of Man*. Among the great writers and thinkers, Voltaire, especially his *Philosophical Dictionary*. Get Parton's *Life of Voltaire*—one of the best biographies ever written.

If you are still delighted with obscure questions read Spinoza and Kant.

The greatest of all is Shakespeare. The man who has read his works thoroughly, and who understands and appreciates them, need care but little for other books.

Yours truly, R. G. Ingersoll

Robert Ingersoll was very fond of Edgar Fawcett, the fine American poet and novelist, and author, among other works, of *The New King Arthur, New York—A Novel*, and *A Gentleman of Leisure*. Mr. Fawcett loved and admired the Colonel with all the warmth of his affectionate and generous nature. Furthermore, he was in full accord with Ingersoll's agnostic views, writing a book entitled *Agnosticism and Other Essays*, for which Ingersoll wrote the Preface. The following is a typical letter from Fawcett to Ingersoll:

[New York] August 10th [1894]

My dear Colonel:

I read your splendid letter in *The World* on " Is Suicide a Sin? " and it made me more loyally fond of you than ever; more devotedly your admirer too. That is truly a great deal for me to say, as you know, since my devotion and admiration are both an old story. . . . You put the whole thing with a superb lucidity and with a gentle eloquence which reminds one of an athlete's hand in a silken glove. . . .

I do so wish that, in all these big questions, literary men would take you more for a guide than they do, or seem to do. You have, of course, an immense constituency; but your love of letters and your deeply poetic spirit render you worthy of a far greater reverence and respect from *writers* than it seems to me that you receive. I want the brilliancy of your thought to penetrate our literature profoundly and permanently. But, of course, that will come. The younger generation of writers cannot escape you any more than the air they breathe. . . . Especially, should the poets love you and sit at your feet. If you die before you see the change, I believe that those who now love you and survive you will see how much of the mere pietistic rubbish in modern poetry has been gradually yet surely swept away by the mighty besom of your fearless and noble intellect.

Ever affectionately, Edgar Fawcett

New York
Mch. 2nd, 1888

C. A. Harvey, Esq.,
Boston.

My dear Sir:
The selection of a Library is such a personal matter, and so depends on the tastes and tendencies of the individual, that one can hardly advise another. Were I going to get a library, I should select, of the

Poets : Shakespeare, Burns, Byron, Shelley, Keats, Mrs. Browning, and George Eliot.

Novelists : Dickens, Thackeray, Hugo, and George Eliot.

History : Draper's *Intellectual Development of Europe* ; Buckle's *History of Civilization in England* ; Motley's *Dutch Republic* ; and Macaulay's *History of England.*

Science : Humboldt, Darwin, Haeckel, Tyndall.

Metaphysics : Spinoza.

Religion : Voltaire's *Philosophical Dictionary* ; Hume's *Essays*, and *The Trial of Theism* by George Jacob Holyoake.

Yours very truly, R. G. Ingersoll

Mr. Paul Blouet, or Max O'Rell (the latter was his *nom de plume*), was a distinguished French author and journalist. He wrote, among other brilliant and popular works, *Jonathan and His Continent*, which was an extensive survey and critique of America and Americans.

Mr. and Mrs. Blouet had a great admiration for Colonel and Mrs. Ingersoll, as well as for their two charming daughters, Eva and Maud; and in *Jonathan and his Continent* Mr. Blouet pays them a handsome tribute which comprises a whole chapter of the book.

Jany 31, '89

My dear Mr. Blouet,
With the greatest pleasure I have read *Jonathan and his Continent*. Every soul in the house has done the same and the verdict is unanimously in your favour. You have hit us hard, but never below the belt. Not one arrow of wit is tipped with malice. We know that our country is a polyglot picnic—that the peculiarities of the world are here—we also know that sudden prosperity shows its joy in wonderful ways. We know that it has been a mighty task to take possession of a continent—to fell the forests—to [bridge ?] the rivers—to plough the fields—to build the towns and the cities—

to construct a hundred and fifty thousand miles of railway—and to feed clothe and educate sixty million of people. The accomplishment of this work has prevented us from reaching the highest point in literature and art. All this you have spoken of and in an exceedingly generous and appreciative way—you have laughingly told us of our faults and your book will do us good.—You are a little hard on the Germans but the reason for that is easy to guess. As a matter of fact, we have no better and no more patriotic citizens than the Germans. They are honest, industrious, and believe in our institutions. But let that go. Your book is filled with the keenest wit, with observation sharp and profound.—I have always insisted that wit is the crystallization of logic.—There is a collision between the facts called flint and steel, and the spark called wit leaps into life. On every page of your book these sparks are found.

And now I come to the hardest part of this letter. I hardly know how to thank you for the beautiful things you have said of me and mine. I was never more astonished than when I read your words of praise. You have placed me under the greatest obligation and I am anxious to pay at least a part of the debt. All unite with me in thanking you again and again for your splendid tribute. I think that it has been published in nearly every paper in the country, and all the " infidels " are on your side. On every side I hear good words for you. . . .

Yours always, R. G. Ingersoll

The hero of Count Tolstoi's novel *The Kreutzer Sonata* Ingersoll considered " one of the vilest and basest of men, suspicious, jealous, cruel, infamous. The wife is infinitely too good for such a wild, unreasoning beast, and yet the writer of this insane story seems to justify the assassin." " If this is a true picture of wedded life in Russia, no wonder that Count Tolstoi looks forward with pleasure to the extinction of the human race." The author appears to attribute all the ills of this world to woman, while Ingersoll thought that " women are better than men; they have greater responsibilities; they bear even the burdens of joy." For him, the desire and love of men and women for one another is " a condition of civilization, progress, and happiness; . . . of everything of real value." Ingersoll's subtle and delicate psychological insight is revealed in this sentence: " There is this profound difference in the sexes: in man . . . desire is the foundation of love, while in woman, love is the foundation of   desire." He held that woman's love alone is enough to justify the existence and perpetuation of the human race.

191

Ingersoll thought that perhaps the most shocking sentiment in *The Kreutzer Sonata* is the sanction of coercion, of force, on the part of the husband against his wife; the idea that a man can compel a woman to love and obey him. " No one can love on compulsion. . . . Love is the perfume of the heart; it is not subject to the will of husbands or kings or of God."

The abject defeatism and pessimism of Tolstoi were indignantly rejected by the healthy, life-loving optimism of Ingersoll. The latter cherished the fond belief that, " on the whole, the race is advancing; that the world is growing steadily and surely better; that each generation enjoys more and suffers less than its predecessor." He said that " the institution of marriage is a failure to the extent, and only to the extent, that the human race is a failure."

Elberon, N. J.
Sept. 17th, '90

My dear Mrs. Myers:

A thousand thanks for your kind and flattering letter. It gave me great pleasure mingled with pain. I thought of the brave and handsome fellows who long ago passed into the twilight—into the silent lands where the best and greatest are.—Let us hope,—hope for the good—and that the great dream will be realized.

I am glad that you like the little article on the Kreutzer Sonata.

From the bottom of my heart I pity wretches who imagine that love is degrading and who try to fill and satisfy their hearts with the love of ghosts.—

The time to be happy is now.

The place to be happy is here.

The way to be happy is to make others so.

Yours sincerely, R. G. Ingersoll

Mrs. Smart, better known as Helen H. Gardener, was a distinguished writer, lecturer, and social worker, active in the Ethical Culture Movement in New York City. Mrs. Gardener was also the first woman Civil Service Commissioner in the U.S.A. Despite the fact that she was the daughter of a clergyman, she became a convinced and outspoken Rationalist and Agnostic, expressing her ideas in *Men, Women, and Gods*, for which Ingersoll supplied the Preface, " Facts and Fictions of Life."

400 Fifth Avenue, March 27, '91

My dear Mrs. Smart,

I am glad that you are having such great success, and hope that you will have even greater. You know that I hope you are to write something born of your artistic feeling unburdened with any moral purpose. A story ought to come free and joyous from your heart—without the limiting and conscious art. My objection to your last book was that it maligned your artistic side—that it was unnatural and lacked the poetry and grace of the ideal.—

I can forgive the language of passion, because passion purifies,—but the same words spoken in the interest of reform touch me like a degradation. You will understand me some day. I know that you look at these things in a different way and that you are governed by your sense of right and duty. And that you are obliged to work in the methods natural to you. I know that you can write stories full of art and feeling—of naturalness and poetry—with deft touches of wit and humour and a foundation of true philosophy. This is the reason I objected to some things in your last book, knowing how much better you can do, *and have done.*

Well, but let all that go.—It is not for me to criticize anybody. All I can say is that I am glad of your success and sincerely hope that you may have fame and wealth.

I am as ever, R. G. Ingersoll

Ingersoll thought Charles Dickens " the greatest novelist who has ever written in the English language "—that " he was the greatest observer since Shakespeare." He placed Dickens far above Thackeray. " Dickens wrote for the home, for the great public," while " Thackeray wrote for the clubs." In Ingersoll's opinion, *The Tale of Two Cities* is " the supreme work of fiction. Its philosophy is perfect. The characters stand out like living statues. In its pages you find the blood and flame, the ferocity and self-sacrifice of the French Revolution."

The three greatest novels of the world he believed to be *The Tale of Two Cities, Les Misérables,* by Victor Hugo, and *Ariadne,* by Ouida. In these examples of literary art Ingersoll found all the qualities which he deemed essential to the most truthful, profound, compassionate, and noble portrayal of human life.

400 Fifth Avenue, Nov. 16, '95

My dear Mr. Scott,

The best novel in the English language is Dickens' *Tale of Two Cities.* It has proportion, pathos, philosophy, and the style is perfect.

The best writers of fiction—the three best—are Dickens, Hugo, and Thackeray.

My favourite books are Shakespeare and Burns, and they have influenced me most.

New York
April 6, '99

My dear Mr. Shanks,

I have been contending for years that what is called prose is the highest form,—higher than rhyme—higher than blank verse. Rhyme and blank verse demand the rise and fall of the voice at *measured* intervals. Prose allows the thought, the emotion to determine the rise and fall. You know the ordinary music is like the hopping of a wren from branch to branch back and forth in accordance with the requirements of time. In Wagner music stops hopping and takes the flight of the eagle.

Yours always, R. G. Ingersoll

The Drama, Acting, and Actors

To Ingersoll, the theatre was " the home of the ideal." He said that the drama was born of the natural love of life and living " People must first be in love with life before they can think it worth representing   When great virtues appear, when magnificent things are done   . then the stage is built, and the life of a nation is compressed into a few hours.   "
He declared that " he who loves the stage has a kind of double life."

Ingersoll tells us that " the drama is a crystallization of history, an epitome of the human heart. The past is lived again and again, and we see upon the stage, love, sacrifice, fidelity, courage—all the virtues mingled with all the follies." He believed that the most important and vital function of the theatre is to cultivate the imagination because " the imagination constitutes the great difference between human beings.
On the stage the real should be idealized, the ordinary should be transfigured; that is, the deeper meaning of things should be given. As we make music of common air, and statues of stone, so the great dramatist should make life blossom on the stage.
. Realism degrades and impoverishes the stage." Ingersoll applied his high and exacting æsthetic and ethical standards as consistently in his judgments of drama and the theatre as in his judgments of all other forms of art. Accordingly, he maintained that " the truly artistic [drama] speaks of per-

fection; that is to say, of harmony, not only of conduct, but of harmony and proportion in everything." It must, above all else, tend to " civilize mankind, to soften the human heart. . . ."

Ingersoll said that " Shakespeare is greatest and best when grandly put upon the stage. There you know the connection, the relation, the circumstances, and these bring out the appropriateness and the perfect meaning of the text. Nobody in this country now thinks of Hamlet without thinking of Booth. For this generation at least, Booth is Hamlet. It is impossible for me to read the words of Sir Toby without seeing the face of W. F. Owen. Brutus is Davenport, Cassius is Lawrence Barrett, and Lear will be associated always in my mind with Edwin Forrest."

Our Critic maintained that no great dramas had been written since Shakespeare; at least, none that could be compared with his.

"America has not failed because life in the Republic is too material. Germany and France, and, in fact, all other nations, have failed in the same way." Ingersoll realized that " there is plenty of material for plays. The Republic has lived a great play—a great poem—a most marvellous drama." However, he felt that " we are beginning. We have found that American plays must be American in spirit. We are tired of imitations and adaptations. Some good work has recently been done, giving great hope for the future." Ingersoll asserted that " the realistic comes first; afterwards the ideal. But . . . love is the eternal passion that will forever hold the stage. . . . It is the sun. All other passions are secondary. Their orbits are determined by the central force from which they receive their light and meaning. Love, however, must be kept pure. The great dramatist is, of necessity, a believer in virtue, in honesty, in courage, and in the nobility of human nature. He must know that there are men and women that even a God could not corrupt; such knowledge, such feeling, is the foundation, and the only foundation, that can support the splendid structure, the many pillared stories and the swelling dome of the great drama.

" In acting, there must be proportion. There are no miracles in art or nature. All that is done—every inflection and gesture —must be in perfect harmony with the circumstances. Sensationalism is based on deformity, and bears the same relation to proportion that caricature does to likeness. . . . In acting there must be natural growth, not sudden climax. The atmosphere of the situation, the relation sustained to others, should produce the emotions. Nothing should be strained. . . . There should be the bud, the leaf, the flower, in natural sequence. There must be no leap from naked branches to the perfect fruit. . . . No one would enjoy a sudden sunset—we want the clouds of gold that float in the azure sea. No one would enjoy a sudden sunrise—we are in love with the morning star, with the dawn that modestly heralds the day and draws aside, with timid hands, the curtains of the night. In other words, we want sequence, proportion, logic, beauty."

Ingersoll said that " the great actor must be acquainted with the heart, must know the motives, ends, objects, and desires that control the thoughts and acts of men. He must be familiar with many people, including the lowest and the highest, so that he may give to others, clothed with flesh and blood, the characters born of the poet's brain. The great actor must know the relations that exist between passion and voice, gesture and emphasis, expression and pose. He must speak not only with his voice, but with his body. The great actor must be master of many arts. . . . Above all, he should be so sincere that he loses himself in the character he portrays. Such an actor will grow intellectually and morally. The great actor should strive to satisfy himself—to reach his own ideal."

At the theatre the Colonel was transported into the fairy-land of the imagination, of ideal beauty. He lived the lives of all portrayed upon the stage; and all the struggles and triumphs, joys and sorrows, follies and crimes, defeats and victories were his own. He seemed gifted with a profound, intuitive awareness and comprehension of the secret springs of human motives and actions; of the rightness and wrongness of psychological situation and behaviour as depicted by dramatist and actor. By " the pathos of the perfect " he was touched to tears; and conversely, he was equally repelled by the counterfeit and debased coinage of heart and mind. Now and again he would make constructive and significant suggestions to his friends of the theatre as to changes and improvements that might be made in the text of a play, or in its interpretation—suggestions that often amazed the professionals because of the deep and subtle dramatic insight they revealed.

Ingersoll had a particularly warm place in his affections for theatrical folk, and he counted among his closest friends many of the foremost actors and actresses of the day. Edwin Booth, Lawrence Barrett, Joseph Jefferson, Edwin Forrest, William Florence, John McCullough, Mrs. Fiske, Julia Marlowe, and William Gillette were frequent guests at the Colonel's home in New York, at his celebrated informal Sunday evening soirées.

Ingersoll was greatly beloved by these people of the stage, and a number of them were of the opinion that the Colonel would have made a superb actor himself, especially in the roles of Hamlet or Lear. Moreover, it was the deep regret of the members of his family that he did not write for the theatre; and Mrs. Ingersoll entertained the unshakable belief that her husband's abilities, interests, and enthusiasms were actually universal and all-embracing.

This Connoisseur was an especially devoted admirer of the surpassing histrionic art of Minnie Maddern Fiske, Julia Marlowe, and Mary Anderson. Adelaide Ristori was Lady Macbeth to him, as well as " the greatest actress he ever saw "; and he was enthusiastic about the artistic genius of Booth, Barrett, Jefferson, Gillette, and Edwin Forrest, whom he considered the greatest King Lear of the stage.

Among Ingersoll's many friends in the world of the theatre none was closer to his affections than Lawrence Barrett. He said that he was " an interpreter of Shakespeare, to whose creations he gave flesh and blood. He began at the foundation of his profession, and rose until he stood next to his friend—next to one who is regarded as the greatest tragedian of our time—next to Edwin Booth." Ingersoll honoured Barrett because " he gave the drama in its highest and most serious form "; because " he shunned the questionable, the vulgar and impure, and gave the intellectual, the pathetic, the manly, and the tragic. He did not stoop to conquer—he soared. He was fitted for the stage. He had a thoughtful face, a vibrant voice, and the pose of chivalry, and besides, he had patience, industry, courage, and the genius of success. He was a graceful and striking Bassanio, a thoughtful Hamlet, an intense Othello, a marvellous Harebell, and the best Cassius of his century."

" In the drama of human life, all are actors," mused Ingersoll, " and no one knows his part. In this great play the scenes are shifted by unknown forces, and the commencement, plot, and end are still unknown—are still unguessed. One by one the players leave the stage, and others take their places. There is no pause—the play goes on. No prompter's voice is heard, and no one has the slightest clue to what the next scene is to be. Will this great drama have an end? Will the curtain fall at last? Will it rise again upon some other stage? Reason says perhaps, and Hope still answers yes. . "

Washington, D. C.
June 14th, 1880

My dear Mr. Barrett:

Had it been possible your kind invitation would have been accepted. Nothing could give me more pleasure than to be where a great actor is honoured. We know that a man able even to understand Shakespeare is great, and that only a genius can clothe in living flesh, filled and thrilled with life's hot blood and passion's flame the mighty offspring of the world's best brain. To us, living in an age approaching civilization, it is amazing that the one complete, perfect man—the one within whose heart all races lived, and in whose brain were stored the fruit of all thought past—the seeds of all to be, was called a "sturdy vagrant" in the English law, while socially he fell below the dullest parson and the half-fed footman of the lowest squire. And yet to him all hearts were open as the sky and Nature told her secrets with his lips. His mind was like a sea to which all rivers run, and from which all the realms of thought receive the dew and rain.

In the drama the highest thought in every age has found expression. While throne and altar forged and fastened chains, the poor slave heard upon the stage the actor curse the injustice of the world, and wept for joy to see, even in a play, the captive free. In all the other walks of life, rogues, hypocrites, and cowards oft succeed, but on the stage, applause greets only those who represent the great, the loving, brave and true, or give to public scorn the very heart of vice. And now the actor takes his place among the benefactors of mankind. Heminge and Condell in their dedication of the Folio of 1623 speak of Shakespeare's works as " these trifles." Yet " these trifles " will outlive the pyramids, and their dust. They will be remembered as long as most things will be forgotten.

Sincerely yours, Robert G. Ingersoll

New York, N. Y.
March 18, 1887

My dear Mary: *

Today, looking over old letters, I happened to find yours of last December, and read again what you say of the likenesses in *The Mirror.* You say that you like Booth and McCullough, but think Forrest's face detestable. This shows how little there is in faces—or rather, in poor pictures of faces.

Forrest was the greatest actor I ever saw. His voice was something miraculous—deep, thrilling, vibrant, magnificent. His whisper filled the largest theatre. He was large and erect, with a fine presence—kingly, imposing, intrepid. In *King Lear* he was simply sublime. Nothing could excel his acting in that part. I have seen hundreds weeping, as he recognized Cordelia.

I do not believe that it is possible for the human race to produce a greater King Lear than Edwin Forrest. In the scene on the heath, insane—a splendid ruin—nothing could have been more touching, nothing truer to nature; and in the last scene of all, one was compelled to hold his breath. I remember perfectly the tones of his voice, when he said:

Why should a dog, a horse, a rat have life,
And thou no breath at all?

and I remember also how, for a moment, my heart stood still.

Hoping you are all happy, and with love to all,

Yours, R. G. Ingersoll

MUSIC

Ingersoll loved music more than all the other arts, with the possible exception of literature. He derived an equal measure of inspiration and joy from the music of Wagner and the dramas of Shakespeare, and these constituted his two principal æsthetic passions in life.

This Critic and Lover of the Arts was peculiarly sensitive to music for the reason that music is the language of the emotions, or, as Ingersoll defined it, " the voice of love "—in a deeper and truer sense than any other medium of artistic expression, and it was on the plane of his heart that he was most susceptible.

He did not know anything about music from the technical point of view—did not even know one note from another; but he had strong likes and preferences in this field of art as in all other æsthetic realms. He declared that he enjoyed music " from the hand organ to the orchestra."

Ingersoll believed that music was " a gradual growth,

* Colonel Ingersoll's younger sister.

subject to the law of evolution," as everything else has been, "with the possible exception of theology." Music is generally loved for its sentimental associations rather than for its intrinsic worth and beauty; and up to the time when he first heard Wagner, Ingersoll himself had appreciated it chiefly on that account.

He maintained that "music may be divided into three kinds: First, the music of simple time, without any particular emphasis—and this may be called the music of the heels; second, music in which time is varied, in which there is the eager haste and the delicious delay   the fast and slow, in accordance with our feelings, with our emotions—and this may be called the music of the heart; third, the music that includes time and emphasis, the hastening and the delay, and something in addition, that produces not only states of feeling but states of thought. This may be called the music of the head—the music of the brain." Ingersoll said that "before man found a name for any thought, or thing, he had hopes and fears and passions, and these were rudely expressed in tones." Of one thing he was certain: "Music was born of love. Had there never been any human affection, there never could have been uttered a strain of music. Possibly some mother, looking into the eyes of her babe, gave the first melody to the enraptured air."

Ingersoll asserted that "language is not subtle enough, tender enough, to express all that we feel; and when language fails, the highest and deepest longings are translated into music. Music is the sunshine—the climate—of the soul, and it floods the heart with a perfect June."

He was also satisfied that "the greatest music is the most marvellous mingling of Love and Death. Love is the greatest of all passions, and Death is its shadow. Death gets all its terror from Love, and Love gets its intensity, radiance, its glory and its rapture, from the darkness of Death. Love is a flower that grows on the edge of the grave."

This Music Lover was irritated by, and regarded as foolish and frivolous, what he called " unmeaning music," such as the old-fashioned type of recitative. To him it was " as though a writer should suddenly leave his subject and write a paragraph consisting of nothing but a repetition of one word like ' the,'

' the,' or ' if,' ' if,' ' if,' varying the repetition of these words, but without meaning—and then resume the subject of his article." However, he liked many of the Old Italian operas in spite of their many passages of recitative; and realized that it had been necessary for music to evolve through all stages and degrees of development, in common with all other forms of art.

Wagner he placed at the topmost pinnacle of musical evolution; and termed him " the Shakespeare of Music." " In his music is the touch of chaos that suggests the infinite." " The funeral march for Siegfried is the funeral music for all the dead. Should all the gods die, this music would be perfectly appropriate. It is elemental, universal, eternal. The love-music in *Tristan and Isolde* is, like *Romeo and Juliet*, an expression of the human heart for all time. So the love-duet in *The Flying Dutchman* has in it the consecration, the infinite self-denial of love. The whole heart is given; every note has wings, and rises and poises like an eagle in the heaven of sound."

I believe that Ingersoll really regarded *Tristan and Isolde* as the greatest of all Wagnerian operas, although on at least one occasion he expressed the opinion that *Lohengrin* is " the sublimest musical composition of the world."

Ingersoll affirmed that " great music is always sad, because it tells us of the perfect; and such is the difference between what we are and that which music suggests, that even in the vase of joy we find some tears." Again, we hear his ever-recurring theme-song—his critical leitmotiv—that true art is the unending, eternal aspiration towards perfection—towards our highest and holiest ideals in being, thought, feeling, and action.

The Colonel declared that " the music of Wagner has colour, and when I hear the violins, the morning seems to slowly come. A horn puts a star above the horizon. The night, in the purple hum of the bass, wanders away like some enormous bee across wide fields of dead clover. The light grows whiter as the violins increase. Colours come from other instruments, and then the full orchestra floods the world with day.

" Wagner seems not only to have given us new tones, new combinations, but the moment the orchestra begins to play his music, all the instruments are transfigured. They seem to utter the sounds that they have been longing to utter. The horns run riot; the drums and cymbals join in the general joy;

the old bass viols are alive with passion; the 'cellos throb with love; the violins are seized with a divine fury, and the notes rush out as eager for the air as pardoned prisoners for the roads and fields." Ingersoll looked upon Wagner as " a sculptor, a painter, in sound. When he died, the greatest fountain of melody that ever enchanted the world ceased. His music will instruct and refine forever," because it " satisfies the brain and heart "; and " it is not only for memory; not only for the present, but for prophecy."

The Colonel's favourite forms of diversion and pleasure outside of his home were attending the opera and the theatre. Most Wagnerian performances at the Metropolitan under the baton of Anton Seidl saw Ingersoll and his family in attendance; and when the great Lilli Lehmann and Jean and Edouard De Reszke were all in the cast together, our Music Lover's satisfaction and delight knew no bounds.

His letters are far too brief and sketchy to convey any comprehensive idea of the range of Ingersoll's musical appreciations. However, it is certain that besides Wagner, he loved the music of Mozart, Liszt, Mendelssohn, some compositions of Schumann and Brahms, and the immortal songs and " Unfinished " Symphony of Schubert he held especially close to his heart, the *Serenade* and the *Ave Maria* representing for him the perfection of beauty.

ART AND ARCHITECTURE

Ingersoll, the connoisseur, was a great lover of art and architecture. Greek sculpture, Italian and Flemish painting, Classic and Gothic architecture gave him the keenest delight and joy. The Venus de Milo represented to him " the supreme idea of the supreme woman. It is a melody in marble. All the lines meet in a kind of voluptuous and glad content." He declared these things to be immortal: " the marbles of the Greeks; the plays of Shakespeare, and the music of Wagner."

The matchless paintings and etchings of Rembrandt set his soul aglow with wonder; the sumptuous colour and gorgeous beauty of the creations of Titian and Rubens; the beatific genius of Raphael; the titantic power and grandeur of Michelangelo; the magnificent realism of Frans Hals, touched responsive chords in the artistic nature of Ingersoll. He particularly loved the delicate, poetic pictures of Corot. Millet's " Angelus " was to him " the perfection of pathos."

Ingersoll's emotions were compounded of quiet rapture, reverence, and exaltation in the presence of the masterpieces of the world of art.

His artistic instincts and powers of observation were so sensitive and true that although he was without any technical training in the field of art he could almost always distinguish between a copy and an original painting.

This Critic was deeply interested in architectural beauty, the Grecian and Gothic forms having the most potent appeal to his æsthetic tastes. In his layman's fashion he was somewhat of a pioneer in his feeling for functional beauty; in his appreciation of the beauty of a bridge or a machine that was perfectly adapted to the purposes it was designed to serve. It was quite a revolutionary conception in Ingersoll's day that a purely utilitarian machine might be, in its own way, as beautiful as a poem, a painting, or a symphony.

Ingersoll's tastes and appreciations in the fine arts, as in literature and all other forms of beauty, were governed by his own very personal standards and ideals of judgment, and these standards and ideals centred around his warm and affluent emotions. These emotions led him to appraise a work of art in the light of its truth to life, its universality of appeal, its power to touch the heart, and to broaden, deepen, and elevate the imagination.

From this group of miscellaneous and unrelated letters we may get a certain insight into a few aspects of Ingersoll, the lover and connoisseur of the arts, which are not to be found in other letters.

The Colonel felt that great art in all its manifestations is an epitome, an *enhancement* and *illumination* of universal human experiences and values. To seek the truth, and " to speak from the heart," are indispensable qualifications for the creative artist, be he novelist, poet, dramatist, painter, sculptor, or musician. Moreover, without the aid of the imagination— which is the supreme civilizing agent of the mind and heart— one may not find the truth, or even know how to set about finding it, nor may one speak correctly or eloquently the language of the emotions.

" Proportion, pathos, philosophy," for content—and " beauty of style," for form—these are among the fundamentals of truly creative art. " Wit is the lightning of the soul . . . a crystallization of logic," hence, one of the surest as well as pleasantest means of " arriving at the [philosophic] conclusion, without the process of thought."

There is a potent element of paradox in Ingersoll's critical thinking: " Rules of art," he says, " are as certain as those in mathematics "—and yet he also assures us that " the prudent is not the poetic; it is the mathematical. Genius is the spirit of abandon; it is joyous, irresponsible . . . careless of conduct and consequence. . . ." But after all, life itself is a paradox, a contradiction, which no one can explain or escape: " In thwarted light leaps colour's flame; the stream impeded, has a song "; and " all these contradictions are higher forms of truth."

Thomas Nast was a celebrated American cartoonist, born in Landau, Germany, but who was taken to the U.S.A. at the age of six. He drew for the *Illustrated London News* and *Harper's Weekly*, picturing the campaigns of Garibaldi in Italy, and the Civil War in the United States. His sympathies were strongly on the side of the North, and Lincoln called him " our best recruiting-sergeant." He later specialized in political cartoons; and was especially noted for his Tammany Tiger. He also won popular acclaim by his modernizations of scenes from Shakespeare.

Mr. Nast caricatured Colonel Ingersoll on several occasions, and was alone among contemporary artists in portraying him as almost unattractive and ugly; all the other cartoonists having given him a benign, beaming, and almost cherubic countenance. However, Nast had no personal malice towards Ingersoll; he merely delineated him as he did every other public figure, in grossly exaggerated, distorted fashion.

New York, Mch 4th, 1889

H. C. Shotwell, Esq.,
Hyde Park, Ill.

My dear Sir:

Accept my thanks for the steel engraving of Abraham Lincoln. It is the best I have ever seen. It is a genuine portrait.

Hundreds of artists have been endeavouring to get the wrinkles out of Lincoln's face, to plaster down his hair, and to make him look like an ordinary, common-place "gentleman." In your engraving, you have Lincoln as he was.

Yours very truly, R. G. Ingersoll

Nov. 8th, 1890

Jno. T. Michan, Esq.

My dear Friend:

Accept my thanks for the *Herald* of Thursday, Oct. 30th, containing a short account of your lecture.

I do not know enough about architecture to say whether you are right or wrong. I have always had an idea, myself, that the really useful, containing only the necessary, is the most beautiful.

Mr. [John] Ruskin says that it is impossible to conceive, for instance, of a beautiful railroad bridge. And yet, I have an idea, that if every beam and wire was in the exact proportion to its strain—that is, just the exact amount of metal at every point necessary—and the same being in harmony—that such a bridge would be beautiful.

So far as a building is concerned, there must be a perfect harmony between its form and use. It must answer to the spirit in which it was constructed, and the purpose for which it was constructed.

I suppose that architecture has been a development along original lines. As for instance, nations or tribes, dwelling in caves, would as they became civilized, make buildings resembling caves. *They might be larger, ampler, better-adapted to their purpose*—but the cave idea, I imagine, would remain predominant.

So I think people who dwell in the woods, would be apt in their architecture to reproduce the old forest in columns of stone. Those who dwell in wigwams would delight in pointed doors and windows.

I am not sure that there is anything in this, but it strikes me as reasonable.

I believe there is a certain harmony between all religions and the temples of these religions—a certain harmony between dwellings, people, and their surroundings; and this harmony cannot be suddenly changed, or rudely violated. It may be slowly changed, but the elemental things remain. After all, beauty is not absolute—it is relative; and what is, or is not, beautiful to a race, or to an individual, depends on the experience of that race or of that individual.

But no matter. I am much obliged to you for the paper and hope to see you when you again visit New York.

Yours very truly, R. G. Ingersoll

PART FIVE

Ingersoll—the Epicure and Bon-vivant

INGERSOLL WAS AN Epicure in the broadest and most inclusive meaning of that term. He was a believer in and
practitioner of the art of good living, if not of "high living."
His Humanism, with its scepticism concerning a future life
in another world, caused him to make the most of life in this
world. Consequently, he appreciated the wisdom of the
ancient, ageless philosophy of the "worldly" people: Eat,
drink, and be merry, for tomorrow ye die. But he was also a
believer in moderation in all things—the golden mean—
knowing that over-indulgence and excess are inevitably self-
defeating; and self-control is the sole climate in which the
amenities can bud and blossom.

Furthermore, since in his philosophy, happiness was the
supreme good, he sought to enjoy and succeed in enjoying life
to the fullest measure. However, by happiness he did not mean
"simply the joys of eating and drinking, the gratification of the
appetite, but good—well-being—in the highest and noblest
sense." And in his opinion, the only way to be happy oneself
is to do all one can to increase the happiness of others; the only
way to keep happiness is to give it away to each and all. Ingersoll believed in "the medicine of mirth"; and "the
longevity of laughter"; and he declared that "every man who
has caused real, true, honest mirth has been a benefactor of the
human race."

He savoured the exquisite satisfaction derived from the
active and fastidious functioning of the five senses—from
colour; music; the touch of loving hands and lips; the taste
of "liquid joys," and luscious victuals; the fragrance of
flowers; the nameless beauty of art and nature—of friendship
and love—of earth and sky.

Ingersoll, the *Bon-vivant*, enormously enjoyed the pleasures
of the palate, of the table. Cooking, he felt, was "one of the
fine arts," and the very "basis of civilization. The man whose

206

arteries and veins are filled with rich blood made of good and well-cooked food, has pluck, courage, endurance, and noble impulses. The inventor of a good soup did more for his race than the maker of any creed." What was more, he entertained a strong suspicion that " the doctrines of total depravity and endless punishment were born of bad cooking and dyspepsia." The Colonel loved a savoury beefsteak done to a turn; but in his opinion, to fry a steak is nothing short of a culinary crime. He insisted that it should always be broiled; and he was a past master of the gastronomic art of beefsteak-broiling, a fact to which all of his family and many of his friends could testify. He also relished a glass of mellow vintage wine; of fine old whisky; or a delicate liqueur; and he derived delectable enjoyment from smoking a flavoursome and fragrant cigar. He even wrote a glowing eulogy to tobacco.

Nearly four centuries ago Columbus, the adventurous, in the blessed island of Cuba, saw happy people with rolled leaves between their lips. Above their heads were little clouds of smoke. Their faces were serene, and in their eyes was the autumnal heaven of content. These people were kind, innocent, gentle, and loving.

The climate of Cuba is the friendship of the earth and air, and of this climate the sacred leaves were born—the leaves that breed in the mind of him who uses them the cloudless, happy days in which they grew.

These leaves make friends, and celebrate with gentle rites the vows of peace. They have given consolation to the world. They are the companions of the lonely—the friends of the imprisoned, of the exile, of workers in mines, of fellers of forests, of sailors on the desolate seas. They are the givers of strength and calm to the vexed and wearied minds of those who build with thought and dream the temples of the soul.

They tell of hope and rest. They smooth the wrinkled brows of pain—drive fears and strange misshapen dreads from out the mind and fill the heart with rest and peace. Within their magic warp and woof some potent, gracious spell imprisoned lies, that, when released by fire, doth softly steal within the fortress of the brain and bind in sleep the captured sentinels of care and grief.

These leaves are the friends of the fireside, and their smoke, like incense, rises from myriads of happy homes. Cuba is the smile of the sea.

The Colonel felt that fashion added a distinct charm and fillip to the all-too-prosaic business of living. He said that it was " the duty of every woman to make herself as beautiful and attractive as she possibly can." Handsome is as handsome does; however, he thought that a woman is "much handsomer if well dressed." Every man, also, should always try to appear at his best, he added. Ingersoll was a hearty advocate of good clothes; and his closets were generously stocked with suits of the finest cut and fabric. Unlike most men, he was an enthusiastic shopper, so much so that he bought more dresses for his wife and daughters than they purchased for themselves. Of course, he bought only the materials for the garments, as all ladies in those days had their dresses made to order.

This Epicurean admired jewellery. He had a notion that the wearing of jewellery is the first evidence the barbarian gives of a wish to be civilized "; and that " the desire for beauty covers the earth with flowers   . . paints the wings of moths, tints the chamber of the shell, and gives the bird its plumage and its song." He advised women to adorn themselves with taste and artistry if they desire the admiration of men; and he gave his own womenfolk many beautiful jewels. Not, however, that they needed these adornments to win and hold the Colonel's affections, or to make themselves attractive in his sight. But he was forever lavishing upon them all manner of presents— the tangible tokens of his abounding love and devotion.

Ingersoll enjoyed life to the utmost, both indoors and out of doors. He knew the happiness that comes from companionship with one's family and friends; and with children, whom he deeply loved, and with whom he was almost invariably able to establish the most satisfying and understanding relationship, because he treated them like self-respecting equals, and because he, too, was a child at heart.

Ingersoll's feeling for nature was primarily emotional; the poet and philosopher in him were aroused and exalted by its beauties, grandeurs, and mysteries. His appreciation of the natural world was on the contemplative, æsthetic, and sentimental, rather than on the analytic and scientific side; although he was quite a student of botany, geology, astronomy, and other natural and physical sciences. He was an ardent lover of mountains, sea and shore, sunrise and sunset, skies and clouds; of trees and birds; the thrilling scents and sounds of spring; and summer's rich fulfilment; of autumn, when "death, poetic death, with hands that colour what they touch, weaves in the   . woods its tapestries of brown and gold "; and of winter, " the mother of industry and prudence," and " above all, of the family relation."

Ingersoll loved the exquisite beauty and fragrance of flowers, particularly of red roses; and on each of his wedding anniversaries, as well as often in between, he presented his wife with a gorgeous bouquet of Jacqueminot roses, his favourite variety. He associated lilies of the valley with Eva, his elder daughter, and accordingly gave them to her on every occasion, to her intense delight. As for his daughter Maud, knowing her preference for things musical, he generally presented her with an album of songs or symphonies, or scores of operas.

A sense of comradeship with animals, especially with dogs and horses, had an important part in the Colonel's enjoyment of life. He admired these animals for their natural grace and beauty; and loved them for their touching and noble qualities of fidelity and devotion, and, in the case of dogs, for their utterly selfless love for human beings. The family was never without several pet dogs of various sizes, and pedigrees and no pedigrees at all; and canine patricians and plebeians dwelt together in harmony and happiness. " Rust," a magnificent, gentle, and loving Irish setter, was probably Ingersoll's greatest favourite among the family dogs. Rust was a real person in his own right, of very superior intelligence and sensitivity. He understood an astonishing number of words, as well as inflections and tones of voice; and between the Colonel and the dog there existed a close and tender bond of friendship, trust, and understanding. The family circle also included a number of cats, which Ingersoll admired for their smooth, subtle grace and charm; and for their unconquerable pride and independence of spirit; and their shamelessly sybaritic ways amused him vastly.

The Colonel in his younger days was an expert horseman. However, after the Civil War he gave up horseback riding, but always enjoyed riding behind a " spanking team " of blacks or bays, with one of his daughters, his son-in-law Walston Brown, or his brother-in-law, Clint Farrell, wielding the reins. After the death of Mr. Farrell's favourite horse, named " Robin," who had lived to an honourable and honoured old age, Ingersoll wrote Clint a letter of condolence, in which he said that for many long years " Robin had driven the family about the town and countryside, and to the end of the trail had been faithful to his trust "; and the Colonel expressed the hope that when his turn came to depart this life as much could be said for him. By way of consolation, he reminded Clint that the beloved old horse had " died full of horse dainties "; and that his existence had been as satisfactory and happy as falls to the lot of members of the equine species.

Our Epicure relished with special appreciation the sweet, serene pleasures of home and fireside: evenings spent in his family circle, with his adored wife and daughters, and a few good friends; reading his favourite books; discussing literature, philosophy, religion, art, and science; listening to lovely duets sung by Eva and Maud; to the incomparable Remenyi playing the violin; and to the great maestro, Seidl, conducting selections from Wagner. The next best thing to spending an evening at home was attending grand opera and the theatre; the music of Wagner and the dramas of Shakespeare being his particular passions. Most Wagnerian performances at the Metropolitan under the magic baton of Anton Seidl saw Ingersoll and his family in attendance; and when the glorious singers, Lilli Lehmann and Jean and Edouard De Reszke, were all in the cast together, the Colonel's delight knew no bounds.

The epicurean aspects of his nature were also evinced in his wide contacts and friendships with interesting people of all sorts—people of the theatre, musicians, artists, poets, novelists, historians, and philosophers, and just plain, everyday, likeable men and women.

Colonel Donaldson was President of the Clover Club, a celebrated Philadelphia club of journalists, whose object was to promote good fellowship between the members of the profession, and representative men in other walks of life. The motto of the Club was:

> While we live, we live in clover
> When we die, we die all over.

It was the privilege and " good fortune of the Clover Club to entertain men who are an honour to literature and the fine arts, to the lyric and dramatic stage, to science, politics, business, and journalism."

Washington, D. C.
January 16, 1883

Colonel Thomas Donaldson,
President, The Clover Club,
Philadelphia.

Dear Colonel Donaldson:

I regret that I cannot be " in clover " with you on the 28th instant. A wonderful thing is clover! It means honey and cream —that is to say, industry and contentment—that is to say, the happy bees in perfumed fields, and at the cottage gate, " boss," the bountiful, serenely chewing satisfaction's cud, in that blessed twilight pause that like a benediction falls between all toil and sleep.

This clover makes me dream of happy hours; of childhood's rosy cheeks; of dimpled babes; of wholesome, loving wives; of honest men; of springs and brooks and violets, and all there is of stainless joy in peaceful human life.

A wonderful word is clover: Drop the " c," and you have the happiest of mankind. Drop the " r," and " c," and you have left the only thing that makes a heaven of this dull and barren earth. Drop the " r," and there remains a warm, deceitful bud that sweetens breath and keeps the peace in countless homes whose masters frequent clubs. After all, Bottom was right: " Good hay, sweet hay, hath no fellow! "

Yours sincerely and regretfully, R. G. Ingersoll

89 Fifth Avenue
Feb. 27th, 1883

My dear [Isaac Newton] Baker,

Whiskey is what you need. After each meal take a good swallow. One swallow will not make a summer but it will make you feel as though summer had come.

Temperance, i.e., total abstinence has killed thousands. It is terrible to die of thirst.—

Eat all you can and the whiskey will see to it that it is all digested. You can have confidence in this prescription because I am not a doctor—never killed people for a living.—

Yours in thirst, R. G. Ingersoll

Washington, D. C., April 26, 1883

Hon. E. J. Sherman,
Lawrence, Mass.

My dear Colonel:

After you went away, the folks commenced. No one man ever received an equal amount of advice in an equal time.

" You must *walk*, Colonel Sherman says that you are liable to fall dead for want of exercise. Do you *hear?* You must *WALK!* "

" Yes," said Grandmother, " the apoplexy is lurking in your blood."

" You are liable to be paralysed," said my wife.

" Or to die in your sleep," said Mrs. Farrell.

" Or after you wake up," chimed in the baby.

" You must walk," said Eva.

" You ought to run," added Maud.

" And never sit down again as long as you live," shouted Clint.

So I started for Georgetown, and walked five miles before breakfast. Then I footed it to the Court, and walked home. After supper I took a stroll in the country, reaching home a little before midnight. The next morning my calves were swollen so that they looked like yearlings. After being rubbed down with whisky and red pepper, and oiling my principal joints, I started out again about daylight, and walked to Bladensburgh—distant about eleven miles. On my return, about half-way home, I was taken with cramps and lock-jaw. I managed by signs to attract the attention of some people on their way to market, and was kindly taken home in a cart laden with garlic, kale, and sassafras.

I was carried in very tenderly by the entire family, all of whom insisted that MORE WALKING was what I needed!

" He stopped and cooled off too suddenly," said Clint.

" Lying down in the road will give anybody the cramps," said Maud.

" I guess Colonel Sherman knows what he is talking about," said Mrs. Farrell.

" Limber him up and start him again," yelled Clint.

So I was put in bed—covered with mustard—my legs straightened out by putting weights on my knees—and my mouth filled with dried apples so as to swell my teeth apart.

As soon as I was able to speak, I sent for Baker that I might dictate a letter to you for further instructions.

Of course it is necessary for you to know my general condition: 1, Both my feet are covered with blisters. 2, The cords in my legs are as tight as the strings of a bass viol. 3, Great pain in the small of my back. 4, Sudden flashes of heat running up and down the spine. 5, Knees badly swollen. 6, Mind wandering. 7, Pulse about 120. 8, Temperature of the body 115 degrees. 9, Fur enough on my tongue to make a sealskin sacque [woman's short coat].

I think I have walked enough. The rest say not. Telegraph your opinion. I am up in bed to sign this letter. I have looked through WALK-er's Dictionary without finding anything on the subject. I have also read " Plato on the *Sole*."

Yours till death, R. G. Ingersoll

The " Clint " to whom the following letter is addressed was Mr. Clinton Pinckney Farrell, Colonel Ingersoll's brother-in-law, and also the only authorized publisher of his works.

"Clint" Farrell and Robert Ingersoll were boon companions, speaking the same language of keen, irrepressible wit and humour.

New York, July 29, 1885

Dear Clint,
—"211 lbs."—That is what the man said as I stepped off the scales today. "211 lbs." is what I said to the folks as we sat down to dinner. "Don't fast any longer," said Maud, "you will be a living skeleton."

I feel first rate—I am going to 200—and then I shall have a feast.— I will give you the menu.

1, Potatoes—fried, not too hard. 2, Green corn—lots of butter. 3, Canteloupes. 4, Hot biscuit & butter. 5, More potatoes. 6, More green corn. 7, Some canteloupes. 8, Glass of cream. 9, A little fried chicken with potatoes. 10, Corn fritters with chicken gravy. 11, Another canteloupe.

The Ingersoll family moved to New York City from Washington, D.C., in November, 1885, a week or two after the following letter was written.

Hoffman House, New York
November 18th, 1885

Dear Folks,
As I telegraphed you, we have rented No. 101 5th Avenue. It is on the East side of the street, on the first block below Chickering Hall. It is a beautiful house, worth $150,000 and it is beautifully furnished. On the 1st floor, a parlour—middle parlour—dining-room—library, closets, butler's pantry, China closet. The walls are covered with paintings, and the mantels and hall with bronzes and marbles. In front parlour between the windows beautiful statue—life-size of Delilah. It is really a work of art. In the middle parlour there is a grand piano.

On second floor, bed rooms, 2 bath rooms, 2 closets—2 wash rooms with closets—beautiful beds—curtains to them. On 3rd floor—just the same, with 2 bath rooms, 2 wash rooms and 2 closets. I never saw wash rooms before. They are just out of the bed rooms, and have two stationary wash bowls in a long marble slab on one side of the room, and on the other, presses for all your clothes. The upper floor has plenty of rooms for servants.

In the basement fine office with billiard table in it. There is all the room I need. Then there are kitchen, laundry, and store rooms. Below basement a cellar for coal & 2 furnaces.

The library is very beautiful all inlaid and frescoed. All the floors are like our parlour. The hall is marble.—In short, it is a beautiful house.

Judge Pierrepont lives next door. The window of Marshall O. Roberts on the corner, Belmont next corner. It is one of the most aristocratic localities in New York. I say this for Sue's benefit. I got it at a splendid bargain—until the 1st of next October. I think that you will all be satisfied. I forgot to say that upstairs there are upright pianos. All the walls are frescoed, and the front parlour has tapestries on the walls. Wait until you see it! I take possession to-morrow.

Love & kisses to and for all. Robert

89 Fifth Avenue, New York
April 16—1887

Walston H. Brown, Esq.*

My dear Friend:

I send you some of the most wonderful whiskey that ever drove the skeleton from a feast or painted landscapes in the brain of man. It is the mingled souls of wheat and corn. There are in it the sunshine and shadow that chased each other over the billowy fields—the breath of June—the carol of the lark—the dews of night—the wealth of Summer and Autumn's rich content—all golden with imprisoned light.

Drink it—and you will hear the voices of men and maidens singing the Harvest Home, mingled with the laughter of children.

Drink it—and you will feel within your blood the star-lit dawns, the dreamy, tawny dusks of many perfect days.

For forty years this liquid joy has been within the happy staves of oak, longing to touch the lips of men.

Yours always, R. G. Ingersoll

New York
December 25th, 1889

Dear Mr. & Mrs. Baker:

Knowing you as a couple of old maids—guzzlers of tea—two gossips whose tongues can be untied by the loquacious leaves from China, the folks send you:

1, Some tea—best in the world. Mackay [Mr. John Mackay] gave it to us. 2, A crane and pot. 3, Two cups and saucers. 4, One pitcher for cream—& 5, One bowl for sugar.

And we all (except myself, as I had nothing to do with it) hope that you will have a good brew tonight—both get *full*, and wake up without a headache tomorrow morning; and that these things will suit you to a T. All send love.

Yours always, R. G. Ingersoll

---

* Ingersoll's future son-in-law, Eva's husband.

Jany 20, 1891

Charles J. Rosebault, Esq.,
Editor's Office of *The Sun*,
City.

Dear Sir:

In answer to your questions with regard to eating and speaking, I think that public dinners are generally too long, and too far apart, and that the average speeches are too long and not far enough apart, that most of the speeches are a little too heavy, so far as manner is concerned, and a little too light in the matter.

I think it is a mistake to put the best speakers last on the list, for the purpose of holding the audience for the worst. I take this occasion, however, to state that this is not always done.

In my opinion, the less speaking and the more eating, the better.

You ask if I can suggest any improvement in the programme of the average public dinner. I think I can. I think they would be far more enjoyable if the women and men dined together. Then I think there would be a little more talking and a little less tippling—more wit and less wine—not quite so heavy, and a good deal happier. And besides all this, each man would have somebody, on whom he could rely, to take him home.

Yours very truly, R. G. Ingersoll

Butte, Aug 26, '91

Dear Walston & Eva,

On my birthday I recd two boxes of cigars tied with olive ribbon [olive was the Colonel's favourite colour]—I knew that they came from you. I had a box of cigars open then and so I waited until that was emptied. Last night I untied the olive ribbon and found just the card with your dear names upon it. Then I opened a box and the aroma of the best filled the air. I lighted a cigar and enjoyed myself. While I smoked I thought of you both, and it gave me joy to think that you love each other and that you will through all the years,—that you will never change with age, but love right on to the very "edge of doom."

I hope that your troubles will all end in smoke & that you may ever be as serene as I was when smoking and thinking of you. I thank you both for having thought of me & for knowing me well enough to know that nothing could be more acceptable than the sacred leaves of Cuba. Good-bye. Love to each and all. I hope to get away from here in ten days at most.—

Yours for ever, Robert

Major Orlando Jay Smith, Civil War veteran, and a strikingly handsome and impressive figure with a wealth of snow-white hair, fresh, florid complexion, aristocratic features, and gracious courtly manner, was one of Ingersoll's closest friends and a neighbour at " Walston." On Sunday morning when Major Smith's more orthodox wife had gone to church, he would come over to " Walston " and sit with Colonel Ingersoll on the porch discussing immortality, religion, and philosophy.

117 East Twenty-first Street,
Gramercy Park
April 14, '99

My dear Major [Orlando J.] Smith,

Today I opened the box of cigars and found your good letter. I read it and said : " He certainly was good to me." I am smoking one now and there steals over me a sense of gratitude, a feeling that I have a friend—that I am not forgotten. Let them say what they will, there is in tobacco the essence, the aroma of friendship. The " Pipe of Peace " is not a savage fancy—it is a civilized and scientific fact. Tobacco is social. It has in it the clasp of comradeship—the soul of confidence. It is a medium of mental exchange. The doctors may say that it shortens life. But the longer life is without it, the worse it is. The preachers say that its use is wicked. The only reason they have for saying so, is that it gives us joy. For my part I had rather smoke one cigar than hear two sermons. In fact I had rather chew " green twist " than read the best chapter in Leviticus. There is solid comfort in tobacco. When I was a boy I used to watch the good old mothers as they smoked. I see them now, crumbling tobacco in their hands—filling the pipes—leaning over and reaching out for a coal—pressing the pipes against the under side of the mantel—sitting slowly down, with the left elbow in the right palm—taking a few quick puffs—then settling down for a good, long smoke. Dear, dear departed days! If the women would smoke now, how peaceful, how perfect homes would be! But whether smoking shortens life or not, whether it puts my soul in peril or not, I send you a thousand thanks for the box of temptations,—temptations from which my sincere prayer is not to be delivered. I love temptations. I will smoke and think of you.

Yours always, R. G. Ingersoll

Miss Sue Sharkey was a devoted and beloved member of the Ingersoll family for over fifty years. She came as a young girl to help care for Eva and Maud when they were babies, and she stayed to care for Eva's children. There was nothing that Sue or " Susie " or " Tuda," as she came to be called later by the Colonel's grandchildren, could not do. She could cook, sew, knit, crochet, can, and preserve all manner of delectable jellies, notably crab-apple jelly, jams, and marmalades. She made dresses and upholstered the household furniture. She told captivating, enthralling fairy-tales and other " tall " tales to the youngsters of three generations.

Eternally young in heart and spirit, most pleasing to look upon, with an opulent wealth of snow-white hair, a pink-and-white complexion, a sympathetic, loving smile, and a boundless capacity for tender sentiment and an irresistible, never-failing wit and sense of humour, her Irish heritage, no doubt, she was indispensable to all the family.

(No dates given.)

Miss Sue Sharkey,

You are hereby invited to be present at the residence of Mr. & Mrs. R. G. Ingersoll on Tuesday, Nov. 4th at 8 o'clock P. M. on the occasion of the marriage of Miss Sue M. Parker and C. P. Farrell Esq.

Pocket handkerchiefs will be furnished for the use of all persons who may be overcome by their feelings.

After the ceremony an opportunity will be given for an examination of the underclothing of the bride. The whole to conclude with music on piano by Maud and Eva Ingersoll and John Brown Esq. will dance a Highland Fling.

Buckets will be set in the back hall to hold tears.

Yours respectfully, Mr. & Mrs. Ingersoll

PART SIX

Ingersoll—Husband, Father, and Friend

LOVE WAS THE fundamental, the central factor in Robert G. Ingersoll's approach to life; love as romance between man and woman, husband and wife; love as sympathy, understanding, and friendship for friends and for all humanity.

Ingersoll, the supreme romantic, declared that " Love is the only bow on life's dark cloud. It is the morning and the evening star. It shines upon the babe, and sheds its radiance on the quiet tomb. It is the mother of art, inspirer of poet, patriot, and philosopher. It is the air and light of every heart— builder of every home, kindler of every fire on every hearth. It was the first to dream of immortality. It fills the world with melody—for music is the voice of love. Love is the magician, the enchanter, that changes worthless things to joy, and makes right royal kings and queens of common clay. It is the perfume of that wondrous flower, the heart, and without that sacred passion, that divine swoon, we are less than beasts; but with it, earth is heaven, and we are gods."

He was the lyric bard and rhapsodist of marriage and family life. It was his belief that " there is no success in life without love and marriage "; and that " you had better be the emperor of one loving and tender heart and she the empress of yours, than to be king of the world." Pure romanticism assuredly reached ultimate expression in these lines: " It is a splendid thing to think that the woman you love will never grow old to you. Through the wrinkles of time, through the masks of years, if you really love her, you will always see the face you loved and won. And a woman who really loves a man does not see that he grows old; he is not decrepit to her; he does not tremble; he is not old; she always sees the same gallant gentleman who won her hand and heart. I like to think of it in that way—I like to think that love is eternal; and to love in that way, and then go down the hill of life together, and as you go down, hear, perhaps, the laughter of grandchildren, while the birds of joy and love sing once more in the leafless branches of the tree of age."

On February 12, 1881, Robert wrote to his brother, Dr. John Ingersoll: "Tomorrow I shall have been married nineteen years, and they have been happy years to me. My wedding day was the most fortunate in my life. No man ever had a better, truer, sweeter wife. She has been the star and anchor of my life. But for her, I should have been a wreck among the rocks. She is dearer to me now than ever before and she will grow dearer as the years go by." And the husband paid supreme tribute in these poetic, tender words to the wife whom he adored:

Ever faithful to the chosen one;
Varying never, constant as the sun.
Artless, honest; every duty gladly done;
Always gentle;
In every act her nature's best—
Nature rising to the top in her
Giving final proof.
Ever giving, asking naught;
Royal in her every thought.
Serenely formed and wrought
Of perfect clay.

The marriage of Robert and Eva Ingersoll might be said to have been " made in heaven," although it was contracted by two religious unbelievers and Agnostics. It marked the beginning of a new epoch in the life of Ingersoll. From the moment that he fell in love with Eva Amelia Parker he became as one transfigured—" re-born." At that moment he attained mature moral stature, his soul burgeoning in new beauty and tenderness. If ever two people were made for each other, Robert Ingersoll and Eva Parker were those two; if ever anything was predestined and inevitable it was that this man and this woman should meet and unite in holy wedlock! Their lives, it seems, had converged since birth, and their hearts and minds and souls as well. Each was a Freethinker, " without superstition "; each was honest, fearless, truth-seeking, and superbly qualified for the good and abundant life; each had that seminal simplicity and goodness which belong to noble natures. Both possessed a rare capacity for happiness and joy, an infinite love for beauty, freedom, and truth. Each was cast in an ample Olympian mould. They complemented and supplemented one another to perfection.

There were three persons who were primarily responsible for the unique and perpetual happiness of Robert Ingersoll: his wife and two daughters, Eva and Maud. To the loving husband and father, they were personifications of paradise; and the " sacred three " returned his love and adoration in full and equal measure.

Ingersoll's deepest contentment and happiness derived from the companionship of his family—from the serene, sweet presence of his wife, and the spontaneous merry laughter of his children and grandchildren.

" The laugh of a child," he wrote, " will make the holiest day more sacred still. Strike, with hand of fire, O weird musician, thy harp strung with Apollo's golden hair; fill the vast cathedral aisles with symphonies sweet and dim, deft toucher of the organ keys; blow, bugler blow, until thy silver notes do touch and kiss the moonlit waves, and charm the lovers wandering ' midst the vine-clad hills.' But know, thy sweetest strains are discords all, compared with childhood's happy laugh—the laugh that fills the eyes with light and every heart with joy. O rippling river of laughter, thou art the blessed boundary line between the beasts and men; and every wayward wave of thine doth drown some fretful fiend of care. O Laughter, rose-lipped daughter of Joy, there are dimples enough in thy cheeks to catch and hold and glorify all the tears of grief."

Ingersoll was the first and almost the sole tutor of his children, as they went to school for a very short period of time, and never attended any college or university. Nevertheless, Eva and Maud were extraordinarily well educated, because they were constantly under the influence of their father. He gave them thorough courses in all major subjects taught in formal centres of learning, and helped them in other fields of knowledge as well. His methods of teaching, though informal and unconventional, were so effective and intelligent, so quickening and stimulating to their processes of thought and imagination, that his children soon found themselves enthralled by history, geography, geology, astronomy, botany, zoology, the physical and social sciences, philosophy, by almost all subjects of study, with the exception of the higher mathematics. Literature and the arts " Papa " made utter enchantment to their eager, receptive young minds. Both girls were intellectually inquiring and adventurous enough to tackle the formidable themes of metaphysics and theology; and the study of comparative religions was one of their favourite occupations. To the Colonel's complete satisfaction and joy, both of his daughters developed honest, courageous, and scientific attitudes of mind towards life. They became as Ingersollian as Ingersoll himself, they were taught to think for themselves, and encouraged to take issue with their father whenever they felt inclined. On most questions, including the question of religion, the Colonel's wife and daughters were in complete accord with his views, and his wife would often laughingly assert that she was a better Agnostic and Freethinker than " Robert " himself.

There was no discipline in the commonly accepted sense in the Ingersoll home; no force or coercion of any kind. Nevertheless, there existed in that home, permeating its atmosphere, a rare kind of discipline—the discipline of perfect freedom—of " the restraining influences of liberty." For the very reason that Ingersoll was so eager to indulge his daughters' slightest wish, constantly urging them to buy more dresses and jewellery, to attend the theatre, concert, and opera more often, Eva and Maud never considered taking advantage of his generosity. Because they were always treated like civilized human beings, his daughters always behaved like civilized human beings. They never caused their father or mother a moment of disappointment or distress, never failed to measure up to their parents' highest hopes and expectations, and always fulfilled their exalted standards and ideals of womanhood.

The Colonel was never so contented and blissful as when spending the evening at home with his family. Seated in his easy-chair before the open fire in the living-room in winter, or on the porch of the country home in summer, he found never-failing satisfaction and delight in conversing with, or in reading aloud to, his two Evas and his Maud; and in listening with rapt admiration to the lovely young voices of his daughters singing the songs of Schubert, Schumann, Mendelssohn, Beethoven, Mozart, Grieg, the Italian operatic masters, and their other favourite composers. Eva was endowed with a heavenly soprano, and Maud with a glorious contralto. Their duets, accompanied on the piano by Mrs. Farrell, were in

Ingersoll's opinion fit entertainment for the Olympian gods. Mrs. Ingersoll loved to hear the girls sing almost as much as did the Colonel, and her favourite selection was Schubert's *Serenade*; but, strange to say, Ingersoll's favourite composition is not known, although it was probably something from *Tristan and Isolde*. Eva studied singing with the noted Italian teacher, Ferronté, who assured her that she was sufficiently gifted to make a brilliant career for herself in concert and opera. Maud was an exceptionally talented pianist and singer, and in the estimation of her family and many of her friends had a touch more delicately beautiful and expressive of the inner spirit of the music she interpreted than was possessed by most professional performers.

Both daughters had a rare genius for appreciation of beauty in all its forms. Both were accomplished in the art of painting, and did charming landscapes and seascapes in oil- and water-colour. However, Eva's greatest passion was Shakespeare, and Maud's was Wagner. Eva could recite almost whole Shakespearean plays by heart, and she had the innate abilities and potentialities of a great actress and a true poet. She could enter into the very being of the marvellous women of Shakespeare—make them come to life before her fascinated listeners. She could read and interpret Shakespeare, Burns, Shelley, Keats, Whitman, and the other noble poets with an appreciation and eloquence scarcely surpassed by her father himself. Her feeling for literary values was creative in a very real sense, as she not only interpreted faithfully the works of the masters, but, like her father, seemed always to add something—to enhance the productions of the genius of the ages.

Eva's interest in architecture led her to a study and active promotion of the cause of town planning; and horticulture and forestry were among her special enthusiasms.

Eva Ingersoll's way of life was the way of beauty; to her family and to all who came into her presence she was Beauty. The classic loveliness of her face and form were matched by the perfection of her character. She was the embodiment of her father's highest ideals; his radiant dreams and aspirations made flesh and blood. Her life was dedicated to the love and service of her family, friends, and humanity.

Maud Ingersoll was also a wonderful woman, of rare,

opulent intellect, brilliant wit, courageous, independent spirit, and great and noble heart. She inherited her father's interest in ideas and love of truth, as well as much of his genius for pithy, epigrammatic expression, his flashes of inspired insight into the core of great questions, his unfailing sense of humour and sparkling wit, and his solid common sense and honest approach to life. She was a true feminist, and she met the most exacting tests of sportsmanship and gallantry of spirit in various experiences in her life with Father. There was something utterly selfless about the way she would pack up and go travelling with the Colonel at a moment's notice, and about the fact that she was never known to show the slightest annoyance at the countless inconveniences encountered on these trips to all sorts of places. Far from feeling any desire to complain, Maud actually revelled in all these salty and savoury adventures. Almost her earliest recollection in life was of sitting patiently in court, hour after hour, at the tender age of four or five, while her father argued endlessly some case. Indeed, all that Maud asked of life was to be constantly at the side of the father who was also her friend, comrade, guide, counsellor, teacher, inspirer, and god.

The two Evas and Maud were not only ornaments and joys in their home, they were also women of vast public spirit, passionately concerned with the important issues of the day and of the age. Every movement for the betterment of humanity found in them eager and generous champions: birth control; child welfare; world peace; woman suffrage, and equality for women in all offices and relations of life; purified politics; slum clearance and model housing; prison reform; social justice; opposition to prejudice, injustice, and cruelty wherever found; intellectual liberty—all these they worked for with true Ingersollian enthusiasm, independence, and moral courage. As active members of the Audubon Society, the Society for the Prevention of Cruelty to Animals, and other humane organizations, they fought continuously for the rights of defenceless animals.

Both Eva and Maud were the recipients of much attention and admiration from many devoted suitors. However, Walston Hill Brown, a prominent and distinguished railwayman and financier, triumphed over all his rivals for the hand of

Eva, and on November 13, 1889, she became his wife. They were married quietly at the Ingersoll home at 400 Fifth Avenue, New York City, in the presence of the family and a few intimate friends. The bride and bridegroom then started on a honeymoon trip which was to have been of several months' duration but ended in two weeks because Eva could not endure the separation from her father and mother any longer. Each day during the fortnight of their absence from home the young couple telegraphed Mr. and Mrs. Ingersoll to say that they were well and to send worlds of love.

At the time of Eva's marriage she made an unwritten agreement with her parents that she and her husband would live with the Ingersolls for one half of the year, and that the Ingersolls would live with the Browns for the balance of the time. This understanding was scrupulously adhered to until the death of Mrs. Ingersoll in 1923.

Walston Brown bought the beautiful country estate at Dobbs' Ferry-on-Hudson, New York, shortly after his marriage to Eva Ingersoll, and presented it to his bride as his most wonderful wedding-gift to her. She lost her heart to "Walston," the place, as she had previously lost it to Walston, the man. The spring of 1890 saw the happy young couple ensconced in their romantic and magnificent new stone mansion country home.

Here for nine serene, smiling summers, lived Colonel and Mrs. Ingersoll, Mr. and Mrs. Brown, Miss Maud Ingersoll, Mrs. Benjamin Weld Parker (Mrs. Ingersoll's mother), Mr. and Mrs. Clinton Pinckney Farrell (sister and brother-in-law of Mrs. Ingersoll), their daughter, Miss Eva Ingersoll Farrell, and Miss Sue Sharkey, a member by adoption of the family. And, in due course, Eva Ingersoll Brown and Robert Ingersoll Brown, the two children of Mr. and Mrs. Walston Brown, came to join the family circle. Thus four generations dwelt together under one roof, with seven or eight in help, which number included a coachman and three or more gardeners; three or four dogs; one or two cats; several canaries; a parrot; six or seven horses; two ponies; five or six cows, many chickens of various varieties, pigeons, guinea hens, turkeys, pet crows, and bees completed the household.

At his fireside the personality of Robert Ingersoll unfolded and flowered in a tenderness, love, contentment, and happiness beautiful beyond imagining. He carried out with complete consistency his professed intention of so treating his wife and children that they could come to his grave and truthfully say: " He who sleeps here never gave us a moment of pain; from his lips, now dust, never came to us an unkind word." To enter the home of Ingersoll was indeed to enter heaven itself, wherein the only realities were idealities, and the eternal verities were personified in the husband and wife, the father, mother, and children.

Robert Ingersoll counted his friends in the thousands. The actual number of those who considered him their friend, in the spiritual sense, was legion; and he, on his side, regarded as his friend, in a real and profound sense, every man and woman who "loved justice, and longed for the right." Ingersoll liked people; and although he was almost incredibly austere and exalted in his own personal standards and ideals, he was, at the same time, almost as catholic and inclusive as nature in his attitude towards common, universal humanity.

Few men ever had a richer or more varied assortment of acquaintances and social contacts than the Colonel. They ranged from Presidents Hayes, Gárfield, and McKinley, through Vice-Presidents, Senators, and Representatives in the Congress of the United States; Judges of the United States Supreme Court and the lower courts; ambassadors and diplomats; men of affairs and men of letters; industrialists, financiers, and labour leaders; ministers of the gospel and atheists; musicians, poets, painters, sculptors, and architects; actors, singers, and scientists; through plain, ordinary men and women, the " respectably " obscure, humble and anonymous, down to the disinherited, destitute, and disreputable: the beggar, the insane, and the outcast.

George Jacob Holyoake called the Ingersolls " the best friends we ever knew in the best household in the world."

Dr. John Lovejoy Elliott, the noble leader of the Ethical Culture movement in America, and successor of Dr. Felix Adler, was one of Ingersoll's most devoted friends and disciples; and a member by adoption of the Ingersoll family. He spoke out of his own intimate personal experience when he thus described the Ingersoll home: " It was to his home, to his wife and children, to all who gathered beneath his roof, that Colonel

Ingersoll owed much of the revelation which he gave to the world. The light of the home founded by Robert and Eva Ingersoll shines out over the world today and makes it a better place. . . What the world owes, what we all owe to this home, cannot easily be overstated. . . . It was in his home that Colonel Ingersoll learned that the great faith of the world is not faith in gods, but faith in men; and he wanted to make room and place for that faith in this world. . . . From his reading of history he knew that the greatest good of the world has come from homes; that the love of men for women and of women for men, the love of parents for children, was the source of that faith in the goodness which lightens the world. . . . He knew that the first law-givers were the founders of the family; and that the state and our laws and institutions are but the imperfect outgrowth and the poor reflection of the most perfect human relations which   . are within the walls of the family. . . ."

He declared that he had " never known a home of such wide and generous hospitality. I have never known a roof where rich and poor   the great and the humble, were so equally welcome. It was as though Robert and Eva Ingersoll had made a home whose spirit was great enough to welcome all the world. Here men and women of all races, all beliefs, all nationalities, were received with a kindness which was equally great and generous for all. . . . Here we have known the actual presence of the spirit of the Brotherhood of Man. Over this house Mrs. Ingersoll presided for over half a century."

Mark Twain was an ardent admirer and friend of Robert Ingersoll. These two men of humour and intellectual emancipation had many things in common, including agnosticism in religion, although the true extent of Mark Twain's heresy was not at that time generally known.

Upon being apprised of the Colonel's death, Mark Twain wrote Ingersoll's niece a nice little note of tender sympathy and sorrow in which he said: ". . Except for my daughter's, I have not grieved for any death as I have grieved for his. He was a great and beautiful spirit; he was a man—all man—from his crown to his foot-soles. My reverence for him was deep and genuine; I prized his affection for me and returned it with usury. . . "

Andrew Carnegie and Ingersoll were brought together through their mutual love of the poetry of Robert Burns, and this gracious and rewarding friendship lasted until the Colonel's death. On July 26, 1899, Mr. Carnegie sent Mrs. Ingersoll a message of sympathy and affection and heart-felt grief for the passing of a well-loved friend: " Seldom has such a pang passed through my heart. .   Truly I feel as if one touching my side had been stricken, so close he seemed to have stood.   No mere acquaintance, or mere friend either, but one of the small circle who went to the core.   I can never cease to regret the loss, nor to reproach myself for opportunities lost to be more in his presence.

" What a record—always right on every issue.   One of the great characters of modern times and the greatest of orators.   A true Tribune of the people.   One who stood for what he saw to be true and noble. . . ."

SOME FAMILY LETTERS

John Livingston Ingersoll was the oldest son of the Rev. and Mrs. John Ingersoll. He lived and practised medicine in Prospect for fifty years, leading the quiet, dutiful existence typical of a small-town physician of those days.

In their early years John was in spirit, as in fact, the elder brother of Robert; however, as time went on the relationship was reversed in the psychological sense, Robert assuming a protective and perpetually solicitous attitude towards John. This was due no doubt to the fact that Robert's material situation in life became more and more prosperous, while that of the Doctor remained static and far indeed from affluent.

The two brothers were deeply and tenderly devoted to each other, although differing widely in temperament and outlook on life. John was more like their preacher-father than any of the five children. While not as devoutly orthodox as the Rev. Mr. Ingersoll, he nevertheless retained throughout his life some measure of religious faith. ' He was also a confirmed believer in, and active worker on behalf of, the cause of prohibition, or temperance as it was then called. His intellectual opinions generally might be said to have been fairly conventional and conformist. However, he was broad-minded enough to feel deep and genuine interest and pride in the career and attainments of his brilliant, radical brother.

The following is the earliest Ingersoll letter on record.

Vandalia, Illinois, Feby 24 (1852)

Dear Bro. John & Sister,

Why don't you answer my letters. Wait a minute you needen't [sic] answer I know it is because I haven't written any, but why hav'nt [sic] you written some then I could have answered them & twould have been all strait. I hope you are getting along well I am at present teaching school but will be through in about five weeks then I will come up north & see you & the rest of the folks. I shall make about 50 dollars this winter or so Do write often Father is well & I heard from Clark * the other day his [sic] is well & Mary † was well the last I heard from her Jno send her a dollar or five she needs it I know she does give my love to your wife God bless you is my prayer I hope I shall see you in a little while tonight I wrote to Ruth ‡ I have no more time so Good-bye from

Your Aff. Bro., Bob Ingersoll

Peoria, Aug. 30th, 1865

My Dear Bro. [John],

I wish that I could be with you that our tears might mingle, and that we might stand side by side at the grave of your little darling. I know that I can say nothing to make your loss appear less, or your great burden easier to be borne. I can only say that my heart is with you my dear brother and that I would gladly share your grief. I did not know until I recd your letter that your little boy was named for me. I hardly knew that you had a babe, and yet I feel as though a part of my own heart almost had gone down to the grave. Death is becoming familiar in our family. Only a few days and we will have to join the dear ones on the other side. Another voice is calling you to heaven. You have one reason less for wishing to live.

Be patient and resigned. Grief is unavailing, and perhaps if you could have seen little Robby's future the angel of death was also the angel of mercy.

I wish I could be with you. Anything that I can write is poor and cold compared to what I feel. Give my best love to poor Teressa. God be with the poor mother that has laid her child in the cradle of death. Think of little Robby as being with our father & mother. He has only ceased to be mortal.

No matter how old you get or your children you will always have a sweet babe in your hearts. The other children will change

* Robert's brother, Ebon Clark Ingersoll.
† Mary Jane Ingersoll, Robert's younger sister.
‡ Ruth Ann Ingersoll, Robert's elder sister.

and to a certain extent grow out of your affections, but Robby will never change.

I can only say May the God of our Father be with you and give you strength to bear your great affliction. Kiss your dear children for me. I send more than love to you my dear brother.

From Robert

The tender relationship between Ebon Clark and Robert Ingersoll is illustrated in the following letter from Clark to his elder brother, Dr. John Livingston Ingersoll. Clark not only adored Robert, but he had a very profound and lively appreciation of his literary, oratorical, and intellectual achievements.

Robert, on his side, was full of enthusiasm for and pride in the career and accomplishments of his lawyer-Congressman brother. Every time Clark made an eloquent speech, or introduced a worth-while bill of resolution in the House of Representatives, the Colonel would dash off a little note to him, overflowing with warm and affectionate praise.

November 15, 1871

Dear Brother:

I want you to read this Oration, without prejudice, and should you not agree with R. (Robert), in his estimation of the character and services of Mr. [Thomas] Paine, you can not but admire the elegance of his diction; the brilliancy of his thought; the splendid and (tonic) irresistible power of his logic; and the vast amount of learning and thought necessary to the production of such an incomparable work.

How infinitely honest, earnest and intense is his brain and how infinitely good is his noble heart is attested on every page.

To me, the words are *pure* gold, set in diamonds! Altogether, it is more than grand, it is *sublime*! I would rather be the author of those 41 pages than to be President of this Republic.

Your aff. brother,
E. C. Ingersoll

Peoria, Nov. 19th, 1871

My dearest Brother [Ebon Clark]:

I am afraid you will flatter me to death. The few lines you wrote to John will be preserved by me as long as I live. I know you have in them said a thousand times more than ought to be said; but . . . every word is precious to my heart. When you open the very doors of your soul and show me the niche occupied by me it is impossible to keep back my tears.

I wish we could be together today. The day is dark, cloudy, damp and cold. There were a few spits of snow last night, and today a little ice clings to the dead and fallen leaves. Nothing is sadder than the leafless trees, except, it may be, the treeless leaves. I wish the snow would come and hide the distress and poverty of the landscape.

Write to me real often, and I will answer. It makes me happy to get a letter from you, no matter how short. It follows me all day like a ray of light.

Am getting along with my business all right. Plenty to do, and no prospect of failing.

I am getting better of my local complaint, but very slowly. Four weeks ago yesterday I stopped using tobacco. Have not smoked or chewed any since.

I was weighed Saturday and weighed 227 lbs. Do not think I will gain any more. I thought maybe tobacco hurt me. Now I drink no tea or coffee or spirits of any kind and use no tobacco, and I am going to continue in the good cause until I satisfy myself whether the effect upon me is good or bad

With infinite love to you

I am as ever Your brother, Robert

The following letter was written to Colonel Ingersoll's elder daughter, Eva Robert, when she was fifteen years of age. Whenever he was away from home the Colonel wrote at least a line or two every day to Eva or Maud, or to Mrs. Ingersoll, or to the whole family together. One or more of the family who remained at home wrote to him every day also.

New Haven
May 14, 1878

My sweet Daughter,

We have had so little correspondence that I hardly know what to say, I hope though that we will write more in future if we are separated, but I hope we will not be separated.

You do not know how proud I am of you and how dear you are to me.

To me you are a perpetual joy. There never was and there never will be a sweeter girl than you.

The future ought to have nothing but joy in store for such a girl. In your sky there never ought to be a cloud of sorrow. If you could only be as happy as I want you to be your life would be infinitely sweet.

You deserve every gift of fortune.

Read as much as you can without hurting your eyes; be careful of them. I want you to know a good deal. All information will be of advantage some time. Now don't study too hard just because I speak about it. Don't be afraid of getting nice things for this summer. I want you to look as well as anybody.

Give my love to your dear Mother—the sweetest woman in

the whole world—and to dear Maud. Love to Sue & the baby and grandmother and Shark [Miss Susie Sharkey].

Be happy every moment, my dear darling daughter.

Good-bye, Robert

On the occasion of the Ingersolls' first trip to Europe in 1875 they visited England, Ireland, and France; and when in Paris they went to the cemetery of Père-la-Chaise, and Ingersoll asked the superintendent of the place where he might find the tomb of Auguste Comte. However, this individual " had never heard even the name of the author of the *Positive Philosophy*."

Ingersoll then inquired if the man had ever heard of Napoleon Bonaparte. " In a half insulted tone, he replied, ' Of course I have, why do you ask me such a question? ' " " Simply," Ingersoll retorted, " that I might have the opportunity of saying, that when everything connected with Napoleon, except his crimes, shall have been forgotten, Auguste Comte will be lovingly remembered as a benefactor of the human race."

Ingersoll detested Bismarck because the " Iron Chancellor " believed in force as the chief instrument of national policy, and because he oppressed the Jews, and suppressed freedom of speech and of the Press in Germany. " The Chancellor has gone so far as to declare that the king is not responsible to the people . . that the king gets his right to govern not from his subjects, but from God."

Ingersoll, in his hatred of the tyranny of government, re-garded " Bismarck as a projection of the Middle Ages; as a shadow that has been thrown across the sunlight of modern civilization, and in that shadow grow all the bloodiest crimes." " Any possible state of anarchy is better than *organized crime* (the italics are mine), because in the chaos of anarchy justice may be done by accident, but in a government organized for the perpetuation of slavery, and for the purpose of crushing out of the human brain every noble thought, justice does not live."

Lewiston, Me.
Oct. 16th, 1872

Dear Clint,*

I am very glad to receive your kind letter—glad that you have read the " Confessions " [of Rousseau]. Of course the author was

* Clinton Pinckney Farrell, the Colonel's brother-in-law.

insane. He was a mental deformity—capable of the best and the meanest actions. He was a lizard with wings—half fiend—half angel. He was, however, a power in his day and did much to awaken the human mind. I have a greater sympathy with, and admiration for the winners of intellectual battles, than for military heroes. I think Voltaire fought more wonderful battles than Napoleon, and to me Auguste Comte seems far greater than Cæsar.

I once thought that Bismarck was a great man. The other day I read his speech on the " Socialist Bill " now before the German Congress, and I found that he knows nothing—that he believes in nothing but brute force. He has no idea of human rights. He thinks they come from the king, not from nature. I am through with him.

I must take his name out of the lecture on Liberty of Man, &c. I will change the next edition.

You and I will have a splendid time this winter reading and talking. There is no more splendid feeling than that you are growing in mind. It gives me a thrill of pleasure to learn a new fact, to get a new idea, to feel that my mind is growing.

Well, good-bye, my dear friend and brother. I love you and yours. Kiss them for me. Love to the dear little baby.

Yours, Robert

Grand Rapids, Michigan
Nov. 8, 1878

My Sweet Daughter,

I recd your charming letter at Cleveland. It was handed me just as I was going on the stage. I made the audience wait until I read it. They are indebted to your letter for a better speech than I could have made without it. That letter filled me with love and gratitude and joy. There never were two sweeter girls.—There never were two as sweet girls & there never will be again as you and Maud.

I must compliment you on your writing. It is real good and your sentences are all constructed well. You will make a great writer. You have brains and heart to spare, and so has that sister.

Sweet Eva you are too generous. Your letter made tears come into my eyes. You and Maud asking Mother to stay with me. You are the best children in the world.

Well, sweet Eva I bid you good-bye. I love you. I carry you tenderly in my heart and your sweet face is always before me.

Love to Maud. Go and kiss her this minute. Kiss them all. I love you—I love you.

Robert

It was on May 30, 1879, that overwhelming sorrow came to Robert Ingersoll on the death of his adored brother, Ebon Clark. All their lives they had shared work and play, dreams, hopes, ambitions and ideals, failures and successes. Their loyalty and mutual affection for each other was without limit.

Washington, D. C.
June 3, 1879

Dear Clint & Sue,

It is all over. The curtain has fallen on the deepest tragedy of my life.

My poor brother lies asleep in that silent chamber that has no window towards the East.

Nothing can be said, nothing can be done.

We love you all.

Yours always, Robert

In fulfilment of a compact made in youth Robert delivered the funeral oration over his brother, amid " one of the largest gatherings of distinguished persons ever seen at a funeral in the national capital."

Ingersoll closed his tender and touching funeral oration with the words: " Life is a narrow vale between the cold and barren peaks of two eternities. We strive in vain to look beyond the heights; we cry aloud, but the only answer is the echo of our wailing cry. From the voiceless lips of the unreplying dead there comes no word; but in the night of death Hope sees a star, and listening Love can hear the rustle of a wing."

Lafayette, Ind.
Dec. 6th, '84

My sweet Eva,

Both your letters reached me yesterday. They have the odour of violets. You love me too much. You give me joy so sharp that it gives me pain. All that is tender, loving and beautiful in nature mingled in you. I am almost afraid of you—afraid that you will sacrifice yourself for those you love—for me. I beg you not to do that. It is natural to form other attachments and I want you to act your nature. I shall be happy when you are. Nothing could make me so miserable as to know that you were denying yourself for me.

Words cannot express the feeling I have for you and Maud and Mother. You are the Trinity that I adore.—All that I am capable of loving I love you. Give my love to all and kiss all for me. We will be together in a few days. Until then, good-bye. I love you.

Yours for ever, Robert

Newburyport, Oct. 1, 1885

Dear Girls,

It is now high noon and we hope that you have been home at least an hour and a half. I felt a little anxious about you and, having recd no dispatch, feel so still.

We are well, my cold is better and Mother feels as well as ever. After we left you Mother took a little cry in the carriage, and has talked about you ever since.

You must enjoy yourselves. Maud, I suppose, is at the piano this very minute and Eva will soon try her hand. I wish you would sing together a good deal. If you knew how I loved to hear your dear voices mingled in song you would make me happy every time you could.

Do not read or work too much. Get a good long sleepy rest. You have been dragged from pillar to post all summer. Now, sleep late in the morning—rest all you can. Be sure & have enough to eat. Live on the fat of the land.

We will see you in a few days. We shall be in New York next Tuesday at 3.30 P.M. If no business requires immediate attention will be home Wednesday morning. Can go to Cleveland from there.

We hope the days are happy.—We send lots and lots of love. Kisses enough to cover your dear bodies.

Yours for ever, Eva & Robert

New York
Oct. 8, 1885

Dear Girls,

I am afraid that I shall not be able to see you before I go to Cleveland. I wish that Secular Union—National League & all in the place spoken of in the Bible. But I cannot get away from this horrible case. I leave poor Mother all alone at the Hoffman. I should think she would hate the place.

Maybe the day will come when we can live together. When the days will be filled with light—serene, tranquil—and we, intoxicated with each other's presence, will feel what heaven is.

Dear Girls—you are wonders. There are none like you. I am too selfish, I love to be with you and have neglected you—that is, I have kept you with me when maybe it would have been better for you to have been at school.

I could not bear to have you *ordered, controlled*—governed by anybody. You must never blame me. I love you both beyond all expression. Good-bye.—Kisses enough to cover your dear bodies.

Yours for ever, Robert

Mrs. Charles Watts, the wife of the celebrated English Rationalist, lecturer, and editor, was also a very distinguished actress in her own right. The Ingersoll family were devoted to

Mrs. Watts, and regarded her as one of their best and most loyal friends. On each of her several visits to the United States she came to have tea or dine with the Ingersolls; and she was always a welcome guest in their home.

Mrs. Watts won all hearts with her great personal charm, vivacious intelligence, wit, and contagious enthusiasm.

400 Fifth Avenue
July 5, 1888

My dear Mrs. Watts,

I hardly know how to thank you for that wonderful speech of yours on the Gladstone article. You are a friend worth having. I was glad to know that you agree with me on the " opinion " argument.

While you have praised me far, far beyond my deserts you have shown me your heart and it is the sincere and noble heart of a perfect friend.—Of course it has been read by the entire family and with one accord the verdict was that Mrs. Charles Watts is one of the best, not only, but the best and bravest of them all. From a literary point of view what you said was marvellous, beautiful, delightful.

We all send love, each of us to both of you.

Yours always, R. G. Ingersoll

Walston Hill Brown, who married Eva Robert Ingersoll, the elder daughter of Colonel and Mrs. Robert G. Ingersoll, on November 13, 1889, was a prominent banker and railway builder. He was born in Cincinnati, Ohio, on June 6, 1842, and died in Riverside, Connecticut, August 3, 1928.

The intellectual background of Robert Ingersoll's son-in-law was an exceedingly liberal one. He was a Unitarian by inheritance and personal conviction, and in later life became a thorough-going Humanist, although he never called himself by that name.

He also came of a family of Abolitionists, his father having operated a station of the " underground railroad " for the assistance of runaway slaves, and Walston was a confirmed Abolitionist on his own account.

400 Fifth Avenue
Nov. 21, '89

Dear Brother [John],

Several days ago I ought to have written you. My only excuse is that I have been far from well, having had the worst cold of my life. Eva as you know was married on the 13th inst and left the same morning for the West. At first they intended going to California—her husband having an interest in lands in that state, but they finally concluded that they would go to Ohio & Michigan—he looking after railroads with which he is connected. They are in Chicago today and we hope that they will be home next Wednesday. We are all satisfied with Eva's choice. Her husband is an excellent man, capable in every way, recognized as a man of intelligence and integrity. The best thing about him is that he is kind and gentle, considerate, generous, and good natured.

I hope that you are all in the best of health, and that the coming winter will bring you nothing but comfort. All send love to each & all.

Yours always, Robert

Butte, Aug. 9, '91

My sweet Eva,

Mother says that you are getting along the best kind and that makes us happy. Dear Eva, you know how I love you and your loving generous husband. You were made for each other and I know that you are going to be happy as long as you both shall live. How poor everything in this world is compared with happy love! What pebbles the rubies are, what common glass the diamonds! I think a hundred times a day about Eva and Walston—and I say to myself, & the words although unspoken make music in my brain—"They are happy—They love each other—He will never give her pain—She will fill his life with joy"—and these unspoken words leave a perfume in my heart. I love you both.

Maud and I are having a good deal of experience—but we are not suffering. Of course we are homesick.

In a little while we shall be home with you in your beautiful place, amid the trees—looking at river sky and hills and better than all at the faces of the ones we love. Maud sends love & kisses to you & Walston and all the family and so do I.

I want you just as soon as you read this to go to Mother—look into her splendid eyes and tell her that I love her, and then give her a good hug and a long kiss for me. Well, sweet daughter, good-bye. You are the perfect one. I love you with all my heart,

And I am yours forever

Robert

Butte, Mont.
Aug. 11th, 1891

My darling Eva,

I cannot allow this day * to pass without telling you how much you have added to the joy of my life—without telling you what a pure and perfect being you have always been.

From the moment of your birth you have been a perpetual delight. I loved you even before you were born. During all the

---

* August 11th was Robert Ingersoll's birthday.

THE LETTERS OF ROBERT G. INGERSOLL

days of your divine life you have been the impersonation of sympathy, of unselfishness, of goodness, and of all there is, or can be, of truth, generosity, beauty, tenderness, devotion, and nobility in human life.—

And so, my dear, dear daughter, on this my 58th birthday, I thank you with all my heart; and love you beyond all words.— Good-night! Love and kisses for you and yours.—

Yours for ever, Robert

Robert Ingersoll was haunted throughout his life by the thought of death. In his early years, this preoccupation with death amounted to a dread that occasionally clouded his otherwise serene and sunny intellectual sky. In later life, however, he became quietly and philosophically reconciled to this " fact in nature," even coming to regard death as a merciful, blessed release from the burdens and sorrows of the world.

July 18, '93

My dear Brother [John],

How are you all? I think of you almost every moment and of your great loss, and of the dear one who fell asleep. I am not foolish enough to think that you can be comforted by words, and yet I cannot help writing as though words might do good. I was greatly impressed by your letter in which you spoke of Father's age, and of Ruth's. How the days and years fly away! In a little while, on the 11th of next month, I shall be sixty years of age, and only a few days ago I was a child. What a riddle it all is. Life and Death, who can tell us what they are? And what is all this for—this living—this suffering—this labour and hope and love—this gold and poverty and after all, this death. Who can tell? Who can guess?

To this mystery there is no key—no clue. We must wait—and bear, and above all—hope. My dear Brother, we must meet as often as we can. We must not waste our lives apart.

Give my love to each and all, and to the dear girls.

Yours always, Robert

Pittsburg, Kansas
May 3rd, 1896

Dear Eva,

I read your beautiful letter and read it with delight. You are not prouder of your father than he is of his daughter. That would be impossible. You have made me happy for many years—every year of your loving life. There never was a better daughter, wife and mother. You seem almost out of place in this cruel and savage world. You ought to live where all is joy. Well, my dear, dear daughter we will be together soon and I shall feel your loving lips on mine. Then we shall forget the separation and all will be

237

happiness once more. I send you thousands of kisses and for your sweet babes.—Love to Walston. Kisses for sweet, perfect Mother and darling Maud.

I love you with all my heart. You are perfect.

Robert

Robert Ingersoll and Andrew Carnegie enjoyed a warm and delightful friendship which centred about their mutual love of Robert Burns. Andrew Carnegie did not confine his admiring friendship to the Colonel, as he was also a great admirer of the beautiful Eva Ingersoll; and before her marriage to Walston Hill Brown he paid persistent and devoted court to her, taking her out to drive, to the opera, and the theatre, sending her magnificent bouquets of flowers; and generally bestowing upon her all sorts of delicate and pointed attentions.

Mr. Carnegie in his *Autobiography* relates the famous story concerning Henry Ward Beecher's introduction to Miss Eva Ingersoll: " Matthew Arnold and his daughter . were our guests when in New York in 1883 . . . so that I saw a great deal, but not enough of him. . . . He expressed a desire to hear the noted preacher, Mr. Beecher; and we started for Brooklyn one Sunday morning.

" Mr. Beecher had been apprised of our coming so that after the services he might remain to meet Mr. Arnold. When I presented Mr. Arnold he was greeted warmly. Mr. Beecher expressed his delight at meeting one in the flesh whom he had long known so well in the spirit. .

" After presenting Matthew Arnold to him, I had the pleasure of presenting the daughter of Colonel Ingersoll, saying, as I did so: ' Mr. Beecher, this is the first time Miss Ingersoll has ever been in a Christian church.' He held out both hands and grasped hers, and looking straight at her and speaking slowly, said: ' Well, well, you are the most beautiful heathen I ever saw.' . . . Then: ' How's your father, Miss Ingersoll? I hope he's well. Many times he and I have stood together on the same platform, and wasn't it lucky for me we were on the same side ! ' "

Mr. Carnegie goes on to comment that: " Beecher was, indeed, a great, broad, generous man, who absorbed what was good wherever found. Herbert Spencer's philosophy, Arnold's insight, tempered with sound sense, Ingersoll's staunch support of high political ends were powers for good in the Republic. Mr. Beecher was great enough to appreciate and hail as helpful friends all of these men."

Andrew Carnegie recalls that he once asked Colonel Ingersoll, "the most effective public speaker I ever heard," to what he attributed his power. He replied, "Avoid elocutionists like snakes and be yourself!"

> 200 Madison Avenue
> Nov. 30, '96

My dear Mr. Carnegie,

I write my first letter to you to thank you for three things—1st for the life of [Fra Paolo] Sarpi that I have read with great interest and with amazement. The wonder is that in one brain there could be such a mingling—such salmagundi of Science and Superstition. How a man can perceive the inalterable succession of facts in Nature and at the same time believe in a supernatural Providence, is beyond my imagination.—2nd I thank you for calling to ask after my health—I know how valuable your time is—and I shall never forget the kindness, and

3rd I thank you for two bottles of spiritual consolation—for a liquid I have held in high esteem since first I read the glorious line—"Freedom and Whisky gang t'gither"—

With best regards to Mrs. Carnegie and your blessed self,

> Yours always, R. G. Ingersoll

> Walston, Dobbs' Ferry-on-Hudson, New York
> Sept 22nd, 1897

Dear Eva,*

Thirty-four years of unbroken kindness, of cloudless sunshine, of perpetual joy, of constant love. Thirty-four years of happy smiles, of loving looks, of gentle words, of generous deeds. Thirty-four years of perfect days—perfect as the heart of June. Thirty-four years, a flower, a palm, a poem, a star; a faultless child, a perfect woman, wife, and mother.

> R. G. Ingersoll

> Mattoon, Ill., Mch 8th, 1899

Dear Eva,†

We recd your sweet letter and the picture of the house you made for us. Grandmother and I are delighted with it. We have picked out our rooms. The parlours are fine and from the bedrooms we can see the river, the sea, or the hills. The air seems

---

* This tender and loving letter was written to his daughter Eva, on her thirty-fourth birthday.

† Robert Ingersoll's little grand-daughter, Eva Ingersoll Brown, the daughter of Mr. and Mrs. Walston Hill Brown, and the editor and author of the original (American) edition of this book.

pure and cool. We are going to plant some ivy that will run all over the sides and some honeysuckles to creep round the windows and fill the rooms with perfume.

Of course you will be there too and dear little Robin* and we will all be happy together in the house that little Eva built. Kiss Robin for us and your dear Mother. Love to Tudy and to your sweet self. We love you.—You are the sweetest girl and Robin the sweetest boy.—Kisses & hugs for you both.

Yours always, Robert & Eva

* Robin was the Colonel's pet-name for his little grandson, Robert G. Ingersoll Brown.

PART SEVEN

Ingersoll—the Humanist

THE SECULAR RELIGION, or ethical philosophy known as Humanism, comes down from the period of Protagoras— the great Greek philosopher of the fifth century B.C.— who proclaimed that " man is the measure of all things."

From that dim and distant past to the present day, this supreme liberating, intellectual, and ethical concept, despite long intervals of eclipse, has inspired and nourished the human spirit. The Roman poet, Terence, seems almost casually and unconsciously to have captured the quintessential significance of Humanism in one memorable phrase that has sounded down the centuries: " I am a man; nothing human is alien to me."

During the Dark Ages it suffered prolonged neglect, but beginning with the fifteenth-century Renaissance with its reaffirmation of the free spirit of man, the flame of Humanism has been kept alive and alight, from generation to generation, by a few fearless heretical thinkers, like Voltaire and the Encyclopædists of the eighteenth century. With the English political and scientific philosophers of the nineteenth century, following the publication of Darwin's *Origin of Species* in 1859, Humanism became a new and inescapable challenge to the intellectual world. For the first time in history the *individual man*, and his human needs, began to be given serious consideration. Humanism centred upon the paramount concern for those human needs. Humanists adhered to what C. F. Potter has called, in his *Humanism a New Religion*, their " faith in the supreme value and self-improvability of human personality." Or as Professor Julian Huxley puts it in his *Religion Without Revelation*, in " human control by human effort in accordance with human ideals " they saw the creation of a more humane and rational world.

Robert G. Ingersoll was the inheritor of this noble Humanist tradition. He realized that for the first time in history the liberating forces of science were making it possible for man to come into his own. Henceforth *man, rather than God, must be the unit and standard of value.* Man's long record of failure and depravity never discouraged Ingersoll, for he realized that only " when men in large numbers have freer access to the best fruits of civilization can we presume to say what they are capable of . . . not until human resources have been organized to bring the best in human nature, whatever it is, to expression, will we be able to decide what men and women have it in them to become " (Max Otto, *The Human Enterprise*).

Since man of necessity must live his life in this world, and, in the course of living, must perforce have contact with his fellowmen, certain basic assumptions are required to establish at least a degree of harmony and understanding among men, to the end that an orderly society may exist. This minimum of agreement concerning fundamental theories and standards of right and wrong is what is traditionally known as the moral code.

Ingersoll found a satisfactory basis for his moral code in Secularism, or Humanism, with its respect for the individual, because he cherished an abiding faith in man and his potentialities. For him, Humanism was " The Creed of Science."

" To love justice; to long for the right; to love mercy; to pity the suffering; to assist the weak; to forget wrongs, and remember benefits. To love the truth; to be sincere; to utter honest words; to love liberty; to wage relentless war against slavery in all its forms. To love wife, and child, and friend; to make a happy home; to love the beautiful in art, in nature; to cultivate the mind; to be familiar with the mighty thoughts that genius has expressed; the noble deeds of all the world; to cultivate courage and cheerfulness; to make others happy; to fill life with the splendour of generous deeds; the warmth of loving words; to discard error; to destroy prejudice; to receive new truths with gladness; to cultivate hope; to see the calm beyond the storm; the dawn beyond the night; to do the best that can be done, and then to be resigned . . ."

Humanism is the moral code which teaches that man is the unit; that he must depend upon himself and himself alone; that there is no benevolent providence to provide for his welfare; that therefore, " man must be the providence of man." He must assume full responsibility for his own life and the lives of his fellows. " If abuses are abolished, man must abolish them. If slaves are freed, man must free them. If new truths are discovered, man must discover them. . . . If justice is done; if labour is rewarded; if superstition is driven from the mind; if the defenceless are protected, and if the right finally triumphs, all must be the work of man," declared Ingersoll, the Humanist.

Likewise, he denied that any person, or any God, can save another, maintaining that each individual must save himself, and do right on his own account—that there can be no such thing as vicarious virtue. Accordingly, to his mind, the Christian dogma of the Atonement represented " a kind of moral bankruptcy." He contended that it allows man " the luxury of sinning upon a credit. . . . Whenever a man is guilty of a wicked action he says, ' charge it.' This kind of (moral) book-keeping tends to breed extravagance in sin."

Ingersoll's own moral code might be summed up in the single sentence: " Give to every human being every right that you claim for yourself." He had infinite respect for the rights and liberties of all men. However, he was careful to explain and to emphasize that the rights and liberties of each individual end where those of another begin. Thus he drew the line between liberty and licence. He believed that liberty is just another name for responsibility—that " where there is no freedom, there can be no responsibility," for where choice is not present, the moral element cannot enter into the situation. Ingersoll declared that " liberty of thought . . . of expression, is of more value than any other thing beneath the stars "; and that " what air is to the lungs, and light is to the eyes, liberty is to the soul of man."

Although he had a superb sense of the wholeness and one-ness of life, Ingersoll was primarily an *individualist*—a believer in the supreme significance and sanctity of individual per-sonality; a nonconformist after Emerson's own heart. In his view, all valid theories and patterns of thought and behaviour centre in the individual. He proclaimed that " it is a mag-nificent thing to be the sole proprietor of yourself." On the other hand, " it is humiliating to know that your ideas are all borrowed.   It is mortifying to feel that you belong to a mental mob, and cry ' crucify him ! ' because the others do.

. . . But there is grandeur in knowing that in the realm of thought you are without a chain . . . that your intellect owes no allegiance to any being, human or divine. . ''

While Ingersoll was relentlessly severe with himself, his belief in humanistic relativism and scientific determinism caused him to be extremely charitable towards the frailties and fallibilities of human beings. He held that before one would be justified in condemning another, one would have to know something of the past, the inheritance, not only of the individual, but something about all his ancestors, back to the very beginnings of human life on the earth! Since all this knowledge is obviously impossible to obtain, *humane understanding* is the only justifiable attitude for each to assume towards all.

The Theist holds that ethical codes, concepts of right and wrong, are derived from an all-wise God. Ingersoll, as a Humanist, contended that ethics are derived from human experience, from reason applied to experience. He passionately repudiated the theological insistence on the moral impotence of man, and affirmed that God, whom man creates, is utterly powerless without man—in fact, is non-existent apart from man —and thus cannot dictate the terms under which man must live. In place of the traditional divine sanctions for morality, Ingersoll believed it necessary to teach mankind the purely *natural origin* and the true nature of morals: that actions are not, as the Theist tells us, right, because God commanded them, or wrong, because he prohibited them, but that they are right because they conduce to the general welfare, or wrong because they tend to injure or destroy the health and happiness of humanity. The Humanist was convinced that our very survival as civilized human beings depends upon our learning to become ethically minded and *man-centred*, rather than to continue to be theologically minded and *God-centred*. He held that we should endeavour to ascertain moral laws and principles in precisely the same scientific spirit in which we seek to discover the facts and truths of chemistry or astronomy. In Ingersoll's opinion, '' all the relations of things to things, of forces to forces, of acts to acts, of causes to effects in the domain of matter, and in the realm of . . . mind, are just as certain, just as unchangeable as the relation between the diameter and circumference of a circle." Accordingly, "even an infinite God cannot change wrong into right, or right into wrong"; or "make ingratitude a virtue, any easier than he could make a square triangle."

The Humanist asserted that Christians would have us believe that Jesus embodied and preached an absolutely unique type of morality; and yet "every great and splendid utterance of Christ was voiced by others centuries before he lived." In many respects Ingersoll admired the teachings of Confucius more than those of any other religious philosopher. But this fact is scarcely surprising, since Confucius was the supreme, non-theistic, humanistic thinker of his time, who affirmed that all duties of man to man could be compressed into the one word "reciprocity," and who was the first to enunciate the Golden Rule, in its negative form: "Do not do unto others, what you would not have them do unto you." Ingersoll also thought Buddha sublimely great of soul, and fully as noble an apostle and exemplar of human brotherhood as was Jesus.

Unlike orthodox religionists, but like all scientific Humanists, Ingersoll was a relativist in his ethical theories—although, despite his disbelief in the Absolute, his conduct was cut to the austere pattern of the very Absolute in whose existence he disbelieved. Knowing man to be fallible, Ingersoll felt that it was fantastically presumptuous to suppose that he could possess the final, absolute truth. But Ingersoll had the spirit of his Humanistic religion which goes on an unending quest for the Good Life—for Wisdom—the blended product of intelligence and goodness. Nevertheless, the forbidding formulas, the intellectually and spiritually snobbish and omniscient systems concerning the unknown, if not the unknowable, which constitute the *letter* of orthodox religion, Ingersoll rejected with characteristic and becoming modesty and honesty.

Theists regard immortality as the fulfilment of human personality; and an eternity of happiness in heaven, as the reward, however disproportionate, for virtue in this life on earth. Humanists, generally agnostic concerning immortality, are inclined to the belief that, like the concept of God, the idea of immortality is the product of the mind and heart and poetic imagination of man. Humanists have no hope or expectation

of an infinite reward for their finite goodness in this world;
however, they hold that

> . . . the weal of the race,
> And the cause of humanity, here and now, are enough
> To give life meaning and death as well   *

However, this is not to say that Ingersoll had no longing for a
life beyond the grave. On the contrary, he ardently desired
to live again, because the thought of eternal separation from
those he loved was fraught with indescribable sorrow to him.
Nevertheless, he appreciated, all too poignantly, that it is
perfectly possible to hope without a shred of evidence to substantiate the hope.

Ingersoll—the Humanist—had as profound a sense of the
sanctities of life as any Christian—or Theist—ever possessed.
His supreme sanctity was *Love*; love of the husband for the wife,
the wife for the husband, and of both for the children; love
of friends and love of humanity. These love relationships
symbolized for him the deepest significance and beauty of
human life.

Beauty in its myriad forms was another of his sanctities.
The wonders and splendours of nature—the unconscious beauty
and grace of animals—the songs and ways of birds—enhanced his
sense of worthful life. The sublime symphonies of Beethoven,
the seraphic songs of Schubert, the glorious harmonies of Wagner
transported his soul to paradise. He was entranced by the
" marbles of the Greeks "; the immortal paintings of Raphael,
Rembrandt, Titian, Leonardo da Vinci; the majestic monuments of man-made and natural architecture. The great poets,
dramatists, novelists, creative artists, thinkers, and scientists
were regarded by Ingersoll as his eternal " creditors," because
of their contributions to the sacred values and verities of the
mind and heart.

Ingersoll felt that the quality of simple *goodness*, wherever
found, was indeed sacred in the truest sense. He believed in
the fundamental soundness and goodness of human nature,
declaring that " there are men and women whom even a God
could not corrupt." He saw the quiet, but epic beauty inherent in the eternal simplicities of life; his imagination
" transfigured the common " things of every day.

* Edgar Lee Masters, "Robert G. Ingersoll" in his *The Great Valley.*

Truth was a sanctity of sanctions to Ingersoll. He affirmed that " nothing is greater, nothing is of more importance, than to find amid the error and darkness of this life, a shining truth. . . . The noblest of occupations is to search for truth. . It is the sacred light of the soul. Every man should be true to himself . . . and in the laboratory of his own mind and for himself alone, should test the so-called facts, the theories of all the world. Truth, *in accordance with his reason,* should be his guide and master."

The sympathy and humane understanding of this Humanist embraced the globe—all sentient life. " He knew all crimes and all regrets; all virtues and their rich rewards." His quality of mercy—of compassion—was consummate; in his spirit human love attained apotheosis. An infinite sensitiveness to suffering crucified his heart upon the cross of man's in-humanity to man. He declared that no perfectly civilized person could be truly happy as long as there remains one oppressed or unhappy being in the universe. His generosity was without bound; he gave freely of his material, mental, and spiritual largesse; and the number of those who appealed to him for financial or other aid was legion. He said that he preferred to be taken advantage of by many undeserving individuals rather than to overlook one deserving person. He put into daily practice the ideal of Keats: he made " his heart the bible of his brain."

The Humanist was certain that all the evil in the world " springs from selfishness . . from cruelty." He pointed out that the single quality which differentiates the civilized from the uncivilized is that of sympathy—compassion. He raised his eloquent voice in uncompromising opposition to every form of cruelty to innocent and helpless human beings and animals. The Humanist did not subscribe to the doctrine that the end justifies the means. He was positive that that doctrine is the essence of immorality, and that it has probably done more to corrupt the mind and heart than all other intellectual rationalizations put together.

As a Humanist, Ingersoll disagreed radically with the ortho-dox theist belief that the goal of life is " to glorify God, and enjoy him for ever." On the contrary, he held that "it is the task of intelligence to ascertain the conditions of (human) happiness, and when found, the truly wise will live in accordance with them "; for " happiness is the only good." And by happiness he meant: " Well-being, in the highest and noblest forms." He said that " wisdom is the science of happiness "; that " the place to be happy is here; the time to be happy is now; and the way to be happy is to make others happy."

His impregnable common sense told him that it is necessary to keep both feet on the ground. He possessed the spiritual sportsmanship which characterizes the true Humanist. He loved life, and lived it with relish and gusto in the midst of a universe which he regarded as utterly indifferent to man, his aims, and aspirations. Enjoying perfect mental and moral health, Ingersoll had no need of the crutches of theology or the illusions of supernaturalism.

The spirit of caste—all artificial barriers which divide men from one another, all prejudices of race, creed, class, or colour—were anathema to him. He was democratic as the sun, yet spiritually fastidious to the core of his being. Ingersoll might be called an uncompromising ethicist, in so far as he himself was concerned, although he was infinitely charitable and lenient towards others. He maintained that the greatest happiness comes from reaching " with thought and deed the ideal in your brain." That it is necessary to be good, to do right, in order to be happy; and that no one escapes the consequences of his actions. His morality was not a thing apart—it was integral to his whole personality—to his every thought, emotion, and action. Yet there was no sense of strain or oppressiveness in the Ingersollian ethics. Instead, there was a spontaneity, a joyousness akin to the laughter of children, or the exfoliation of summer leafage.

Ingersoll had implicit faith in science; in the education of the mind, together with the education of the heart. He believed that the most essential of all education is the *culture of the heart*—the building of honest and unselfish character. He was convinced that when the heart becomes educated along with the mind, many seemingly difficult if not insoluble individual and social problems may well become automatically adjusted and settled. " Intelligence, guided by kindness, is the only possible saviour of mankind," he held.

In his appreciation and glorification of science he took it

for granted, as did almost all his contemporaries, that science would be placed at the service of human needs and well-being, not prostituted to the uses of destruction and death. He was sufficiently the social and economic radical to say that those who use the instruments of production should own them as well, to the end that all men should share in the wealth and abundance of the world.

This, of course, is good Socialist doctrine; and the undoubted fact is that Ingersoll did entertain some unmistakably socialistic ideas, notwithstanding his aversion to Socialism as he understood it. To him, it meant regimentation and the consequent destruction of individual liberty and independence, which, in his sight, was indeed the ultimate heresy. Socialism signified to his mind, rightly or wrongly, what Totalitarianism means to us today.

The whole intellectual approach of Ingersoll to practical social problems was drastically different from the Socialist approach. For the Humanist had little or no faith in legal and legislative panaceas and remedies for re-making the world, feeling that law and government can help almost exclusively in negative ways to better the lot of the average man. He had no faith in ready-made nostrums of any sort. He was an evolutionist—a gradualist; was never deluded into believing that the millennium would arrive overnight. But he did believe that something very like it might come some day, provided that we wish and work for it hard and intelligently enough.

Children had no greater champion than Robert Ingersoll. He declared that they should be allowed to develop like flowers in the sunlight; and insisted that they should never be coerced or punished. "Let the children have liberty. Be honest and fair with them; be just and tender, and they will make you rich in love and joy." He was a bitter enemy of child labour, as of all forms of exploitation of and cruelty to children.

Ingersoll contended that "every good man, every good woman, should try to do away with war, to stop the appeal to savage force." He realized that war is a desecration of all moral values; and he knew that if it is ever to be abolished, nations, like individuals, must be compelled to submit their differences to a disinterested third party—a world court of justice; and that the decisions of this court must be absolutely binding upon the nations involved. " This court should be in perpetual session. Its members should be selected by the various governments to be affected by its decisions, and at the command and disposal of this court, the rest of Christendom being disarmed, there should be a military force sufficient to carry its judgments into effect. There should be no other excuse, no other business for an army or navy in the civilized world."

Good practical idealist that he was, most of our current welfare programmes and laws, such as old-age pensions, work-men's compensation, maternity, health, accident, and un-employment insurance, higher wages and shorter hours, were anticipated and endorsed by Ingersoll. He stood for a more equitable distribution of wealth, better relations between capital, management, and labour. He felt that wealth should be regarded as a public trust, and insisted that there is something wrong with a society " where those who do the most, have the least."

Through such basic reforms growing out of the humanistic attitude towards life, " we are laying the foundations of the grand temple of the future—not the temple of all the gods, but of all the people—wherein, with appropriate rites, will be celebrated the religion of Humanity. We are doing what little we can to hasten the coming of the day when society shall cease producing millionaires and mendicants—gorged in-dolence and famished industry—truth in rags, and superstition robed and crowned. We are looking for the time when the useful shall be the honourable, and when *Reason* throned upon the world's brain, shall be King of Kings, and God of Gods."

BIRTH CONTROL

Perhaps the surest way to achieve true civilization, he thought, would be " for woman to become the mistress of herself "—of her own body and her own spirit. Through the emancipation of woman, " ignorance, poverty, and vice " might " stop populating the world. . . . Science must put it in the power of woman to decide for herself whether she will or will not become a mother "; and " intelligence " must become " the master of passion." Through the intelligent practice of birth control and voluntary parenthood, disease and crime may yet be prevented from conquering the world.

New York, December 7th, 1886

Hon. Ralph Plumb,
Streator, Illinois.

My dear Friend:

As you say, the people have been educated, and they are now able to discuss with their so-called superiors, all questions affecting the welfare of mankind. There is one thing that troubles me, and that is this: Thousands and thousands of people are incapable of taking care of themselves. The world is filled with deformities. Poverty and want and vice beget children. In the great cities, the gutter is a nursery. The tendency to commit crime is transmitted. This is one of the terrible facts. We must have, before the world is saved, a religion of the body. There must be a public sentiment, so strong, so powerful, that disease will not perpetuate itself; and there must be a public sentiment so strong, that . . . criminals will not be allowed to perpetuate themselves.

This, however, is a great subject, and a letter must of necessity be too short for discussion. . . .

Society must protect itself; but before it does, or can, it must know enough to know that everything is naturally produced—that today is the child of yesterday, and the mother of tomorrow.

Yours very truly, R. G. Ingersoll

TOLERATION

Although Ingersoll appreciated the genius of George Washington, his admiration for him was tempered by important reservations. Ingersoll never forgave Washington for his refusal to rescue Thomas Paine when he was imprisoned and under sentence of death in France because he had had the moral courage to vote in the French Convention to spare the life of Louis XVI. Nor did the Humanist approve Washington's advocacy of an established church in Virginia, which was defeated chiefly through the active opposition of Thomas Jefferson.

John Russell Young, to whom the following letter is addressed, was a distinguished American writer and journalist (1841–99).

New York, March 26th, 1888

Mr. John Russell Young,
Herald Office, City.

My dear Friend:

I have read with great pleasure your reply to the article, " The Genius of Battle."

I agree with you perfectly, that Washington led an army that

251

fought for political independence, and not for the liberty of the individual, or for liberty as a principle.

Of course, every man in jail is in favour of liberty, as a prejudice,—but it takes a far grander man who is not in jail to fight and suffer for a man who is.

I agree with you also in your statement that what gives dignity and splendour to the victory of the government in the Civil War is that it was a victory for liberty. Personally, I think far more of the liberty of the individual, than I do of the political independence of a nation. If the individuals are not free, it makes but very little difference who the master is. I think your answer complete.

Yours very truly, R. G. Ingersoll

A warm and long-standing friendship existed between Colonel Ingersoll and Mr. Courtlandt Palmer, urbane man of the world, publicist, and Freethinker; each enjoyed the other's emancipated, liberal outlook on life and things. Ingersoll participated in several meetings of the celebrated Nineteenth Century Club, of which Mr. Palmer was the Founder and President.

On May 8, 1888, when the club met in the Metropolitan Opera House, Ingersoll was one of three speakers taking part in a discussion on the subject of " The Limitations of Toleration," the two other speakers being the Hon. Frederic R. Coudert and Ex-Governor Stewart L. Woodford.

Apropos of this debate, Robert Ingersoll's irrepressible and ever-admiring friend, Walt Whitman, had this to say: " Ingersoll uses them both up as a matter of course—does it easily, nonchalantly—sits back in his chair—I should imagine this way —shuts his eyes: as easily as this, sweeps them right and left with a movement of his arm."

The Colonel delivered the eulogy at the funeral services for Courtlandt Palmer.

March 26 (?), 1888

My dear Palmer:

On the question of " Limitations of Toleration," I shall insist:

1. That thought is a necessary, natural product—the result of what we call " impressions," made through the medium of the senses upon the brain—not forgetting the effect of heredity.

2. That no human being is accountable to any being—human or divine—for his thoughts.

3. That human beings have a certain interest in the thoughts

of each other, and that if one being undertakes to tell his thoughts to another, he should be honest.

4. That all have an equal right to express their thoughts upon all subjects.

5. That for one man to say to another, " I tolerate you," is an assumption of superiority, and is not a disclaimer, but a waiver, of the right to persecute.

6. Each man has the same right to express to the whole world his ideas, that the rest of the world has to express their thoughts to him.

Very truly yours, R. G. Ingersoll

CENSORSHIP

When the Rev. Alexander Clark, an orthodox minister, died, Col. Ingersoll paid him the following glowing tribute, out of gratitude for the Reverend Mr. Clark's spirit of friendliness and fair play.

A Tribute to the Rev. Alexander Clark.

Washington, D. C., July 13th, 1879

Upon the grave of the Reverend Alexander Clark I wish to place one flower. Utterly destitute of cold, dogmatic pride, that often passes for the love of God; without the arrogance of the elect; simple, free, and kind—this earnest man made me his friend by being mine. I forgot that he was a Christian, and he seemed to forget that I was not, while each remembered that the other was at least a man.

Frank, candid, and sincere, he practised what he preached, and looked with the holy eyes of charity upon the failings and mistakes of men. He believed in the power of kindness, and spanned with divine sympathy the hideous gulf that separates the fallen from the pure. Giving freely to others the rights that he claimed for himself, it never occurred to him that his God hated a brave and honest unbeliever. He remembered that even an Infidel has rights that love respects; that hatred has no saving power, and that in order to be a Christian it is not necessary to become less than a human being. He knew that no one can be maligned into kindness; that epithets cannot convince . . . and that the finger of scorn never points towards heaven.

For this man I felt the greatest possible regard. In spite of the taunts and jeers of his brethren, he publicly proclaimed that he would treat Infidels with fairness and respect; that he would endeavour to convince them by argument and win them with love. He insisted that the God he worshipped loved the well-being even of an Atheist. In this grand position he stood almost alone A few more such clergymen might drive calumny from the lips of faith. . . .

The heartiness and kindness with which this generous man treated me can never be excelled. He admitted that I had not lost, and could not lose, a single right by the expression of my honest thought. . . .

His sympathies were not confined within the prison of a creed, but ran out and over the walls like vines, hiding the cruel rocks and rusted bars with leaf and flower. He could not echo with his heart the fiendish sentence of eternal fire. In spite of book and creed he read between the lines the words of tenderness and love, with promises for all the world. Above, beyond, the dogmas of his church—humane even to the verge of heresy—causing some to doubt his love for God because he failed to hate his unbelieving fellow-men, he laboured for the welfare of mankind, and to this work gave up his life with all his heart.

Washington, D. C., July 24th, '78

Rev. Alexander Clark.

My dear Friend:

In the first place, I thank you from the bottom of my heart, for the kind and generous things you have been pleased to say concerning me.

I have not been used to this kind of treatment by the clergy, and I hardly know what to say. For assault, for calumny, for misrepresentation, I am armed, and endeavour to keep every weapon in the arsenal ready for use. But to be appreciated by a clergyman who extends the hand of friendship, who has upon his face a smile, and who speaks to me as though I had the rights of a human being, astonishes me to that extent that I hardly know what to say.

After all, humanity is above all the creeds, above all the dogmas. These doctrines, these theories, through all ages have begotten hatred. After all, the man is more than the theologian, and one good action is better than a thousand beliefs.

I believe you, by nature, to be a frank, free, generous, and humane man. You are not, in my judgment indebted to religion but religion is indebted to you. You are, I know, perfectly honest in your opinions, and yet you allow to others the liberty you claim for yourself.

Now, I wish to convince you that you are not kind, and truthful, and generous because of your religious belief; and to do this, I need only call your attention to what happened since you were kind enough to speak of me, in your paper, as one having the rights of a human being.

I want to convince you that real religion has nothing to do with belief. That a very bad man can be an exceedingly good theologian. That a man may believe every word of the bible, and never do a good action.

But I did not intend to say as much as I have upon this subject.

I want simply to thank you for your kindness, and to assure you that I shall always hold you in the highest respect.

There is one thing about which you make a mistake. I never signed any petition that obscene matter be allowed to go in the United States mails. I simply want the law, so that the right of conscience, and of the press, shall not be interfered with. That is all. No man living despises the publishers of and dealers in literature that tends to pollute the imaginations of men, more thoroughly than I do. I want the laws so that pure men may publish pure thoughts, upon any and all subjects, and that all such publications be admitted to the mails. I do not want a system of espionage established. I do not want some clerk to say whether or not a book of mine can be carried through the mails. You will at once see my position. . . .

Well, I have written enough. If you ever visit Washington, come and see me. We certainly can exchange thoughts without bitterness; and each can frankly tell the other what he really thinks, and remain, notwithstanding all this, friends.

It seems very strange that I should thank an orthodox minister; but I do. Strange that I should really feel as though I wanted to know one better; but I do.

Yours truly, R. G. Ingersoll

CAPITAL PUNISHMENT

Ingersoll believed that there is reason to hope for the reformation of criminals, and for the reduction of crime, through changing conditions in radical and realistic fashion. He conceded that the criminal is a dangerous individual, and that " society has the right to protect itself " against him. But Ingersoll's idea was that the prison, instead of being a place of punishment, " should be a school. The convicts should be educated " in right thinking and right doing. Prisoners should be permitted to work, and should be paid a reasonable sum for their labour. He felt that only a superior type of men should be placed in charge of prisons; that they should be " philanthropists and philosophers . . The prisoner, having been taught, we will say, for five years—taught the underlying principles of conduct, of the naturalness and harmony of virtue, of the discord of crime; having been convinced that society has no hatred, that nobody wishes to punish, to degrade, or to rob him; and being at the time of his discharge paid a reasonable price for his labour; being allowed by law to change his name, so that his identity will not be preserved, he could go out of the prison a friend of the government."

However, Ingersoll thought that congenital, hopeless criminals should either " be imprisoned for life; or they should be put upon some island, some place where they can be guarded, where it may be that by proper effort they could support themselves, the men on one island, the women on another. Such people should not populate the earth. Neither the diseases nor the deformities of the mind or body should be perpetuated. Life at the fountain should not be polluted."

New York, Jan'y 9, 1889

J. M. Frost, Esq.,
388 Broadway, City.

My dear Sir:
I do not know how Mr. Jones came to address me on the subject of the execution of criminals by the application of electricity. I know nothing of the subject except in a very general way, and have had no correspondence with those having the matter in charge, or with those engaged in experiments for the purpose of ascertaining the best and most painless method.

I agree with you, however, that the execution should be as painless as possible. I do not believe that the State should be revengeful. I think the treatment of criminals in all nations, that I know anything about, has been and is barbarous, and that the tendency has been and is to produce crime.

Yours truly, R. G. Ingersoll

New York, April 29th, '90

Gen'l Newton M. Curtis,
Albany, N. Y.

My dear Friend:
I have read with a great deal of interest your speech in the General Assembly, on the abolition of the death penalty—and I believe it will do great good.

I agree with you that capital punishment debases and demoralizes the public conscience. It destroys, or tends to destroy, a regard for human life. At the same time, I believe that before the death penalty can be abolished, we must destroy the foundation on which it now rests. As long as people believe in the inspiration of the Bible, they will quote, "whoso sheddeth man's blood, by man shall his blood be shed"; and it is very hard to conceive how a God who expects to burn a majority of his children for ever, could object to a few beings hanged in this world.

Your friend, R. G. Ingersoll ·

Nov. 29th, '90

Col. W. E. Horn,
The Tribune,
Rome, Ga.

My dear Sir:
    Accept my thanks for " An Appeal to Humanity."
    The treatment of convicts, in many of the states [of the U.S.A.] is infamous beyond the power of words to express. It is a system that not only compels the keepers to become criminals, but sows the seeds of crime on every hand. The tendency is to beget in tender hearts a hatred of authority, and of what is called law.

Yours very truly, R. G. Ingersoll

CHILDREN

If there was anything that aroused Ingersoll's burning indignation more than all else, it was unkindness and cruelty to children. He said that throughout history until comparatively recent times, women have been slaves; but that children have been the slaves of slaves.

He insisted that " children have the same rights that we have, and we ought to treat them as though they were human beings "; that they should be " reared with love, with kindness, with tenderness, and not with brutality. When your little child tells a lie, do not rush at him as though the world were about to go into bankruptcy. Be honest with him. A tyrant father will have liars for his children. . . . A lie is born of tyranny upon the one hand and weakness upon the other; and when you rush at a poor little boy with a club in your hand, of course he lies." Ingersoll declared that he thanked Mother Nature that she had " put ingenuity enough in the brain of a child, when attacked by a brutal parent, to throw up a little breastwork in the shape of a lie." Some people, he claimed, " acted as though they thought that when the Saviour said, ' Suffer little children to come unto me, for of such is the kingdom of heaven,' he had a raw-hide under his mantle, and made that remark simply to get the children within striking distance."

A Milwaukee merchant wrote to Colonel Ingersoll asking his ideas as to the training and treatment of children.

Washington, D. C., April 21st, 1885

Dear Sir:
    In reply to your inquiry, I am very sorry that the prevalent ideas on the government of children are wrong. Children are

" governed " too much. We expect too much from them, and use them too much as the subjects of our moral experiments. Victims of virtuous vivisections, we notice too closely all the unruly acts of children, sit over them constantly as inspectors and spies. They should have freedom of action, even if they now and then abuse it.

In time they will learn better if we do not elevate their little faults and peccadilloes into awful acts of moral delinquency and distinguished examples of total depravity. By constantly showing our horror at their conduct and emphasizing our disapprobation, by threatening them with punishment and inflicting it, we stir up the worst that is in them and keep alive the fires of opposition and insubordination. In time the evil propensities of children will die out if they are not everlastingly noticed and punished. As to your two-year-old boy, " throwing everything he can lay his hands on " at somebody or some thing, take a good deal of trouble to keep things out of his reach, and when you fail to do this, let him throw. He will soon get tired, cease to think it fun, and stop of his own accord if you do not notice him too much, and if no one throws back. As to his " striking when he is angry," let him strike, but see that no one strikes back. His little blows cannot do much harm, and he will tire of striking when no one makes any account of it. This plan may take a good deal of time and patience. Of course it will. The parent who cannot give these is not fit to have children.

A child is worth infinitely more than any business or any money, and properly treated will pay a handsome dividend every time.

As to punishment by the rod, no good came of it, or ever will. It appeals to the lowest animal instinct, to brutish fear. The use of the whip fosters hypocrisy, deceit, lying, and fawning. It is the tyrant's weapon, the slave's inheritance. It is the lazy resort of power to command obedience that should only come of love; at least obedience that is good for anything to the child or the parents. I would infinitely rather my children should grow up " unruly " and " disobedient " than be feared by them, a tyrant in my own house. I should expect them to improve upon my example and be tyrants over others. I would rather die than strike my child, even with my hand, much less with whip or rod. My children never had from me an unkind word, and they never gave me an unkind word. Depend upon it, the Bible idea of using the rod is born of barbarism. Reject it as tyrannical, contemptible, detestable, and let your child grow up in the atmosphere of loving kindness always.

Yours very truly, R. G. Ingersoll

FREEDOM OF THOUGHT

Ingersoll received innumerable letters from young men all over the country and from Europe, Asia, and Africa, expressing interest in and enthusiastic agreement with his ideas and teachings. These letters never failed to bring the Agnostic keen pleasure, and a psychological "lift" which was much appreciated.

Washington, D. C.
July 31, 1879

Chas. E. Cochran, Esq.,
Philadelphia.

My dear Sir:
I know of no better religion than for a man to live in accordance with his highest ideas. The man who retains his own self-respect through life need have nothing to fear after death. If there is a God, I am satisfied he cannot afford to damn an honest man.

I hope you will be absolutely true to yourself, not only in the world of thought, but in that of action as well. Nothing pleases me more than to receive letters from young men who have made up their minds to do their own thinking and to break the fetters of custom and superstition.

Yours truly, R. G. Ingersoll

Toronto, Canada
January 8th, 1887

Mr. Charles Watts, Editor
Secular Thought,
London, England.

A liberal paper should be edited by a liberal man. And by the word liberal I mean not only free, not only one who thinks for himself, not only one who has escaped from the prisons of custom and creed, but one who is candid, intelligent, and kind— that is to say, liberal towards others.

This liberal editor should not for ever play upon one string, no matter how wonderful the music. He should not have his attention for ever fixed upon one question—that is to say, he should not look through a reversed telescope and narrow his horizon to that degree that he sees only one thing.

To know that the Bible is the literature of a barbarous people, to know that it is uninspired, to be certain that the supernatural cannot and does not exist—all this is but the beginning of wisdom. This only lays the foundation for unprejudiced observation. To kill weeds, to fell forests, to drive away or exterminate wild beasts —this is preparatory to doing something of greater value. Of course the weeds must be killed, the forests must be felled, and the beasts must be destroyed before the building of homes and the cultivation of fields.

A liberal paper should not discuss theological questions alone. Intelligent people everywhere have given up most of the old superstitions. They have pretty well made up their minds what is false, and they want to know something that is true. For this reason a liberal paper should keep abreast of the discoveries of the human mind. No science should be neglected; no fact should be overlooked. Inventions should be described and understood. And not only this, but the beautiful in thought, in form and colour, should be preserved. The paper should be filled with things calculated to interest thoughtful, intelligent, and serious people. There should be a column for children as well as for men.

Above all, it should be perfectly kind and candid. In discussion there should be no place for hatred, no opportunity for slander. A personality is always out of place. An angry man can neither reason himself nor perceive the reason of what another says. The orthodox world has always dealt in personalities. Every minister can answer the argument of an opponent by attacking the character of the opponent. This example should never be followed by a liberal man. Nobody can be bad enough to prove that the Bible is uninspired, and nobody can be good enough to prove that it is the word of God. These facts have no relation.

Nothing should be asserted that is not known. Nothing should be denied, the falsity of which has not been, or cannot be, demonstrated. Opinions are simply given for what they are worth. They are guesses, and one guesser should give to another guesser all the right of guessing that he claims for himself. Upon the great questions of origin, of destiny, of immortality, of punishment and reward in other worlds, every honest man must say " I do not know." Upon these questions, this is the creed of intelligence. Nothing is harder to bear than the egotism of ignorance, and the arrogance of superstition. The man who has some knowledge of the difficulties surrounding these subjects, who knows something of the limitations of the human mind, must of necessity be mentally modest. And this condition of mental modesty is the only one consistent with individual progress.

Above all, and over all, a liberal paper should teach the absolute freedom of mind, the utter independence of the individual, the perfect liberty of speech. We should remember that the world is as it must be; that the present is the necessary offspring of the past; that the future must be what the present makes it, and that the real work of the reformer—of the philanthropist—is to change the conditions of the present, to the end that the future may be better.

Yours always, R. G. Ingersoll

New York
March 18th, 1888

F. E. Ormsby, Esq.,
Dubuque, Iowa.

My dear Friend:
I did not happen to read your letter of the 15th, until a moment ago, and did not, for a moment, dream that you had been placed in an unpleasant position growing out of the publication

of my letter to you in regard to the attack made upon me by the Rev. C. O. Brown.

Of course I should not think of wasting time to answer the calumnies of the pulpit. Life is too short to answer them all, and eternity would be somewhat cramped.

. . . I never signed the petition in question, [but] I would have signed it had it been presented to me—because I think it of immense importance to the people that the mails should be free—that they should not be tampered with—and the petition asks for a repeal of the laws, unless they can be so amended as not to interfere with the rights of conscience.

Anyone not filled to overflowing with prejudice, can see the correctness of this position. Of course, I never was, and never can be, in favour of allowing obscene literature to be sold or sent through the mails. I have said this on many occasions, and everyone who knows anything about me, knows my views.

But I despise any system of espionage. I despise all the fraudulent and deceitful means adopted to catch people in some offence. I hate decoy letters, and the thousand methods employed in the name of virtue, for leading others into temptation. It would be ten thousand times better to have all laws on the subject repealed, than to have the ones enforced by such men as have been engaged in that business.

Books, papers, instruments—plainly obscene, should be destroyed—and the persons who make them, or vend them, or print them, should be punished. But you know that there is a vast difference of opinion as to what is moral, or immoral. Thousands of people regard the greatest, the noblest, and the purest works of art, as immoral. Ministers regard the works of Shakespeare as obscene—look upon the theatre as immoral—regard the opera as the enemy of virtue.

Of course it is not desirable to have laws that can be enforced in such a way as to destroy the beautiful. Neither do we want hypocrites and prudes clothed with the power to decide such questions.

Every Minister who has charged me with being in favour of the dissemination of obscene literature, knew that he told a falsehood—knew that he was simply a slanderer and calumniator.

For instance: Thousands of people are opposed to Capital Punishment—but they are not in favour of murder. Many good men believe that there should be no laws for the collection of debts—yet they are honest men, and pay their debts, and they are not for the repeal of present laws to the end that men may have the opportunity of cheating their neighbours, but they really believe that more debts would be paid—that it would be important then to each person to make and maintain a good character, to the end that he might have credit.

Many people are in favour of granting divorces for many causes, and yet they are not the apologists, or the friends, of vice—they believe that a marriage without love, is immoral—they believe that children born of parents who hate each other, are victims, and pay the penalty of the faults of others.

Many people believe that liberty is of great importance. Some are so bigoted that they would blot the sun from the sky, simply to keep weeds from growing, and would charge all persons opposed to the destruction of the sun, with being friends of weeds—when the truth is, they are simply the friends of corn and wheat, of sunshine and life.

Some of the best people in this country regarded the legislation in respect to the mails, as dangerous . . . believed that it was dangerous to clothe irresponsible agents with the power of saying what should, or should not, be carried in the mails. Personally, I occupied a middle ground. I wanted the law so that infidel works should not be classed with the immoral and obscene. In all the old English Statutes the immoral, the obscene, the blasphemous, were all classed together. Paine's great work called *The Rights of Man* was embraced in these Statutes, and was denounced as immoral, because it was infidel. Decisions of the same character have been made in this country, and our Statutes are substantial copies of the old English Statutes.

Certainly, nothing can be more absurd than to call atheistic or infidel works, "immoral." The works of Voltaire, of Thomas Paine, and some of my own lectures, were not allowed to pass through the Custom Houses in Canada, the decision being that they were embraced by the words of a Statute substantially like our own.

Under our Statute, some of the most beautiful works of art have been condemned, and men have been fined and imprisoned for selling photographs of the purest and most beautiful creations of the brush and chisel.

As I said before, I have always occupied a middle ground—that is to say, I have been in favour of punishing any man who sent obscene things through the mails—and I have always been in favour of the destruction of such matter. But where the books, or the pictures, were not clearly obscene, I have always been opposed to clothing any agent with the power of making a final decision of questions that should be submitted only to the refined, the cultivated, and the competent. And as to books and pamphlets in which the religion of the day is attacked, these I have always insisted should be as freely carried as works written on the other side.

One word more. The petition about which all this fuss has been made, emphatically called attention to the fact that the rights of conscience were being ignored, and asked for a modification of the law. The petition also stated that if the law could not be modified so as not to interfere with the rights of conscience, then it ought to be repealed . . . .

The ministers, the clergy, the parsons—being utterly and entirely unable to answer my arguments against the miraculous character of their religion, and against the authenticity of their sacred volume ! —have endeavoured to revenge themselves by attacking my character. Nothing is more natural than for a defeated priest to resort to calumny. . . .

Yours very truly, R. G. Ingersoll

The Improved Man

A three-cornered symposium on *The Improved Man*, conducted by Colonel Ingersoll, Judge Albion Winegar Tourgee, and Dr. Daniel Bennett St. John Roosa, was held in the columns of the New York *World* in February, 1890. The following article was Ingersoll's contribution.

The Improved Man will be in favour of universal liberty—that is to say, he will be opposed to all kings and nobles, to all privileged classes. He will give to all others the rights that he claims for himself. He will neither bow nor cringe, nor accept bowing and cringing from others. He will be neither master nor slave, neither prince nor peasant—simply man.

He will be the enemy of all caste, no matter whether its foundation be wealth, title or power, and of him it will be said: " Blessed is that man who is afraid of no man and of whom no man is afraid."

The Improved Man will be in favour of universal education. He will believe it the duty of every person to shed all the light he can, to the end that no child may be reared in darkness. By education he will mean the gaining of useful knowledge, the development of the mind along the natural paths that lead to human happiness.

He will not waste his time in ascertaining the foolish theories of extinct peoples nor in studying the dead languages for the sake of understanding the theologies of ignorance and fear, but he will turn his attention to the affairs of life, and will do his utmost to see to it that every child has an opportunity to learn the demonstrated facts of science, the true history of the world, the great principles of right and wrong applicable to human conduct—the things necessary to the preservation of the individual and of the state, and such arts and industries as are essential to the preservation of all.

He will also endeavour to develop the mind in the direction of the beautiful—of the highest art—so that the palace in which the mind dwells may be enriched and rendered beautiful, to the end that these stones, called facts, may be turned to statues.

The Improved Man will believe only in the religion of this world. He will have nothing to do with the miraculous and supernatural. He will find that there is no room in the universe for these things. He will know that happiness is the only good, and that everything that tends to the happiness of sentient beings is good, and that to do the things—and no other—that add to the happiness of man is to practise the highest possible religion. His motto will be: " Sufficient unto each world is the evil thereof." He will know that each man should be his own priest, and that the brain is the real cathedral. He will know that in the realm of mind there is no authority—that majorities in this mental world can settle nothing—that each soul is the sovereign of its own world, and that it cannot abdicate without degrading itself. He will not bow to numbers or force, neither to antiquity nor custom. He, standing under the flag of nature, under the blue and stars, will decide for himself. He will not endeavour by prayers and supplications, by fastings and genuflections, to change the mind of the " Infinite " or alter the course of nature, neither will he employ others to do these things in his place. He will have no confidence in the religion of idleness, and will give no part of what he earns to support parson or priest, archbishop or pope. He will know that honest labour is the highest form of prayer. He will spend no time in ringing bells, or swinging censers, or in chanting the litanies of barbarism, but he will appreciate all that is artistic—that is beautiful—that tends to refine and ennoble the human race. He will not live a life of fear. He will stand in awe neither of man nor ghosts. He will enjoy not only the sunshine of life, but will bear with fortitude the darkest days. He will have no fear of death. About the grave there will be no terrors, and his life will end as serenely as the sun rises.

The Improved Man will be satisfied that the supernatural does not exist—that behind every fact, every thought and dream is an efficient cause. He will know that every human action is a necessary product, and he will also know that men cannot be reformed by punishment, by degradation or by revenge. He will regard those who violate the laws of nature and the laws of states as the victims of conditions, of circumstances, and he will do what he can for the well-being of his fellow-men.

The Improved Man will not give his life to the accumulation of wealth. He will find no happiness in exciting the envy of his neighbours. He will not care to live in a palace, while others who are good, industrious, and kind are compelled to huddle in huts and dens. He will know that great wealth is a great burden, and that to accumulate beyond the actual needs of a reasonable human being is to increase not wealth, but responsibility and trouble.

The Improved Man will find his greatest joy in the happiness of others, and he will know that the home is the real temple. He will believe in the democracy of the fireside, and will reap his greatest reward in being loved by those whose lives he has enriched.

The Improved Man will be self-poised, independent, candid, and free. He will be a scientist. He will observe, investigate, experiment, and demonstrate. He will use his sense and his senses. He will keep his mind open as the day to the hints and suggestions of nature. He will always be a student, a learner, and a listener—a believer in intellectual hospitality. In the world of his brain there will be continuous summer, perpetual seed-time, and harvest. Facts will be the foundation of his faith. In one hand he will carry the torch of truth, and with the other, raise the fallen.

Robert G. Ingersoll

Walston, Dobbs' Ferry-on-Hudson
July 31st, '93

My dear Traubel,

You are in the Ideal—that lovely realm where there are no petty jealousies and ambitions, spites and hatreds—where the lowest do not insist on having the highest places. So, in your wonderful lines on *A Face*, you are in the ideal world. Such *A Face* you have seen only within yourself. It is subjective, and yet I am greatly flattered that it has been dedicated to me. The lines are as elemental—as cosmic as Whitman. .

It does seem to me that every man seeks his own good. The way he goes, the means he uses depend on his idea of good—and on the kind of man he is, and on his surroundings. If he is intelligent in the highest sense he will be good, and if good and intelligent he will know that his highest good can be attained only through the happiness of others, and by means that tend to better the condition of the race. It seems to me that intelligence (enough of it) will cause the selfish and the generous to act in the same way. Some men are so, that they find delight in giving happiness to others, and some are so that they find delight in inflicting pain. What is the real difference between these men? Shakespeare says that there is no darkness but ignorance. But this does not explain the difference in men. There are temperament, disposition, deformity of brain. In other words, some, most it may be, are born failures and nothing can redeem them—nothing for them but to pass away. The first thing is to be born right—the next, to grow up in the climate of kindness and refinement, and the next, to be " really " educated—taught the useful. The living failures cannot be saved. This is the reason that the work of raising the race seems so enormous and the time for its accomplishment so long. This is why I say that one man can do so little no matter how great he may be. Still, I believe that the world is slowly advancing in spite of theology, superstition, and the countless vagaries and vices of mankind. I want to do the little that I can to increase the light and to scatter the seeds of kindness. I feel grateful to the great souls who have given us the light and liberty that we enjoy—to those who have battled king and priest and prejudice and ignorance. But think of what remains to be done! Think of how millions still kneel before the idols of wood and stone—before the altars of ignorance and hypocrisy.

This country is far better than when I was a boy, but the eagerness with which men lynch and mob their fellows makes me almost despair of the Republic. And yet I am sure that the world is growing better. And I am also sure that men like you are sowing good seed and that the harvest will come some time. . . .

Perhaps Civilization and Savagery pursue each other like light and darkness around the globe. Perhaps after a time the soil occupied by a nation—a people—wears out and the nation goes down mentally and physically, and then the land lies idle for centuries getting ready for a better race. But whatever the fact may be I know that our duties are all within our reach and that each can do a little towards hastening the coming of the better day.

Yours always, R. G. Ingersoll

Walston, Dobbs' Ferry-on-Hudson
Aug. 17th, '93

My dear Traubel,

I read your beautiful letter in which you so wonderfully overestimate the little I have done or can do.

You are wrong: I can do but little—not enough to talk about. Here is a case in point; we are in the midst of financial and industrial disaster. Thousands of men are being thrown out of employment—banks are closing and on every hand is disastrous failure. Now, what can one man do?—The wisest cannot tell what the causes are of this condition—neither can they suggest a cure. Countless forces are at work—forces below the surface—forces that we do not perceive and these forces determine the destiny of the individual and the nation. It is, when I think of the complexity and secrecy of these forces, that I feel helpless—and conclude that he who plants the seed will never see a leaf or bud. And yet I believe in doing—in the blessed gospel of work. And I believe that all our duties are here, in this world. But the work seems so vast and endless. It is said that the "Banks" off Newfoundland were made by the dirt and rocks that fell from icebergs as they journeyed South. But think of the millions of years all this required. It may be that the distance from protoplasm to man was not as great as it will be from man to gentleman. And yet I am full of hope for the future, although I know that the day will not come until many centuries after I am dead. Yet I am willing and anxious to do what I can to teach people to think and to destroy the phantom of superstition.

The "Plan" of Nature I detest. Competition, and struggle, the survival of the strongest, of those with the sharpest claws and longest teeth. Life feeding on life with ravenous, merciless hunger —every leaf a battlefield—war everywhere. No wonder that man has believed in devils.

And yet in this darkness there has been a little light, the light of love and virtue. And in every age some heroic man has carried the torch. We have certainly advanced in the years that are dead, and we are certainly going forward now, and I firmly believe that the pace is growing swifter day by day.

266

But I am depressed by the weakness of the individual—one man can do so little and the harvest is so far away.

Sometimes I almost despair of the race. When I see thousands of people, some of them educated, kissing a supposed bone of St. Anne, now, at the close of the nineteenth century, here, in the United States, I feel that the minds of millions are still in the dens and caves of savagery. Is it not wonderful that all people do not see that the Catholic Church is the fortress of ignorance, superstition, and hypocrisy—an organization that seeks to govern by exciting the fears of the ignorant and the hopes of the foolish? How that Church—that impudent beggar—lives and thrives. It has murdered many millions—it has committed all crimes, and yet millions bow at its altars. From this we can see how little one man can do—and how little millions can do. The Catholic Church with its celibacy—an insult to the world—with its confessional that destroys manhood and womanhood—with all its absurdities and crime, lives and flourishes here, in the Great Republic.

Still, I have confidence in the final victory of reason, of education, and civilization. I shall do what I can to hasten the day of deliverance.

I am yours always, R. G. Ingersoll

KINDNESS TO ANIMALS

Henry Bergh, Sen., who is referred to in the paragraph below, "did as much good as any man who has lived in the nineteenth century" for the cause of kindness, in the opinion of his friend and admirer, Robert Ingersoll. Mr. Bergh was the outstanding philanthropist of his day, founder and president of the American Society for the Prevention of Cruelty to Animals and of the American Society for the Prevention of Cruelty to Children.

" The gospel of kindness is not only preached but practised. Such has been the result of this advance of civilization of this bursting into blossom of the flower called pity, in the heart—that we treat our horses (thanks to Henry Bergh) better than our ancestors did their slaves, their servants, or their tenants. The gentlemen of today show more affection for their dogs than most of the kings of England exhibited towards their wives. The great tide is towards mercy. "

LAND OWNERSHIP

Colonel Ingersoll was acquainted with Henry George, the famous author of *Progress and Poverty*, in which is set forth the theory of the Single Tax. Ingersoll was deeply interested in many of George's ideas, while entertaining doubts of the practicability of certain of his theories; but above all, he admired the humane and noble spirit of the man.

New York, N. Y.
Oct. 17th, 1886

Henry George, Esq.
My dear Friend:
    It so happened that I did not see your letter until late this afternoon—too late to attend the lecture. I regret that I was deprived of the privilege of hearing your views on the celebrated deliverer of the Jewish people.
    While I may not entirely agree with your theories—probably because I am not well acquainted with them—still, I am satisfied that the children of Nature are entitled to the essentials of life— that is to say, to water, to air, and to land. I am satisfied that the time will come—and I have been long of this opinion—when no man will be allowed to own land that he does not use. It is not to the interest of any country to have a few landlords and millions of tenants. I am a believer in homes, and believe that patriotism is born by the fireside. We do not want a nation of tenants—that is to say, of serfs.
    Some people say that the idle should not live on the labour of the industrious; that nothing can be more infamous than for those who do not produce, to make those divide who do. And yet, this is exactly what happens in every monarchy of the world. The idle do live on the labour of the industrious, and those who do not produce, make those who do, divide with them. The worst possible definition of Socialism is a perfect description of Germany, Austria, England, Spain, Italy, and in fact of almost every government in the world. Admit that the Nihilists are as bad as any human being has ever described them, or charged them to be: put them in power, and would their government be worse than that which now exists in Russia?
    For a great many years the world has been hearing about " the brotherhood of man." For centuries, poverty was declared to be a virtue. The world was taught to rely on the goodness of the gods, and the charity of the rich. At last, people are beginning to find that they must rely upon themselves; that charity is not what they want; that, as a rule, the giver becomes arrogant, and the taker, servile, cringing, and doubly helpless. The world should be governed on a scientific basis. We should turn our attention, not so much to the relief of the individual cases as to the prevention of want. The world should be so governed, that a healthy man should have no excuse for wanting bread. The rich should become intelligent enough to know, that nothing is as costly, nothing as extravagant, as to reduce wages below a liberal living point. The

value of the property in the City of New York depends on the prosperity of the people. If the people are satisfied; if in the homes of the poor you find plenty of food—you find contentment. That contentment is the basis of values. Let that be destroyed; let the multitude be hungry; let them feel that they have been robbed —that the rich are their enemies, that wealth is a slave-driver, that capital is heartless—then what will the palaces be worth? A man to be truly prosperous, and to be secure in that prosperity, should live among prosperous people.

The time has come for the world, as I have said, to be controlled by science—that is to say, by wisdom, by intelligence, by justice. No man can be rich enough to be independent of his fellows, and no man can be so poor as to absolve his fellows from all responsibility towards him.

There was a great ship disabled at sea, and there were on board a thousand steerage passengers and one hundred in the cabin. The food began to grow scarce in the steerage, for they only had enough to last during an ordinary voyage. There was plenty in the cabin—plenty, not only for the hundred there, but for the thousand below. For a few days the steerage passengers depended on charity, and a few generous souls gave them a little meat and bread. Some gave them crumbs, others, advice; some talked about vested rights, and a couple of clergymen, travelling for their health, gave them prayers. But the demand grew greater than charity supplied. Advice was not food. Prayers did not satisfy hunger. At last the cry was raised: "We will help ourselves." When the ship reached shore, everybody said the steerage was right.

After all, this world is only a great ship making its annual trips through the ocean of ether around the sun, and if the steerage passengers grow hungry, and if they can truthfully say that they have by their labour, by their toil, produced all the food in the cabin, shall they be allowed to die for lack of bread?

In my judgment, the cabin will become intelligent enough to divide, and the steerage will become intelligent enough to be satisfied with its share.

I am not an Anarchist, a Nihilist, or a Socialist. I am simply a human being willing to give to all other human beings every right that I claim for myself.

Yours truly, R. G. Ingersoll

MARRIAGE AND DIVORCE

Dr. R. Greer,   November 15th, 1888
Chicago, Illinois.

Dear Sir:

I am a believer in marriage, and I do not think the trouble in marriage is caused by the institution, but by a lack of civilization in the men and women who marry.

Yours truly, R. G. Ingersoll

In the autumn of 1889 the *North American Review* propounded the following questions:

" 1, Do you believe in the principle of divorce under any circumstances? 2, Ought divorced people to be allowed to marry, under any circumstances? 3, What is the effect of divorce on the integrity of the family? 4, Does the absolute prohibition of divorce, where it exists, contribute to the moral purity of society? "

These questions were answered in the November, 1889, issue of *The Review*, by Cardinal Gibbons, Bishop Henry C. Potter, and Robert G. Ingersoll.

Cardinal Gibbons, in upholding the orthodox Catholic position that divorce is inadmissible under all circumstances, declared that " God instituted in Paradise the marriage state and sanctified it. . . He established its law of unity and indissolubility." Bishop Henry C. Potter, of the Protestant Episcopal Church, assumed a less uncompromising position in his statement that " according to Episcopal law no minister is allowed, as a rule, to solemnize the marriage of any man or woman who has a divorced husband or wife still living. But if the person seeking to be married is the innocent party in the divorce for adultery, that person, whether man or woman, may be married by a minister of the Church. . "

Ingersoll commenced his contribution to the symposium with the statement that " the world for the most part is ruled by the tomb, and the living are tyrannized over by the dead. Old ideas, long after the conditions under which they were produced have passed away, often persist in surviving. Opinions on the subject of divorce have been, for the most part, inherited from the early Christians, who believed that the world was about to be destroyed "; and therefore "discouraged all worldly pursuits, except the soliciting of alms. There was no time to marry, no time to build homes and have families. All their thoughts were centred upon the heaven they expected to inherit. . . . Human love was spoken of with contempt. ' Let the dead bury their dead. Follow thou me.' Marriage was discouraged. It was regarded as only one degree above open and unbridled vice, and was allowed only in consideration of human weakness. . . The exceedingly godly, the really spiritual, believed in celibacy, and held the opposite sex in a kind of pious abhorrence. And yet with that inconsistency so characteristic of theologians, marriage was held to be a sacrament."

Whether a contract or a sacrament, marriage, in this Humanist's opinion, " is the most important, the most sacred, agreement that human beings can make. A true marriage is a natural concord and agreement of souls, a harmony in which discord is not even imagined. When two beings thus love, thus unite, this is the true marriage of soul and soul. That which is said before the altar, or minister, or magistrate . . is only the outward evidence of that which has already happened within; it simply testifies to a union that has already taken place. . . . The idea of contract is lost. Duty and obligation are instantly changed into desire and joy, and two lives, like uniting streams, flow on as one.

" The question then arises, Should this marriage, under any circumstances, be dissolved? In this contract of marriage, the man agrees to protect and cherish his wife. Suppose that he refuses to protect; that he abuses, assaults, and tramples upon the woman he wed. He has violated the contract. . . . Is she bound by the contract he has broken? If so, what is the consideration for this obligation? Must she live with him for his sake? Or, if she leaves him to preserve her life, must she remain his wife for his sake? No intelligent man will answer these questions in the affirmative.

" If, then, she is not bound to remain his wife for the husband's sake, is she bound to remain his wife because the marriage was a sacrament? Is there any obligation on the part of the wife to remain with the brutal husband for the sake of God? Can her conduct affect in any way the happiness of an infinite being?

" It must be admitted that the peace of society will be promoted by the separation of such people. . . . Even married women have a right to personal security. They do not lose, either by contract or sacrament, the right of self-preservation; this they share in common, to say the least of it, with the lowest living creatures. It may be said that the woman is free to go, and that the courts will protect her from the brutality of the man who promised to be her protector; but where shall the woman go? She may have no friends; or they may be poor;

her kindred may be dead. Has she no right to build another home? . . . Is there no future for her? . Can she never sit by her own hearth, with the arms of her children about her neck, and with a husband who loves and protects her? Is she to become a social pariah, and is this for the benefit of society?—or is it for the sake of the wretch who destroyed her life? "

Question (2). Ought divorced people to be allowed to marry, under any circumstances?

To this the Colonel replied: "This depends upon whether marriage is a crime. If it is not a crime, why should any penalty be attached? Can any one conceive of any reason why a woman obtaining a divorce, without fault on her part, should be compelled as a punishment to remain forever single? Why should a man who faithfully kept his contract of marriage, and who was deserted by an unfaithful wife, be punished for the benefit of society? There is still another view. We must remember that human passions are the same after as before divorce. To prevent remarriage is to give excuse for vice."

Question (3). What is the effect of divorce upon the integrity of the family?

"The real marriage is back of the ceremony, and the real divorce is back of the decree. When love is dead, when husband and wife abhor each other, they are divorced. The decree records in a judicial way what has really taken place, just as the ceremony of marriage attests a contract already made. . If we wish to preserve the integrity of the family, we must preserve the democracy of the fireside, the republicanism of the home, the absolute and perfect equality of husband and wife. . . Real homes can never be preserved through force, through slavery, or superstition. Nothing can be more sacred than a home, no altar purer than the hearth."

Question (4). Does the absolute prohibition of divorce, where it exists contribute to the moral purity of society?

Ingersoll answered this by saying that "we must define our terms. What is moral purity? The intelligent of this world seek the well-being of themselves and others. They know that happiness is the only good; and this they strive to attain. To live in accordance with the conditions of well-being is moral in the highest sense. To use the best instrumentalities to attain the highest ends is our highest conception of the moral."

He continued, saying that " in true marriage men and women give not only their bodies, but their souls. . They who give their bodies, but not their souls, are not married, whatever the ceremony may be; this is immoral. . . . If this be true, upon what principle can a woman continue to sustain the relation of wife after love is dead? Is there some other consideration that can take the place of genuine affection? Can she be bribed with money, or a home, or position, or by public opinion, and still remain a virtuous woman? Is it for the good of society that virtue should be thus crucified between church and state? Can it be said that this contributes to the moral purity of the human race? "'

He further inquired whether a higher standard of virtue— of morality—obtains in countries " where divorce is prohibited than in those where it is granted? Where husbands and wives who have ceased to love cannot be divorced, there are mistresses and lovers."

" The sacramental view of marriage," he contended, " is the shield of vice." There is nothing more immoral than " for a husband to insist on living with a wife who has no love for him." This is " a perpetual crime. Is the wife to lose her personality? Has she no right of choice? Is the man she hates the lord of her desire? Has she no right to guard the jewels of her soul? Is there a depth below this? And is this the foundation of morality? . This the arch that supports the dome of civilization? Is this pathetic sacrifice on the one hand, this sacrilege on the other, pleasing in the sight of heaven? "

He concluded his article with a moving and tender tribute to motherhood: " To me, the tenderest word in our language, the most pathetic fact within our knowledge, is maternity. Around this sacred word cluster the joys and sorrows, the agonies and ecstasies, of the human race. The mother walks in the shadow of death that she may give another life. Upon the altar of love she puts her own life in pawn. When the world is civilized, no wife will become a mother against her will. Man will then know that to enslave another is to imprison himself."

New York, N. Y.
March 27th, 1890

Sydney D. Fisher, Esq.,
Philadelphia.

My dear Sir:

Accept my thanks for your essay. *The Cause of the Increase of Divorce.*

I think you are right in saying that a great change has taken place in the position of women, that " they no longer believe in the endurance of suffering which accomplishes nothing," and that they believe in lives of utility and sense and do not intend to be held in the snare " simply because the Canonists think that the marriage ceremony is supernatural."

Divorces have increased because women have become more and more womanly and more and more intelligent, and consequently will not suffer, in the name of marriage, indignities that were formerly borne by slaves.

I am always delighted when I read anything that appeals from the supernatural to the natural, and from the will of God to the well-being of man.

Yours truly, R. G. Ingersoll

Dobbs' Ferry, N. Y.
August, 1894

To the Editor of
The Conservator.

My dear Traubel:

The death of love is the end of marriage. Celibacy is the essence of vulgarity. It tries to put a stain upon motherhood, upon marriage, upon love—that is to say, upon all that is holiest in the human heart. Why should we desire the destruction of human passion? Take passions from human beings, and what is left? The great object should be, not to destroy passions, but to make them obedient to the intellect. To indulge passion to the utmost is one form of intemperance—to destroy passion is another. The reasonable gratification of passion under the domination of the intellect is true wisdom and perfect virtue. Love is a transfiguration. It ennobles, purifies, and glorifies. In true marriage two hearts burst into flower. Two lives unite. They melt in music. Every moment is a melody. Love is a revelation, a creation. From love the world borrows its beauty and the heavens, their glory. Justice, self-denial, charity, and pity are the children of love. Lover, wife, mother, husband, father, child, home—these words shed light—they are the gems of human speech. Without love all glory fades, the noble falls from life, art dies, music loses meaning and becomes mere motions of the air, and virtue ceases to exist.

R. G. Ingersoll

Miss Lily Farrell, to whom the following letter was written, was the only sister of Clinton Pinckney Farrell, brother-in-law of Colonel Ingersoll.

Dobbs' Ferry, New York
October 19th, 1894

My dear Lily,

Clint told me the other day. I do not know whether to congratulate you or not.

Marriage is splendid for man—but for woman? Well, I hardly know. The one thing in its favour is that it is natural and has been for a long time. It is probably best to travel the regular road. People, like weeds and oysters and ants, act the drama—the comedy—the tragedy—called life, and the best thing for each is to play his little part until Nature rings down the curtain. So, after thinking it all over, I congratulate you and wish you many, many years of glad content. And I also congratulate the young man.

Do not expect too much, Lily, men are not very good—just tolerable—and you must not get the ideal *too* ideal—just ideal enough. If he really loves you and wants to make you happy—that is, and always will be, enough.

Yours always, R. G. Ingersoll

PROHIBITION

On May 22, 1876, Colonel Ingersoll delivered his celebrated "Address to the Jury," in the Munn trial, which concerned a revenue officer charged with illicit dealings in whisky. Ingersoll was the attorney for the defence, and succeeded in securing his client's acquittal. His address is chiefly noted for its arraignment of alcohol, or rather, of the evils produced by the abuse of alcohol.

This attack on liquor so deeply impressed some temperance advocate that, a year later, he appropriated it bodily, together with another passage written by an unknown person, and published the whole as his own. The Colonel wrote the following letter of refutation and explanation.

Peoria, October 10, 1877

Editor, *Terre Haute Saturday Courier*.

Dear Sir:

If you published any speech upon the subject of temperance in which there was anything about "God and Heaven," and attributed the speech to me, you made a mistake. I never made a speech of that kind.

In what is known as the Munn trial at Chicago, I did make a few remarks upon alcohol. The remarks were as follows:

" I believe, gentlemen, that alcohol to a certain degree demoralizes those who make it, those who sell it, and those who drink it. I believe that from the time it issues from the coiled and poisoned worm of the distillery, until it empties into the hell of crime, dishonour, and death, that it demoralizes everybody that touches it, from its source to where it ends. I do not believe that anybody can contemplate the subject without becoming prejudiced against that liquid crime.

" All we have to do, gentlemen, is to think of the wrecks upon either bank of this stream of death—of the suicides—of the insanity —of the poverty—of the ignorance—of the destitution—of the little children tugging at the faded dresses of weeping and despairing wives asking for bread—of the men of genius it has wrecked—of the millions struggling with imaginary serpents produced by this devilish thing; and when you think of the jails—of the alms houses —of the asylums—of the prisons and of the scaffolds. . . . I do not wonder that every thoughtful man is prejudiced against that damned stuff called alcohol."

This is the only temperance speech I ever made. If that is in the book of Dr. Gunn he obtained it from me. I never saw the Doctor nor his book. I do not borrow ideas. I have a factory of my own. Your postal-card friend is an idiot.

Yours truly, R. G. Ingersoll

Robert Ingersoll did not believe in the principle of prohibition, or in any so-called sumptuary laws. He said that "few people understand the restraining influence of liberty. Moderation walks hand in hand with freedom." By this he did not mean, " the freedom springing from the sudden rupture of restraint. That kind of freedom usually rushes to extremes." He felt convinced that true temperance must come through a gradual process of education; and that if laws are placed on the statute books which cannot be enforced because the majority of people are not intellectually, emotionally, and morally ready for them, a condition of dishonesty and demoralization inevitably results. He insisted that " unpopular laws make hypocrites, perjurers, and official shirkers of duty."

New York, May 16th, 1887

Maurice Gross, Esq.

My dear Friend:

I never was a Prohibitionist—never have believed in sumptuary legislation, but have always advocated the greatest individual liberty. . . .

The trouble with Prohibition is that it fills the country with spies—makes neighbours suspicious of each other—fills the community with meddlers—with people who poke their impudent noses into the business of others.

Besides, prohibition does not prohibit—it does not even prohibit the Prohibitionists.

Yours truly, R. G. Ingersoll

June 3rd, 1887

Howard C. Tripp, Esq.,
Queen City, Texas.

My dear Sir:

I did write the letter on the subject of prohibition . . . and I say to you, I never was a Prohibitionist. I have never believed in sumptuary legislation. I do not believe in putting out the sun to keep weeds from growing. Neither do I think it wise to interfere with the liberty of men, to prevent the few going to excess.

People will become temperate as they become civilized. Through the countless direct influences of education, art, music—everything that tends to enlighten and to ennoble will, at the same time, tend to make men temperate in all things. . . .

I do not believe that wine and beer are injurious to the world. I think that life is made a little richer, a little better, and the joy of the world increased, by the blood of the grape.

I also think that what is good for the man is good for the woman, and what is good for men and women is good for children. If wine is used, it should be used at the table. It should add to the kindness, the sociability, and the joy of the hearth.

I do not believe in destroying that which is good, because a few abuse it. In other words, I am a believer in individual liberty.

The Government should protect its citizens from fraud—from violence—and should enforce honest contracts. It should protect people from foreign invasion, and from insurrection—and with these exceptions, American citizens should be allowed to take care of themselves.

Yours truly, R. G. Ingersoll

New York, N. Y.
July 6, 1887

T. B. Murdock, Esq.,
Eldorado, Kansas.

My dear Friend:

I remember you perfectly, and remember you with pleasure. The fact is, however, that I am not a Prohibitionist. I would rather be free than to be happy, if I had to purchase happiness with liberty. In other words, I can conceive of no happiness without freedom. I would not want to be shut up in the place that I really wanted to be in. I would rather be loose in a country that I desired to leave. Of course I believe in temperance.

Hoping that you are getting rich, and keeping sober.

Yours truly, R. G. Ingersoll

Miss Frances Willard dedicated her life to the cause of social reform, particularly to that of temperance and prohibition. She was Secretary, and, later, President of the Women's Christian Temperance Union, and in 1884 helped to organize the Prohibition party.

In 1889 she sent the Colonel a copy of her autobiography, *Glimpses of Fifty Years*.

New York
Oct. 30, '89

Miss Frances E. Willard.

My dear Madam:

Accept my thanks for the book . . I shall read the story of your life with the greatest interest. The fact that you believe nearly everything that I do not, will make no difference with me. Long ago the conclusion was forced upon my mind that we all do as we must—that we are all just as bad and just as good as we can be. This conclusion has at heart kept me from hating those who fail to agree with me. I hope to have the pleasure of meeting you, and when we " define our terms " it may be that our greatest differences will consist of words. There are words that divide like walls—like chasms—people who should work together ior the good of all.

Sincerely yours, R. G. Ingersoll

RACIAL INTOLERANCE

Ingersoll abhorred race and religious prejudice. He wanted to " substitute humanity for superstition, the love of our fellow-men for the fear of God." He maintained that we should be " great enough and grand enough to know that the rights of the Jews are precisely the same as our own"; that we "cannot trample upon their rights without endangering our own rights; and no man who will take liberty from another is good enough to enjoy liberty himself." Ingersoll felt that when one considers what the Jewish people have suffered throughout the centuries, " it is amazing that every one of them does not hate with all his heart and soul and strength the entire Christian world." The Colonel asserted that " intellectually and morally

278

the Jews are the equal of any people." And with characteristic common sense, he declared that good Jews are strangely like good Gentiles; and that bad Jews are in no noticeable sense different from bad Gentiles. In a word, this Humanist held that one should always judge people as individuals, and as individuals only.

Washington, D. C.
July 26th, 1879

Hon. J. J. Noah.

My dear Friend:

As a matter of course, I am utterly opposed to the oppression of any class, and regard the action of the proprietors of the Manhattan Beach Hotel in reference to the Jews as bigoted, mean, and disgraceful. Such action belongs to the Dark Ages. The persecution of the Jews should bring a blush to every Christian cheek.

Nothing is more infamous than the oppression of a class. Each man has the right to be judged upon his own merits. To oppress him, or to hold him in contempt on account of religion, race, or colour, is a crime. Every man should be treated justly and kindly, not because he is, or is not a Jew, or a Gentile, but because he is a human being, and, as such, capable of joy or pain. If, at any hotel a man fails to act in a decent and becoming manner, let him be put out, not on account of the nation to which he belongs, but on account of his behaviour. Any other course is unjust and cruel.

It will not do for the keepers of public houses to brand an entire race as unfit to associate with them.

Some of the leading men of the world are Jews. These wonderful people, although dispersed, despised, and for many ages persecuted in all countries where people loved their enemies and returned good for evil, have contributed to every science, and enriched every art. He who has heard the music of Mendelssohn and Meyerbeer, who has studied the grand philosophy of Spinoza, and has seen upon the stage Rachel, mistress of Passion, will hardly unite in the condemnation of the race to which these prodigies belonged.

Neither should it be forgotten that the Jews furnished their persecutors with a religion, and that they are the only people, according to the dogmas of our day, with whom the Almighty ever deigned to have any intercourse whatever.

When we remember that God selected a Jewess for his mother —passing by the women of India, Egypt, Athens, and Rome, as well as the grandmothers of Mr. Corbin—it is hardly in good taste for the worshippers of that same God to hold the Jews in scorn.

We should also remember that the Jews were the only people "inspired." All the "sacred" writers—all the "prophets" were of this race, and while Christians almost worship Abraham, notwithstanding the affair of Hagar, and his willingness to murder his own son; and while they hold in almost infinite respect David the murderer, and Solomon the Mormon, it certainly is not perfectly consistent to denounce men and women of the same race who have committed no crime.

The Christians have always been guilty of this inconsistency with regard to the Jews:—They have worshipped the dead and persecuted the living. I think it would be much better to let the dead take care of themselves, while we respect and maintain the rights of the living.

I cannot forget that during the Revolution the Jews prayed in their synagogues for the success of the Colonies. I cannot forget that during our Civil War, thousands of them fought for the preservation of the Union, many of them rising from the ranks to the most important commands. Neither can I forget that many of the Jews are, today, among the foremost advocates of intellectual liberty; that they have outgrown the prejudices of race and creed, and believe in the universal brotherhood of man. And in this connection it may not be out of place to speak of your father. He was a man who adorned every position he held, and who, as lawyer, judge, essayist, and philanthropist, was an honour to his race, and to my country.

It will not do in this, the second century of the United States, to insult a gentleman because of his nation.

We are, at last, a great, rich, and prosperous people. Greatness should be just. Wealth should be generous, and prosperity should at least beget good manners.

Every American should resist every insult to humanity; for while the rights of the lowest are trampled upon, the liberties of the highest are not safe.

While for the ancient myths and legends of your people I have not the respect entertained by Christians, I still hold the rights of Jews to be as sacred as my own.

Yours respectfully, R. G. Ingersoll

New York, N. Y.
April 4th, 1890

To the Editor of
The American Hebrew.

Dear Sir:

When I was a child, I was taught that the Jews were an exceedingly hard-hearted and cruel people, and that they were so destitute of the finer feelings that they had a little while before that time crucified the only perfect man who had appeared upon the earth; that this perfect man was also perfect God, and that the Jews had really stained their hands with the blood of the Infinite.

When I got somewhat older, I found that nearly all people had been guilty of substantially the same crime—that is, that they had destroyed the progressive and the thoughtful; that religionists had in all ages been cruel; that the chief priests of all people had incited the mob to the end that heretics—that is to say, philosophers

—that is to say, men who knew that the chief priests were hypocrites—might be destroyed.

I also found that Christians had committed more of these crimes than all other religionists put together.

I also became acquainted with a large number of Jewish people, and I found them like other people, except that, as a rule, they were more industrious, more temperate, had fewer vagrants among them, no beggars, very few criminals; and in addition to all this, I found that they were intelligent, kind to their wives and children, and that, as a rule, they kept their contracts and paid their debts.

The prejudice was created almost entirely by religious, or rather, irreligious, instruction. All children in Christian countries are taught that all the Jews are to be eternally damned who die in the faith of Abraham, Isaac, and Jacob; that it is not enough to believe in the inspiration of the Old Testament—not enough to obey the Ten Commandments—not enough to believe the miracles performed in the days of the prophets, but that every Jew must accept the New Testament and must be a believer in Christianity— that is to say, he must be regenerated—or he will simply be eternal kindling wood.

The Church has taught, and still teaches, that every Jew is an outcast; that he is today busily fulfilling prophecy; that he is a wandering witness in favour of " the glad tidings of great joy "; that Jehovah is seeing to it that the Jews shall not exist as a nation —that they shall have no abiding place, but that they shall remain scattered, to the end that the inspiration of the Bible may be substantiated.

Dr. John Hall of this city, a few years ago, when the Jewish people were being persecuted in Russia, took the ground that it was all fulfilment of prophecy, and that whenever a Jewish maiden was stabbed to death, God put a tongue in every wound for the purpose of declaring the truth of the Old Testament.

Just as long as Christians take these positions, of course they will do what they can to assist in the fulfilment of what they call prophecy, and they will do their utmost to keep the Jewish people in a state of exile, and then point to that fact as one of the cornerstones of Christianity.

My opinion is that in the early days of Christianity all sensible Jews were witnesses against the faith, and in this was excited the hostility of the orthodox. Every sensible Jew knew that no miracles had been performed in Jerusalem. They all knew that the sun had not been darkened, that the graves had not given up their dead, that the veil of the temple had not been rent in twain—and they told what they knew. They were then denounced as the most infamous of human beings, and this hatred has pursued them from that day to this.

There is no chapter in history as infamous, as bloody, as cruel, as relentless, as the chapter in which it is told the manner in which Christians—those who love their enemies—have treated the Jewish people. The story is enough to bring the blush of shame to the cheek, and the words of indignation to the lips of every honest man.

Nothing can be more unjust than to generalize about nationalities, and to speak of a race as worthless, or vicious, simply because you have met an individual who treated you unjustly. There are good people and bad people in all races, and the individual is not responsible for the crimes of the nation, or the nation responsible for the actions of the few. Good men and honest men are found in every faith, and they are not honest or dishonest because they are Jews or Gentiles, but for entirely different reasons.

Some of the best people I have ever known are Jews, and some of the worst people I have known are Christians. The Christians were not bad simply because they were Christians, neither were the Jews good because they were Jews. A man is far above these badges of faith and race. Good Jews are precisely the same as good Christians, and bad Christians are wonderfully like bad Jews.

Personally, I have either no prejudices about religion, or I have equal prejudice against all religions. The consequence is that I judge of people not by their creeds, not by their rites, not by their mummeries, but by their actions.

In the first place, at the bottom of this prejudice, lies the coiled serpent of superstition. In other words, it is a religious question. It seems impossible for the people of one religion to like the people believing in another religion. They have different gods, different heavens, and a great variety of hells. For the followers of one god to treat the followers of another god decently, is a kind of treason. In order to be really true to his god, each follower must not only hate all other gods, but the followers of all other gods.

The Jewish people should outgrow their own superstitions. It is time for them to throw away the idea of inspiration. The intelligent Jew of today knows that the Old Testament was written by barbarians and he knows that the rites and ceremonies are simply absurd. He knows that no intelligent man should care anything about Abraham, Isaac, and Jacob, three dead barbarians. In other words, the Jewish people should leave their superstition, and rely on science and philosophy.

The Christian should do the same. He, by this time, should know that his religion is a mistake, that his creed has no foundation in the eternal verities. The Christian certainly should give up the hopeless task of converting the Jewish people, and the Jews should give up the useless task of converting the Christians. There is no propriety in swapping superstitions—neither party can afford to give any boot.

When the Christian throws away his cruel and heartless superstitions, and when the Jew throws away his, then they can meet as man and man.

In the meantime, the world will go on in its blundering way, and I shall know and feel that everybody does as he must, and that the Christian, to the extent that he is prejudiced, [is so] by reason of his ignorance, and that consequently the great lever with which to raise all mankind into the sunshine of philosophy, is intelligence.

Yours truly, R. G. Ingersoll

June 18th, 1891

A. Leo Weil, Esq.,
Pittsburgh, Pa.

My dear Sir:

I received and read your letter on " Anti-Semitism."

Undoubtedly the Jews, when they had a nation, separated themselves from others by means of their religion. They believed that they were " The Chosen People " of Jehovah, and that Jehovah was the biggest God of all, and when he had anything like a fair chance could put any heathen deity " to sleep " in the third round. The Jewish people, without doubt, were honest in this.

After the start of the Christian religion, the Jews who became Christians were the bitter enemies of Jews who did not become Christians. The early Christians pretended that certain great wonders took place in Jerusalem, and the Jews, not Christians, who were in Jerusalem at the time, were honest enough to say that no such things happened, and their children were candid enough to repeat what their fathers said. In this way every Jew not a Christian, became a witness against the Christian religion and was consequently hated by Christians.

Of course, the Christians did all they could to prejudice pagan converts against the Jews. The Jews had to defend each other. That is, being surrounded by hatred, they huddled in the centre, together—and, as you say, all the Christian children have been taught that the Jews killed God, and as a consequence the Christian children hated the Jews, and they were considered lawful prey for many centuries.

The history of their persecution is in my judgment, the saddest and most infamous in the world.

There is, of course, another fact, and that is, that the Jews were not allowed to compete with the barbarian Christians in the trades or professions, or even in the cultivation of the land. The consequence was that they were driven to trade, and the result was that they became the best traders in the world.

I do not think, as a matter of fact, that the Jewish religion is any better than the religion of their persecutors. The Jews persecuted when they had the power. Neither do I think that the people of the Middle Ages were any more superstitious than the Jews. It would be hard for anybody to be more superstitious than a real believer in the Old Testament—a real worshipper of Jehovah.

Undoubtedly the Jews—many of them—were and are better educated than their Christian persecutors, and undoubtedly there were among them writers and physicians and men of considerable science. They were and are a people of great talent. They were persecuted on account of religion, and will be persecuted until their persecutors become civilized, and until the Jews themselves become civilized. I hope to see the day when Christianity and Judaism will be remembered as superstitions, and as nothing else.

I believe in equal rights for all. I believe in giving to the Hebrew every right that I claim for myself, and I hope for them what I hope for others—liberty of body and mind.

I do not agree with you that the Jewish race has " a mission," any more than any other nation has " a mission." Neither do I agree with you in the idea that the " One God " dogma is of any importance. The Greeks, with thousands of Gods, were a wonderfully intelligent and happy race. Of course it is better to have only one God like ours—only one like Jehovah.

You will, I know, understand me perfectly. I give to every man —no matter of what race—all the rights that I claim for myself. I abhor all tyranny, I hate all persecution, and I execrate, beyond the power of words to express, the spirit of caste.

Yours always, R. G. Ingersoll

SCHOOLS

Ingersoll was passionately opposed to sectarian domination of education. He pleaded constantly for free institutions of learning, devoted to " the science of eternal truth," in which every teacher would be told " to ascertain all the facts he can . . . to be infinitely true to himself and to us; to feel that he is without a chain, except the obligation to be honest. . . Instead of dismissing professors for finding something out," we should " discharge those who do not. Let each teacher understand that investigation is not dangerous for him; that his bread is safe, no matter how much truth he may discover. . . ."

He approved of the kindergarten system, for " attending school is then a pleasure—the children do not run away from school, but to school."

He was one of the earliest advocates of vocational schools; however, he would never have favoured the supplanting of all general, cultural education with mere training in technology. He felt, for instance, that familiarity with Shakespeare was an absolute essential to true culture of the mind and heart.

This Humanist realized the vital importance of securing the highest type of teachers for our children and youth; and that the only way to obtain the services of superior teachers is to pay them well—pay them salaries commensurate with the value of their work. He said that " we should not collect taxes to pay people for guessing. The common school is the bread of life for the people, and it should not be touched by the withering hand of superstition."

Mr. Sidney Edgerton (1818–1900), to whom the following letter is addressed, was a prominent judge and politician, an abolitionist, and an Agnostic.

Washington, D. C.
December 20, '84

Dear Mr. Edgerton,

I just finished reading your address which you were kind enough to send me. I agree with you. This is not a Theocracy. It is a government of the people—of this world and for this world. We are no longer subject to the aristocracy of the air—and theology has nothing to do with government and has no place, or should have none, in the schools.

All power comes from the consent of the governed.—We have retired the gods—all of them—from politics. Now we want them out of education—out of morality—out of charity.—They are of no use in this world. If we should put God in the Constitution there would be no room left for man.

Your speech states the whole question and states it well. Theology has nothing to do with facts,—nothing to do with science. It is nonsense to talk about Methodist mathematics—Baptist botany, Catholic chemistry, Presbyterian physiology. The sciences are not sectarian. Men should teach something that is known—something that may be or is of value in this world. There is going to be a struggle to destroy or debauch our public schools. They are now preserved by the hatred that churches have for each other, and we may be able to keep them. As it is now the Protestants are willing to keep their hands off—if Catholics will do the same. But all the disciples of superstition feel that schools where no religion is taught are their enemies. They are right. Keep the bible out of the school—prevent the teaching of any creed, and the next generation will be freethinkers. But no matter what the consequences are, the public schools should be secular. Religion should neither be taught nor attacked. Each church must depend on itself to make converts.

Yours truly, R. G. Ingersoll

October 29th, 1888

Frank A. Bruce, Esq.,
Boston, Mass.

My dear Sir:

Much obliged to you for your kind letter. So far as the schools are concerned, my idea is that nothing should be taught in a school that somebody does not know. Taxes should not be collected to pay people for guessing.

I am opposed to all religious instruction in schools—that is to say, I am opposed to filling the minds of children with superstition. The school is the place in which children should be taught—not to believe, but to think, to investigate, and to examine for themselves. A child should not be treated like a waste-basket.

Yours truly, R. G. Ingersoll

SUICIDE

The publication of Robert G. Ingersoll's first letter on the subject of suicide, entitled " Is Suicide a Sin ? " in the New York *World*, of August 31, 1894, created a great sensation among the general public, and a storm of theological controversy. Numerous clergymen, in particular, attempted to answer the Colonel's arguments, chiefly with vilification and personal abuse. In a second letter to the *World*, Ingersoll replied to his clerical and lay critics, and summarized in brief and forceful fashion his views on this highly inflammatory subject.

" In the article written by me about suicide, the ground was taken that, ' under many circumstances a man has the right to kill himself.' This has been attacked with great fury by clergymen, editors, and the writers of letters," said Ingersoll. " These people contend that the right of self-destruction does not and cannot exist. They insist that life is the gift of God, and that he only has the right to end the days of men; that it is our duty to bear the sorrows that he sends with grateful patience. Some have denounced suicide as the worst of crimes—worse than the murder of another."

Ingersoll went on to consider the *first* question, as to whether a man has the right to take his own life under any circumstances whatever. By way of bringing home the point of his argument, he gave several vivid and, to his mind, unassailable illustrations of the justifiability of suicide under certain conditions. " A man is being slowly devoured by cancer—his agony is intense—his suffering all that nerves can feel. His life is slowly being taken. . . . This man . . . is of no use to himself. His life is but a succession of pangs. He is of no use to his wife, his children, his friends, or society. . . . Has he the right to render himself unconscious? Is it proper for him to take refuge in sleep? " The Colonel asserted that he could not believe " that a good God . . . takes pleasure in the sufferings of men." On the contrary, he was convinced that " If there be a good God, he will, to the extent of his power, lessen the evils of life." Therefore, the Humanist insisted that " the man being eaten by the cancer—a burden to himself and to others, useless in every way—has the right to end his pain and pass through happy sleep to dreamless rest." However, Ingersoll said that his critics would tell this unfortunate man that it is his " duty to be devoured "; that " the good God " wishes him to suffer; that his " life is the gift of God," and that he " holds it in trust," and has " no right to end it. The cancer is the creation of God," and it is his " duty to furnish it with food."

Ingersoll posited another imaginary case. " A man has been captured by savages in Central Africa. He is about to be tortured to death. His captors are going to thrust splinters of pine into his flesh and then set them on fire. He watches them as they make the preparations. . . . There is no hope of rescue, of help. He has a vial of poison. He knows that he can take it and in one moment pass beyond their power, leaving to them only the dead body. Is this man under obligation to keep his life because God gave it, until the savages by torture take it? . . . Has he no right to defend himself? . . . What would any man of ordinary intelligence do in a case like this? Is there room for discussion? " the Colonel queried. He continued: " If the man took the poison, shortened his life a few moments, escaped the tortures of the savages, is it possible that he would in another world be tortured forever . . .?

" Suppose another case: In the good old days, when the Inquisition flourished, when men loved their enemies and murdered their friends, many frightful and ingenious ways were devised to touch the nerves of pain. Those who loved God . . . would take a fellow-man who had been convicted of ' heresy,' lay him upon the floor of a dungeon, secure his arms and legs with chains . . . so that he could not move, put an iron vessel, the opening downward, on his stomach, place in the vessel several rats, then tie it securely to his body. Then these worshippers of God would wait until the rats, seeking food and liberty, would gnaw through the body of the victim. Now, if a man about to be subjected to this torture had within his hand a dagger, would it excite the wrath of the ' good God,' if with one quick stroke he found the protection of death?" Ingersoll said that "to this question there can be but one answer."

"If, in the cases I have supposed, men would have the right to take their lives," Ingersoll continued, "then I was right when I said that 'under many circumstances a man has a right to kill himself.'"

The *second* question at issue was as to whether persons who committed suicide are physical cowards. Ingersoll denied that they are. He said that "they may lack moral courage; they may exaggerate their misfortunes, lose the sense of proportion, but the man who plunges the dagger in his heart, who sends the bullet through his brain, who leaps from some roof and dashes himself against the stones beneath, is not and cannot be a physical coward. So, the man, forced to a choice of evils, choosing the less is not a coward, but a reasonable man."

Third.—Ingersoll took the position that "some suicides were sane; that they acted on their best judgment . . . and were in full possession of their minds." He said that "most of the persons who have tried to answer me have taken the ground that suicide is not only a crime, but some of them have felt that it is the greatest of crimes. Now, if it be a crime, then," the Colonel contended, even according to the critics' own reasoning, "the suicide must have been sane"; for, "under the law, an insane person is incapable of committing a crime."

Fourth.—Ingersoll contended that "suicide was and is the foundation of the Christian religion"; because "if Christ were God, he had the power to protect himself without injuring his assailants"; and "having that power it was his duty to use it, and that failing to use it, he consented to his own death and was guilty of suicide." He said that to this "the clergy answer that it was self-sacrifice for the redemption of man, that he made an atonement for the sins of believers." He asserted that "these ideas about redemption and atonement are born of a belief in the 'fall of man,' on account of the sins of our first 'parents,' and of the declaration that 'without the shedding of blood there is no remission of sin.'" However, Ingersoll felt that "no intelligent person" believes any longer in the "fall of man" dogma.

But if, on the other hand, "Christ were a man, and attacked the religion of his time because it was cruel and absurd; if he endeavoured to find a religion of kindness, of good deeds, to take the place of heartlessness and ceremony, and if, rather than to deny what he believed to be right and true, he suffered death, then he was a noble man—a benefactor of his race." However, " if he were God, there was no need of this. . . . If he had only made himself known, all knees would have touched the ground. If he were God it required no heroism to die. He knew that what we call death is but the opening of the gates of eternal life. If he.were God there was no self-sacrifice. He had no need to suffer pain. He could have changed the crucifixion to a joy," Ingersoll argued.

He asserted that " even the editors of religious weeklies see that there is no escape from these conclusions—from these arguments—and so, instead of attacking the arguments, they attack the man who makes them."

Fifth.—Ingersoll denounced the law of New York State making an attempt to commit suicide a crime. He felt that the unfortunates who seek death as a release from intolerable agony and suffering should be pitied rather than punished.

Sixth.—The Colonel said that this controversy had brought out " a curious thing. For several centuries the clergy have declared that . infidelity is a bad support, a wretched consolation, in the hour of death. They have, in spite of the truth, declared that all the great unbelievers died trembling with fear, asking God for mercy, surrounded by fiends, in the torments of despair. . . . At the same time, these ministers admitted that the average murderer could meet death on the scaffold with perfect serenity, and could smilingly ask the people who had gathered to see him killed to meet him in heaven." But now, Ingersoll added, " this has all changed, and . . . the clergy, in their sermons answering me, declare that the atheists, the freethinkers, have no fear of death—that to avoid some little annoyance, a passing inconvenience, they gladly and cheerfully put out the light of life. It is now said that infidels believe that death is the end . . . that it is without pain—that therefore they have no fear . . . and that when life becomes a burden they carelessly throw it away." Ingersoll declared that " this certainly is a great change," and he congratulated himself " on having forced the clergy to contradict themselves."

Seventh.—The Colonel charged the clergy with taking the

position that " the atheist, the unbeliever, has no standard of morality—that he can have no real conception of right and wrong. They are of the opinion that it is impossible for one to be moral or good unless he believes in some Being far above himself." To this, Ingersoll retorted that " we might ask how God can be moral or good unless he believes in some Being superior to himself?" The Humanist maintained that morality " is the best thing to do under the circumstances." And, " what is the best thing to do under the circumstances? That which will increase the sum of human happiness—or lessen it the least."

Eighth.—Ingersoll said that many of his opponents in this discussion had held that suicide is the basest of all crimes—that a murderer is superior to one who destroys himself. The reason for this attitude seems to lie in the belief that " the suicide dies in an act of sin." Therefore, " probably he would commit a lesser crime if he would murder his wife or mother," declared Ingersoll, brandishing his sharpest blade of sarcasm. To the Humanist's mind, it seemed perfectly clear that it is far better " to injure yourself than another . . . better to kill yourself if you wish to die, than murder one whose life is full of joy."

Ninth.—The Colonel said that nearly every one who had tried to answer him had been " exceedingly careful " to misquote him, and then answer something that he never uttered. " They have declared that I have advised people who were in trouble, or somewhat annoyed, to kill themselves; that I have told men who have lost their money, who have failed in business, who were not in good health, to kill themselves at once, without taking into consideration any duty that they owed to wives, children, friends or society." However, this was the very opposite of his position, since he believed that " no man has a right to leave his wife to fight the battle alone, if he is able to help. No man has a right to desert his children if he can possibly be of use to them."

Ingersoll said that after all, the instinct of self-preservation is predominant in the human race; " people do not kill themselves on the advice of friends or enemies." Everyone desires to be happy, to enjoy life to the uttermost; and " as long as life gives joy, the idea of self-destruction never enters the human mind." It is the " oppressors, the tyrants, those who trample on the rights of others; the robbers of the poor, those who put wages below the living point; the ministers who make people insane by preaching the dogma of eternal pain . . . who drive the weak, the suffering and the helpless down to death," Ingersoll asserted. He ridiculed the theological doctrine that " God has appointed a time for each to die," declaring that no evidence has ever been produced to prove that " any God takes any interest in the affairs of men." He said that " even the clergy admit that their God, through all ages, has allowed his friends, his worshippers, to be imprisoned, tortured, and murdered by his enemies."

Tenth.—Ingersoll never ceased to marvel at the extraordinary, the endless, and inexhaustible patience and endurance of the overwhelming majority of mankind; at the fact " that so many, in spite of ' age, ache, and penury,' guard with trembling hands. the spark of life."

New York, N. Y.
June 2nd, 1890

[To One Contemplating Suicide]
My dear Sir :
    If I were you, I would stay in the world a while longer. I think we are going to have a pleasant summer; and if you can find a cool place, I really think you would enjoy yourself better living than you will dead.

No man should kill himself as long as he can be of the least use to anybody, and if you cannot find some person that you are willing to do something for, find a good dog and take care of him. You have no idea how much better you will feel.

I send you back your papers, with the hope that this letter will make you feel a little better,

Truly your friend, R. G. Ingersoll

SEX EQUALITY

Robert Ingersoll was an ardent champion of the rights of women. He declared that " they have all the rights that I have, and one more—the right to be protected." He believed absolutely that women are the equals of men in innate capacity; and that, given time and opportunity, they will become the equals of men in achievement in all fields of human endeavour.

However, until comparatively recent times, " women have been the slaves of slaves," Ingersoll said; and " it took millions of ages for women to come from the condition of abject slavery up to the institution of marriage." He held orthodox religion very largely accountable for the lowly status of women throughout the centuries; because nearly every religion has blamed all the evil, crime, and suffering in the world upon the transgression of Eve, or her prototype by another name.

Ingersoll was, indeed, a thorough-going feminist; he believed in the right of women to engage in all professions and occupations short of those too hazardous " to life and limb "; and in their right to vote and to hold political office. He maintained that " in every field where woman has become a competitor of man she has become, or has given evidence that she is to become, his equal."

The Colonel asserted that St. Paul admonished women to look to their husbands as the fount and source of all knowledge; and " for many centuries they have followed this advice; and of course they have not learned a great deal, because their husbands could not answer their questions. Husbands, as a rule, do not know a great deal, and it will not do for every wife to depend on the ignorance of her worse half."

Ingersoll said that " the women of today are the great readers, and no book is a great success unless it pleases the women. As a result of this, all the literature of the world has changed, so that now in all departments the thoughts of women are taken into consideration; and women have thoughts, because they are the intellectual equals of men."

He realized and rejoiced that " in all departments women are advancing; some of them have taken the highest honours at medical colleges; others are prominent in the sciences; some are great artists; and there are several very fine sculptors." Ingersoll was also a firm believer in women's clubs and organizations devoted to philanthropic, welfare, and public interests of all sorts. Furthermore, he entertained the opinion that women's professional, business, and public activities, so far from interfering with their duties as wives and mothers, would aid, supplement, and complement the domestic ties and obligations. Said he: " The greater the brain, the greater the power to love, the greater the power to discharge all duties and obligations "; accordingly, he had no fear of the future, in so far as it related to the emancipation of women.

Ingersoll not only detested the domination of women by men, he also passionately opposed the leadership principle, in theory and practice, as he felt that it represented a constant source of danger to the healthy functioning of democracy. If the masses of the people look to an all-powerful, all-wise leader to think and act *for* them, they almost inevitably abdicate their individual responsibilities and judgments, and become intellectual, if not physical, serfs and slaves.

New York, Nov. 30, '92

Horace L. Traubel, Esq.,
Camden, New Jersey.

Dear Friend:

I read your article about " Woman's Rule and Women's Rights," with the greatest pleasure.

Your ideas are not only right, but they are most beautifully expressed. I believe, with you, that women are not *things* to be battled for; that idea came from savagery. There is something higher for woman than to wait, like the tigress, until two tigers, by tooth and claw, have settled the question of her ownership. So I agree with you that love does not ask for condescension. Neither is woman a step lower than man. Between those who love each other, the question of superiority, or as to who has the right to control, can, by no possibility, be raised. Tyranny lives only in mean minds; only he has the right to rule who limits this right to himself.

I would like to see two classes of people abolished—leaders and followers. When this is done, then, in your words, " all that is in us will run to music." There is one line in your article which should be read by the whole world: " It is irrational to expect to raise free children of slave mothers."

Yours truly, R. G. Ingersoll

A warm and admiring friendship existed between Mrs. Elizabeth Cady Stanton and Robert G. Ingersoll; each was always enthusiastic in praise of the other's capacities as thinker, orator, feminist, and humanist.

Elizabeth Cady Stanton (1815–1902), the great woman suffrage champion, was the leader among the brave little band of pioneers who signed the call to the first Woman's Rights Convention, held at Seneca Falls, New York, in 1848. This Convention made the first formal demand for the extension of the suffrage to women. Mrs. Stanton became the President of the

National Woman Suffrage Association, which was organized at that time, and remained in that office until 1893. In 1868 she was a candidate for Congress.

New York, March 8th, 1894

My dear Mrs. Stanton:

I am in favour of giving every right to women that I claim for myself, and I shall vote to do that if I ever have the chance.

True, I have done but little for what you call " the cause of woman "—I have had other fish to fry. I thought it of more importance to get superstition out of her head than to put a ballot in her hand.

Besides, woman suffrage has had great leaders—you and Miss Anthony and many others have done great work and great good, and have said all that was worth saying. There was no need of me. In fact, I would have excited prejudice on account of my religious opinions.

Rest assured, I am on your side, and will vote your way and will give you aid and comfort—and let you do the speaking.

Yours always, R. G. Ingersoll

VEGETARIANISM

New York
July 6th, 1887

Mr. James Andrew,
Walworth Road,
London, England.

My dear Sir:

I read your pamphlet on Vegetarianism with great interest. Probably the time will come when man will be civilized enough not to kill and eat his fellow creatures. We have at least made some advance—we have stopped eating each other, and the next step may in the far future be taken.

I do not approve of the plan of this world. I do not see how a devil could have done worse. This world is so that all life feeds upon life. Even the animals that devour grass crush unconsciously millions of living things, and it may be that the little things have just as intense feeling as the big ones.

There is one thing, however, about which I fear you are mistaken. People who live on vegetables, and animals that live on vegetables, are no more merciful, so far as I know, than the ones that live on meat. I find that people who live on rice torture each other, and now and then flay their fellow citizens alive. I find that a Jersey bull, living on grass, will fight, so to speak, at the drop of a hat; and if there is anything that an old ram, full of clover, won't butt, I have never seen it.

I have no time to follow the subject, but I must admit that

the eating of meat—when I think about it—is shocking, and that I am somewhat ashamed to look into the peaceful and trusting eyes of cattle.

Yours truly, R. G. Ingersoll

New York
February 21st, 1890

W. H. Gibbs, Esq.,
Lyons, Iowa.

My dear Sir:
. . . The truth is, that men like other animals, live on each other. Your book on usury only shows that cannibalism has taken a different form. We have stopped boiling and roasting our fellow-men. We have stopped eating them in slices—but we live on them just the same.

Yours very truly, R. G. Ingersoll

VIVISECTION

Colonel Ingersoll maintained that no civilized person will voluntarily inflict unnecessary pain. " He will see that his horse has food, if he can procure it, and if he cannot procure the food, he will end the sufferings of the animal in the best and easiest way."

Ingersoll quoted Dr. Lawson Tait, at that time the foremost surgeon of England, as saying that " vivisection has done harm instead of good " to humanity; that " the vivisectors have hindered the progress of surgery." And, according to Dr. Tait, similar views were entertained by many other leading men of science and medicine.

The Colonel believed that " vivisection should be controlled by law. No animal should be allowed to be tortured. And to cut up a living animal not under the influence of chloroform or ether, should be a penitentiary offence."

New York, N. Y.
May 27th, 1890

Philip G. Peabody, Esq.,
Boston, Mass.

My dear Friend:
Vivisection is the Inquisition—the Hell—of Science.

All the cruelty which the human—or rather the inhuman—heart is capable of inflicting, is in that one word. Below this there is no depth. This word lies like a coiled serpent at the bottom of the abyss.

U 295

We can excuse, in part, the crimes of passion. We take into consideration the fact that man is liable to be caught by the whirlwind, and that from a brain on fire the soul rushes to a crime. But what excuse can ingenuity form for a man who deliberately—with an unaccelerated pulse—with the calmness of John Calvin at the murder of Servetus—seeks with curious and cunning knives, in the living, quivering flesh of a dog, for all the throbbing nerves of pain? The wretches who commit these infamous crimes pretend that they are working for the good of man; that they are actuated by philanthropy; and that their pity for the sufferings of the human race drives out all pity for the animals they slowly torture to death. But those who are incapable of pitying animals are, as a matter of fact, incapable of pitying men. A physician who would cut a living rabbit in pieces—laying bare the nerves, denuding them with knives, pulling them out with forceps—would not hesitate to try experiments with men and women for the gratification of his curiosity. To settle some theory, he would trifle with the life of any patient in his power. By the same reasoning he will justify the vivisection of animals and patients. He will say that it is better that a few animals should suffer than that one human being should die; and that it is far better that one patient should die, if, through the sacrifice of that one, several may be saved.

Brain without heart is far more dangerous than heart without brain. Have these scientific assassins discovered anything of value? They may have settled some disputes as to the action of some organ, but have they added to the useful knowledge of the race?

It is not necessary for a man to be a specialist in order to have and express an opinion as to the right or wrong of vivisection. It is not necessary to be a scientist or a naturalist to detest cruelty and to love mercy. Above all the discoveries of the thinkers, above all the inventions of the ingenious, above all the victories won on fields of intellectual conflict, rise human sympathy and a sense of justice.

I know that good for the human race can never be aecomplished by torture. I also know that all that has been ascertained by vivisection could have been done by the dissection of the dead. I know that all the torture has been useless. All the agony inflicted has simply hardened the hearts of the criminals, without enlightening their minds. . . .

The human race might be physically improved if all the sickly and deformed babes were killed, and if all the paupers, liars, drunkards, thieves, villains, and vivisectionists were murdered. All this might, in a few ages, result in the production of a generation of physically perfect men and women; but what would such beings be worth,—men and women healthy and heartless, muscular and cruel—that is to say, intelligent wild beasts?

Never can I be the friend of one who vivisects his fellow-creatures. I do not wish to touch his hand.

When the angel of pity is driven from the heart; when the fountain of tears is dry,—the soul becomes a serpent crawling in the dust of a desert.

Very truly yours, R. G. Ingersoll

WORLD UNITY

Although upon the whole Robert Ingersoll was in drastic disagreement with the general philosophy of Tolstoi, he fully shared the illustrious author's abhorrence of war and believed that it should be outlawed as an instrument of national policy; and that a world court of justice should be established with compulsory jurisdiction over all disputes between nations.

October 13th, 1887

Bayard Wyman, Esq.,
Perry, Ohio.

My dear Sir:
I have read a few pages of Tolstoi. The man has great talent, but I cannot convince myself that he is entirely sane. His doctrine of non-resistance is to me the infinite of absurdity. Neither do I believe that the ignorant of this world can be helped by the educated bringing themselves down. It is far better to lift the ignorant —to raise them up—to make them dissatisfied with their condition.

I believe that there ought to be an International Court—a Court to settle questions between nations—a Court having the control of an army to carry its decrees into effect. In this way, war could for the most part be prevented.

Yours very truly, R. G. Ingersoll

New York, N. Y., Sept. 12th, 1889

Charles Watts, Esq.

My dear Friend:
I take this occasion to congratulate you on the success of your labours in Canada, and through you all labourers who have in any way assisted.

People are seeing a little clearer, every day, that the only good, the only sensible object in life, is happiness, and they are also seeing that happiness is not the result of what is known as belief— that it does not follow from subscribing to a creed, or from the performance of certain ceremonies or the saying of certain prayers.

Whoever is in harmony with the conditions of happiness will be happy. Man must have food and raiment, he must have friends, and these can only be obtained by honest labour.

Intelligence ascertains the conditions of well-being, and wisdom lives in accordance with these conditions.

We want to educate the world to the point that passions and

prejudices will not disregard the discoveries of intelligence, but that man, knowing that his own well-being is in some way dependent upon the well-being of the world, will do what he can, not only for himself, but for others.

I regard knowledge, that is to say, science, that is to say, intelligence, as the true saviour of mankind. So I believe in attending to the affairs of this world—in giving our time, our attention, our labour, to the accomplishment of some object in our reach; for the attainment of an end that we can understand; and I hail with joy the coming of that time when the world will be fed and clothed, educated and civilized—a world without want, without beggary and misery—a world without superstition or slavery, without famine and pestilence; and above all, a world without fear.

Very truly your friend, R. G. Ingersoll

To Robert Ingersoll the ideals embodied in the Declaration of Independence and the Bill of Rights were a very real part of his religion of Humanism. Self-government, individual liberty, equal rights, and justice for all, special privileges for none, the " Four Freedoms," the universal human right to the " pursuit of happiness "—these were fundamental, vital articles of his living social faith. He believed with his whole heart and mind in the American form of government, in representative republican institutions—that the American political system is the best that has ever been devised. He realized, of course, that it is not fool-proof, but that, all things considered, it functions for the greatest good of the greatest number more effectually than any other system of government in the world.

In connection with the celebration of the great Chicago World's Fair in 1891, Mr. John McGovern, editor of the *Illustrated World's Fair*, wrote to Col. Ingersoll for a contribution to his magazine on the subject of the general significance and world-wide importance of the Fair. Ingersoll wrote the following letter, which was published as an article in the December, 1891, issue.

New York, N. Y.
November, 1891

Dear Mr. Editor:

The Great Fair should be for the intellectual, mechanical, artistic, political, and social advancement of the world.

Nations, like small communities, are in danger of becoming provincial, and must become so, unless they exchange commodities, theories, thoughts, and ideals. Isolation is the soil of ignorance, and ignorance is the soil of egotism; and nations, like individuals who live apart, mistake provincialism for perfection, and hatred of all other nations for patriotism. With most people, strangers are not only enemies, but inferiors. They imagine that they are progressive because they know little of others, and compare their present, not with the present of other nations, but with their own past.

Few people have imagination enough to sympathize with those of a different complexion, with those professing another religion or speaking another language, or even wearing garments unlike their own. Most people regard every difference between themselves and others as an evidence of the inferiority of the others. They have not intelligence enough to put themselves in the place of another if that other happens to be outwardly unlike themselves.

Countless agencies have been at work for many years destroying the hedges of thorns that have so long divided nations, and we at last are beginning to see that other people do not differ from us, except in the same particulars that we differ from them. At last, nations are becoming acquainted with each other, and they now know that people everywhere are substantially the same. We now know that, while nations differ outwardly in form and feature, somewhat in theory, philosophy and creed, still, inwardly—that is to say, so far as hopes and passions are concerned—they are much the same, having the same fears, experiencing the same joys and sorrows. So we are beginning to find that the virtues belong exclusively to no race, to no creed, and to no religion; that the humanities dwell in the hearts of men, whomever and whatever they may happen to worship. We have at last found that every creed is of necessity a provincialism, destined to be lost in the universal.

At last, Science extends an invitation to all nations, and places at their disposal its ships and its cars; and when these people meet—or rather, the representatives of these people—they will find that, in spite of the accidents of birth, they are, after all, about the same; that their sympathies, their ideas of right and wrong, of virtue and vice, of heroism and honour, are substantially alike. They will find that in every land honesty is honoured, truth respected and admired, and that generosity and charity touch all hearts.

So it is of the greatest importance that the inventions of the world should be brought beneath one roof. These inventions, in my judgment, are destined to be the liberators of mankind. They enslave forces and compel the energies of nature to work for man. These forces have no backs to feel the lash, no tears to shed, no hearts to break.

The history of the world demonstrates that man becomes what we call civilized by increasing his wants. As his necessities increase, he becomes industrious and energetic. If his heart does not keep pace with his brain, he is cruel, and the physically or mentally strong enslave the physically or mentally weak. At present these inventions, while they have greatly increased the countless articles needed by man, have to a certain extent enslaved mankind. In a savage state, there are few failures. Almost everyone succeeds in hunting and fishing. The wants are few, and easily supplied. As man becomes civilized, wants increase; or rather, as wants increase, man becomes civilized. Then the struggle for existence becomes complex; failures increase.

The first result of the invention of machinery has been to increase the wealth of the few. The hope of the world is that through invention man can finally take such advantage of these forces of nature, of the weight of water, of the force of wind, of steam, of electricity, that they will do the work of the world; and it is the hope of the really civilized that these inventions will finally cease to be the property of the few, to the end that they may do the work of all for all.

When those who do the work own the machines, when those who toil control the inventions, then, and not till then, can the world be civilized or free. When these forces shall do the bidding of the individual, when they become the property of the mechanic, instead of the monopoly, when they belong to labour instead of what is called capital, when these great powers are as free to the individual labourer as the air and light are now free to all, then, and not until then, the individual will be restored, and all forms of slavery will disappear.

Another great benefit will come from the Fair. Other nations, in some directions are more artistic than we, but no nation has made the common as beautiful as we have. We have given beauty of form to machines, to common utensils, to the things of every day, and have thus laid the foundation for producing the artistic in its highest possible forms. It will be of great benefit to us to look upon the painting and marbles of the Old World. To see them is an education.

The Great Republic has lived a greater poem than the brain and heart of man have as yet produced, and we have supplied material for artists and poets yet unborn; material for form and colour and song. The Republic is today Art's greatest market.

Nothing is so well calculated to make friends of all nations as to really become acquainted with the best that each has produced. The nation that has produced a great poet, a great artist, a great statesman, a great thinker, takes its place on an equality with other nations of the world, and transfers to all of its citizens some of the genius of its most illustrious men.

This great Fair will be an object lesson to the other nations. They will see the result of a government, republican in form, where the people are the source of authority, where governors and presidents are servants—not rulers. We want all nations to see the Great Republic as it is, to know that here, under our flag, are sixty-five millions of people and that they are the best fed, the best clothed, and the best housed in the world. We want them to know that we are solving the great social problems, and that we are going to demonstrate the right and power of man to govern himself. We want the subjects of other nations to see a land filled with citizens—not subjects; a land in which the pew is above the pulpit; where the people are superior to the state; where legislators are representatives and where authority means simply the duty to enforce the people's will.

Let us hope above all things that this Fair will bind the nations together closer and stronger; and let us hope that this will result in the settlement of all national difficulties by arbitration instead of war. In a savage state individuals settle their own difficulties by an appeal to force. After a time these individuals agree that their difficulties shall be settled by others. This is the first great step towards civilization. The result is the establishment of courts. Nations at present sustain to each other the same relations that savage does to savage. Each nation is left to decide for itself, and it generally decides according to its strength, not the strength of its side of the case, but the strength of its army. The consequence is that what is called the Law of Nations is a savage code. The world will never be civilized until there is an international court. Savages begin to be civilized when they submit their difficulties to their peers. Nations will become civilized when they submit their difficulties to a great [world] court, the judgments of which can be carried out, all nations pledging the co-operation of their armies and their navies for that purpose. If the holding of this great Fair will result in hastening the coming of that time, it will be a great blessing to the whole world.

And here let me prophesy. The Fair will be worthy of Chicago, the most wonderful city of the world—of Illinois, the best State in the Union,—of the United States, the best country on the earth. It will represent the progressive spirit of the Nineteenth Century. Beneath its ample roofs will be gathered the treasures of art and the accomplishments of science. At the feet of the Republic will be laid the triumphs of our race, the best of every land.

Yours truly, R. G. Ingersoll

On January 11, 1896, a special dispatch was sent to all the important papers of the country, and copied from them into the secular and religious sheets, that Colonel Ingersoll had " renounced " his infidelity and joined the church. The special dispatch began as follows:

" Kalamazoo, Mich.—

" Robert G. Ingersoll, during his lecture on ' Lincoln ' here last night, created a sensation. In the middle of his discourse he . . . spoke of his visit to the People's Church, and said ·

' It is the grandest thing in your state, if not in the whole United States. If there were a similar church near my home, I would join it, if its members would permit me ' "

Regarding the real facts of his visit to the People's Church, the Colonel wrote this letter to Mr. E. M. Macdonald, editor of *The Truth Seeker*:

New York, N. Y., Jan. 23, 1896

My dear Mr. Macdonald:

So many foolish things have been published about my visit to the " People's Church " at Kalamazoo that it occurred to me, for the enlightenment of our friends, to tell you the story.

A few days ago, at the request of the pastor, Miss Caroline J. Bartlett, I visited the People's Church. This Church has no creed, and those who support it may, or may not, be believers in the existence of God, the inspiration of the Bible, or the immortality of the soul. This Church has nothing to do with the supernatural, or miraculous. It is for the good of people in this world—to increase happiness this side of the tomb. It desires to increase knowledge, to develop the brain, to give light, and heat, and soil to all the seeds of good that can be found within the human heart. It takes no interest in the miracles of ignorant antiquity, but is delighted with the truths of our day and the facts of all time. It teaches the little children of the poor, reforms abuses, protects the weak, and sides with the suffering and unfortunate. Its only object is to do good—to add to the sum of happiness. It does not ask you to believe right, but to do right. The pastor of this church is earnest, enthusiastic, and self-sacrificing. The dream of her heart, the ambition of her soul, is to do good. Of course the orthodox ministers are her enemies, and denounce her work as contrary to the religion of Christ. These ministers may be right, and yet I think her work is good, and that she will accomplish more for the benefit of man than all the orthodox churches in the world.

Yours always, R. G. Ingersoll

INDEX

Lightning Source UK Ltd.
Milton Keynes UK
UKOW05f1902081216
289534UK00013B/358/P